Truth may seem, but cannot be:
Beauty brag, but 'tis not she;
Truth and beauty buried be.

To this urn let those repair
That are either true or fair;
For these dead birds sigh a prayer.

Bacon

A HISTORY OF
THE JEWS IN ENGLAND

NOTE

The authors of all volumes published by the Jewish Historical Society of England accept full and sole responsibility for the views expressed by them.

TO

THE MEMORY OF

My Mother

PREFACE

THE Jewish population of the British Isles has never formed any but a numerically insignificant proportion of the Diaspora. Yet, despite this relative insignificance of Anglo-Jewry, the story of the Jews in this country is of supreme importance to the student of the philosophy of Jewry and of Jewish history. The adage that history repeats itself is well worn, but none the less true. The history of the Jews in England is the history in miniature of the Diaspora. Since the opening of the Christian era the story of the Jews has everywhere been the same—continual alternations of prosperity and persecution. With nations as with individuals the wheel of fortune ever revolves, but with the Jews its progress seems to have been more rapid, for the alternations have been more numerous than with any other race. But with the Jews the wheel lingers during the period of depression and hurries through that of elation in order to recover the time that has been lost. The story told in the following pages shows all the vicissitudes common these two thousand years to the lot of Jewry. The times of prosperity in England have been among the happiest in the annals of the race. At other seasons Anglo-Jewry has reached the lowest depths of despair, when but a step seemed to separate the community from annihilation. Yet that step here as elsewhere has never been taken. The history of the Jews throughout the Diaspora seems to point the moral that the mission of Israel is to suffer—and to persist.

But the story of the Jews in England is something more than a mere illustration of the general fortunes of the Jews. The unparalleled preservation of mediæval records in England enables the historian to trace more clearly than elsewhere the peculiar position of the Jews under the Feudal System. Then, again, the stages in Jewish emancipation in England are very accurately marked. We see the Jews earning by civic virtues the claim for political rights. Emancipation in England was not granted in obedience to abstract principles ; it was a practical concession made by practical men. In other ways, too, the story told in this book has its importance not merely as a record of the past but as a guide and hope for the future. The tale unfolded may not be brilliant, but the moral pointed is inspiring.

In the preparation of this volume I have been indebted to many friends for valuable assistance and advice. First to be mentioned is Mr. Lucien Wolf, for whose suggestions for the period after the Re-Settlement I am under great obligations. I should also at this point like to acknowledge the assistance I received throughout the preparation of the book from a volume of which no mention appears in the bibliographies—I refer to the *Bibliotheca Anglo-Judaica*, for which Mr. Wolf and Dr. Joseph Jacobs are jointly responsible. Mr. Israel Solomons and Mr. Elkan Adler read the whole of the proofs and favoured me with much valuable criticism. Mr. Lionel Abrahams and Dr. H. P. Stokes very kindly read the chapters dealing with the Pre-Expulsion period, and their criticisms, as well as those of Mr. H. S. Q. Henriques, the author of " The Return of the Jews to England,"

(Macmillan & Co., 1905), who read the chapter dealing with the legal changes that occurred between
the Expulsion and the Re-Settlement, proved of great
value.

Use has been made of Mr. Henriques's book, but
the permission of the author for such use has been
previously obtained. The living writers, however,
whose works proved of most assistance in the preparation of the volume are Mr. Lionel Abrahams, the
Very Reverend the Haham Dr. M. Gaster, Dr. Joseph
Jacobs, and Mr. Lucien Wolf. Mr. Abrahams, in his
masterly monograph on the Expulsion, has not only
proved a great aid : one might almost say that in the
absence of his pioneer work the narrative of the
Expulsion and of the century that preceded it would
have been little more than a bald statement. Dr.
Gaster's researches into the history of his Community
have been practically the only source of several chapters in the present volume. Without his assistance
the inner history of Anglo-Jewish Sephardism would
have been almost, if not altogether, a blank page.
Dr. Joseph Jacobs has collected into his "Jews of
Angevin England" almost all the contemporary references to Jews in this country during that period.
The task of dealing with this especially difficult
era, and of weaving the available material into one
connected narrative, has in consequence been appreciably lightened. Mr. Wolf's writings on the Re-
Settlement and the years immediately subsequent to
it are so well known as hardly to need mention.
To one curious of estimating the extent and value
of his work in this sphere a comparison between his
"Menasseh ben Israel" and Kayserling's essay on
the same subject would prove enlightening. To Mr.
Israel Abrahams I am indebted for seeing the volume
through the press.

The bulk of Chapters XVII. to XXI. first appeared in the Re-Settlement Number of the *Jewish Chronicle*, by the kindness and courtesy of whose proprietors and editor I have been permitted to incorporate them in the present volume. With regard to the illustrations, which were selected in consultation with Mr. Elkan Adler and Mr. Israel Solomons, I must express my acknowledgments of the assistance rendered by Mr. Gustave Tuck. The greater number of the illustrations are reproduced from rare engravings in the possession of Mr. Israel Solomons. To Mr. Elkan Adler I am indebted for the portrait of his late father, Dr. N. M. Adler, and to Mrs. James H. Solomon for that of her late uncle, Mr. Lionel L. Cohen. The photographs of the House of Aaron of Lincoln and of Clifford's Tower, York, were taken by Mr. Frank Haes.

April 1907.

CONTENTS

CONTENTS

CHAPTER IV

RICHARD I.'s CORONATION
(1154-1190)

CHAPTER V

THE MASSACRE AT YORK
(1190)

CHAPTER VI

THE EXCHEQUER OF THE JEWS
(1194-1216)

CHAPTER VII

PROTECTION AND PERSECUTION
(1216-1241)

CONTENTS

CHAPTER VIII

TALLAGES, SPOLIATION, AND IMPRISONMENT
(1238-1251)

CHAPTER IX

LITTLE ST. HUGH OF LINCOLN
(1253-1268)

CHAPTER X

THE LAST PHASE
(1262-1279)

CHAPTER XI

THE EXPULSION
(1282-1290)

CHAPTER XII

PRE-EXPULSION JEWRY

CONTENTS

CHAPTER XIII

THE MIDDLE PERIOD
(1290–1550)

CHAPTER XIV

THE DOMUS CONVERSORUM
(1213–1609)

CHAPTER XV

QUEEN ELIZABETH'S JEWISH PHYSICIAN
(1581–1650)

CHAPTER XVI

THE TRANSLATION OF THE BIBLE

CHAPTER XVII

ENGLISH ELEMENTS IN THE RE-SETTLEMENT
(1630–1649)

CONTENTS

CHAPTER XVIII
THE CRYPTO-JEWS
(1643-1655)

CHAPTER XIX
MENASSEH BEN ISRAEL
(1648-1654)

CHAPTER XX
THE WHITEHALL CONFERENCE
(1650-1655)

CHAPTER XXI
THE RE-SETTLEMENT
(1655-1658)

CONTENTS

CHAPTER XXVII

FROM THE REVOLUTION TO THE GEORGIA SETTLEMENT
(1655–1750)

CHAPTER XXVIII

THE NATURALISATION CONTROVERSY
(1690–1753)

CHAPTER XXIX

THE SEPHARDIM
(1699–1784)

CHAPTER XXX

THE ASHKENAZIM
(1765–1797)

CHAPTER XXXI

THE OPENING OF THE NINETEENTH CENTURY
(1792–1824)

CONTENTS

CHAPTER XXXII

THE REFORM MOVEMENT
(1802-1885)

CHAPTER XXXIII

THE DISABILITIES OF THE JEWS
(1830-1855)

CHAPTER XXXIV

POLITICAL EMANCIPATION OBTAINED
(1830-1866)

CHAPTER XXXV

GROWTH AND REORGANISATION OF THE COMMUNITY
(1840-1906)

ILLUSTRATIONS

A HISTORY OF
THE JEWS IN ENGLAND

CHAPTER I

THE EARLIEST LEGENDS
(BEFORE 1066)

MANY opinions have been expressed regarding the Solomon and Britain. date of the first connection of Jews with the British Isles. The earliest period which has been suggested for a Jewish settlement, either temporary or permanent, is that of the era of Solomon and Hiram, King of Tyre, when the fleets of the allied nations sailed westward from Palestine for purposes of commerce. It is in the highest degree probable that the "Tarshish" to which Solomon's subjects voyaged was Spain, and it may well be that Tyrians and Phoenicians, accompanied by Israelites, ventured to pass through the Straits of Gibraltar, and to sail as far as the Cornish coast in order to bring back supplies of tin, for which, in very early times, the south-west corner of England was famous. The evidence on which this theory rests is philological rather than historical. A Semitic origin is found for the name Britain in the Phoenician words *Berat-Anach* ("the country of tin"), and for the well-known Cornish place names, Marazion ("Bitterness of Zion") and Market Jew. Resemblances have been traced between

A

the Hebrew and Cornish languages; and it has been
pointed out that Jewish names were once common
among the inhabitants of Cornwall. Whether the
names and words in question are really to be regarded
as evidence of Jewish influence is, of course, a matter
of doubt; and the controversy on the subject has
been inconclusive. It may be that they are instances
of purely accidental coincidences; it may be that they
are due to Jewish intercourse with England during
the reign of Solomon. It is possible also that they
may date from a later period.[1]

It has been suggested that Julius Cæsar, whose
favourable disposition towards the Jews is undoubted,
may have been accompanied by soldiers of that race
on his visits to Britain, and may have settled some of
them there. Again, a few decades later, Jews may
have been settled in Britain by the Romans, but in far
different circumstances. On the capture of Jerusalem
numbers of Jews were sold as slaves and scattered in
all parts of the then known world. Possibly some
may have come to Britain. Vague legends are related
of the mission of Peter to Britain, and since his efforts
were directed to Jewish rather than Gentile converts,
his alleged visit to the island is quoted as a proof of
the existence of Jews there.[2]

A still less probable early connection between

[1] For the controversy regarding the Jews in Cornwall see F. Max
Müller, "Chips from a German Workshop," vol. iii. (1870); the Rev. John
Bannister, "Jews in Cornwall," and "Marazion," *Journal of the Royal
Institution of Cornwall* (1867). Besides the advocates of this early Jewish
settlement in Cornwall and their opponents, there is another school which
holds the view that the alleged traces of Jewry are due to Jewish connections during the period of admitted Jewish settlement in England.

[2] The strongest argument in favour of the presence of Jews in Roman
Britain seems to have been the discovery of a curious Roman brick during
some excavations in Mark Lane, London, about 1650. The brick, which
was the keystone of an arched vault full of burnt corn, bore on one side
a raised representation of Samson driving the foxes into a field of corn.
The Roman Samson, Hercules, was the guardian of granaries, and it is
suggested that as the story of Samson could hardly have been known to
the Romans at the period to which the brick referred, the vault was probably erected by some Jews settled under the Roman ægis.

Judæa and the British Isles is related in some of the legends that have clustered around the Coronation Stone now in Westminster Abbey. This relic, which is claimed to have been Jacob's pillow on the occasion of his famous dream, and later one of the corner-stones of Solomon's Temple, is said to have been saved from the *debâcle* on the destruction of the first Temple, and to have been included among the treasures of some Danite refugees who, taking ship, fled west-wards. Their goal, it is suggested, was the Cassiterides or Tin Islands of Cornwall, but driven slightly out of their course some of the refugees were wrecked on the coast of Ireland. Among the salvage was the corner-stone of the Temple. Included either among the survivors of the wreck or in a subsequent ship-load of refugees were a princess of the house of Judah and the scribe Baruch. The prophet Jeremiah is also held by some to have been among the company. A marriage was contracted between the Jewish princess and a native chieftain, and the sacred stone used for their coronation. From this alliance, the legend continues, sprang the present royal house of Britain.[1]

The Coronation Stone legends.

Even if, however, those who advocate the theory of Jewish settlements in Britain in these early days are in the right, the Jews to whom they refer were little more than wayfarers. It is certain that they were in no sense the founders of a permanent Jewish settlement, and whatever Jews may have been in the country, before or immediately after the opening of the Christian era, either speedily left it again or were merged in the surrounding population. In the racial sense the settlement, if there was one, existed; in the religious sense there was none. Between this early supposed settlement and the later

No permanent Jewish settlement.

[1] For the Coronation Stone legends see William F. Skene, "The Coronation Stone"; Albert M. Hyamson, "The Coronation Stone and its Legendary Jewish Connection," *Jewish Chronicle*, August 8, 1902.

one there was no sort of connection whatsoever. The Jews of Cornwall or of Ireland must have been but an isolated fragment glistening for a moment in the firmament of history, but to pass into perpetual darkness.

The Lost Ten Tribes and the English.

There is a third legendary Israelitish connection with early Britain, if possible more visionary than those already noted. It amounts to an Israelitish origin for both the ancient Britons and their Saxon conquerors. The advocates of the Anglo-Israel theories — or to be more exact, both the Brito-Israelites and the Anglo-Israelites — claim that the inhabitants of England are the descendants of the Lost Ten Tribes of Israel, who were taken into captivity by the Assyrians on the final destruction of the Kingdom of Israel. The historical connection between the Ten Tribes and the English is briefly as follows : Contemporary with the exile of the Israelites in Halah and Habor, by the river of Gozan and the cities of the Medes, appeared in the same districts the Scythians, a branch of the Khumri. The Scythians or Scutai—whence Scots—wandered toward the west, and ultimately settled in Britain as well as in other parts. From them the Celtic inhabitants of the island were descended. Another branch of the Khumri, the Sacai, afterwards Saxons (Sons of Isaac), subsequently followed the lead of the Scythians, and formed many republics on the Israelitish pattern in northern and central Europe ; one of their branches ultimately invaded Britain, where they settled.[1]

Setting aside all the legendary traditions, the question of the date of the first settlement of Jews in England is still clothed in mystery not yet fully penetrable. So slight and inconclusive are the few

[1] For Anglo-Israelism see "Jewish Encyclopedia," article by Joseph Jacobs; and Hastings' "Dictionary of Ethics and Religion," article by Albert M. Hyamson.

extant references to Jews in pre-Norman England, that a large number, probably the majority, of historians are of opinion that, with the exception of occasional wayfarers, especially Gallo-Jewish slave-dealers, there were no Jews settled in England until after the Norman Conquest. Of the presence of Jewish slave-dealers in Northern Gaul there can be no question, and it is very probable that some of these were indirectly responsible for the conversion of Britain to Christianity. The British slaves who, in the Roman market-place, attracted the attention of Gregory, and directed it towards Britain, were most probably introduced into Italy by Jewish merchants.

Jews and the introduction of Christianity.

The earliest references to Jews appear in the *Liber Pœnitentialis* of Archbishop Theodore of Canterbury (A.D. 669). These ecclesiastical enactments are directed against the intercourse in certain specified instances between Christians and Jews. Especially is the celebration, with the Jews, of Easter or Passover forbidden under penalties. Christians were not allowed to take food with Jews, to sell Christian slaves to them, or to celebrate mass where Jews were buried. A century later these anti-Jewish prohibitions were repeated by Egbert, Archbishop of York, in his *Excerptiones*. Against these enactments as evidence of a Jewish settlement, it has been pointed out that not a single reference to Jews can be found in Bede's or the other old English Chronicles, nor in the contemporary charters. Moreover, it has been suggested that the references quoted may not refer to Jews at all, and, if they do, may only have been copied from continental codes. Some of the enactments relate to Judaising practices rather than to Jews, and regarding the former there was a burning controversy in the Church at the time. These enactments may, therefore, have been directed against heretics rather than against Jews.

The earliest Jewish reference.

The next piece of evidence regarding a pre-Norman Jewish settlement is of a more definite nature. In a Hebrew work, *Emek Habacha*, by Joseph Cohen (1575), it is stated, under the year 810, that in consequence of continued warfare and a general condition of unsettlement in Germany, many Jews fled thence to Spain and England. This evidence is not contemporary, nor is it corroborated. A contemporary document,[1] however, which, if authentic, would almost decide the question in favour of a Jewish settlement in England at that date, relates that in the year 833, Whitglaff, King of the Mercians, having been defeated by Egbert, took refuge in that Abbey, and, in return for the protection and assistance rendered him by the abbot and monks on the occasion, granted a charter confirming "to them all lands, tenements, and possessions, and all other gifts which had at any time been bestowed upon them by his predecessors or their nobles, or by any other faithful Christians or by Jews."[2] Accepting this statement it would appear that not only were Jews in the country at the time, but they had apparently been settled there for a number of years. It has even been contended that the statement proves Jews were qualified to hold lands. Other property than lands is, however, mentioned in the charter, and this claim can hardly be deduced from the record.[3]

Finally there is the evidence of the so-called Laws of Edward the Confessor, wherein it is declared: "That the Jews, wheresoever they be, are under the King's guard and protection; neither can any one of them put himself under the protection of any rich

A supposed Jewish immigration in the ninth century.

The Laws of Edward the Confessor.

---

[1] Ingulphus, "History of Croyland Abbey."

[2] The authenticity of this historical record has been very strongly contested and is now accepted by very few scholars.

[3] At the beginning of the eleventh century, according to Basnage, the Jews were expelled from England. Unfortunately no authority is given for the statement.

man without the King's licence, for the Jews, and all they have, belong to the King; and if any person shall detain them or their money, the King may claim them, if he please, as his own." These laws, although attributed to Edward the Confessor, were compiled in their present form at a much later date, when Jews were admittedly settled in the country. Whether this distinct reference to Jews was to be found in the earliest version cannot be stated. In its present form it sums up the position of the Jews under the Feudal System both in England and on the Continent. Although that System was not fully introduced into this country until the Norman Conquest, the penultimate of the Saxon kings had been imbued with sufficient of the spirit of the Norman Government to have rendered the adoption of such legislation possible. The evidence concerning the pre-Norman settlement of Jews in England is inconclusive. Whatever exists must, however, be reinforced by the probability of the penetration of Jews, perhaps not in considerable numbers, to Saxon England, and, fortified by the combination of all these stray supports, the historian is justified in concluding that Jews were not unknown in England before the Norman Conquest.

In 1062 appears the first more or less reliable mention of Jews in connection with Ireland. In that year it is said[1] two Jews came oversea to Ireland bringing presents to Fairdelbach. They were not, however, permitted to remain.

Jews visit Ireland.

AUTHORITIES :—Joseph Jacobs, "The Jews of Angevin England" (1893), "When did the Jews first settle in England?" (*Jewish Quarterly Review*, vol. i. 1888); J. M. Rigg, "Select Pleas . . . from the Rolls of the Exchequer of the Jews" (1902); J. E. Blunt, "The Jews in England" (1830); A. Neubauer, "Notes on the Jews in Oxford" (*Oxford Historical Society's Publications, Collectanea*, 1890); John Caley, "The Origin of the Jews in England" (*Archæologia*, vol. viii. 1787).

---

[1] *Annales Inisfalenses :* O'Conner, *Rerum Hibernicarum*, ii. p. 81.

CHAPTER II

UNDER THE NORMANS
(1066–1146)

Immigration under William I. WHETHER Jews were settled in England before the Conquest or not, it is certain that a Jewish immigration into England took place early in the reign of William the Conqueror. The exact date of their settlement is again unknown, but they came from Rouen, and their advent was one of the direct consequences of the Conquest.

England at the period of the Norman invasion was inhabited almost entirely by land-holders of various grades, villeins, and Churchmen. A small proportion of the population was engaged in trades, but the commercial class was entirely unrepresented. The country was divided between the upper and lower classes, while of the middle there was as yet neither representatives nor substitutes. So long as the English were content to remain at home, either on their estates or in their villages, and took no practical interest in external affairs, the ordinary produce of the soil and district was sufficient to supply their wants, and the baron, his retainers, and villeins lived at home in plenty, and found sufficient to enable The need for a middle class. them to visit their neighbours on either friendly or hostile errands. When, however, the desire to leave that somewhat narrow orbit arose, other needs came. Payment in kind when attempted beyond the smallest limits becomes so cumbersome as to be hardly practicable, and the wider one's interests spread the more pressing becomes the necessity for a reliable and convenient means of exchange. To satisfy the requirements of the advance in the state of civilisation that marked the advent of the Normans to England, in the first place coin, and in the second the machinery of commerce, were required. Both could be supplied by the Jews. Driven by persecution from almost all other callings in life, the Jews of Europe had perforce been compelled to devote themselves more and more to finance and trade. In these twin occupations, reinforced by their superior intelligence, due doubtless to the continual sharpening by persecution that Jewry had even then undergone, the Jews of the Middle Ages excelled. In the economy of Norman England the Jews were well fitted to take the place of the middle class, then lacking, and in the natural course, whether at the special invitation of the king or on their own initiative, the Jews must inevitably have found their way into the country. *The need for the Jews.*

It has been suggested that a large sum of money was paid by the Jews to William so that he should permit them to settle in England. To such an extent, however, was it to the interest of the king that they should cross the Channel that it is not likely there was any need to bribe him. William was specially anxious that the feudal dues should be paid him in coin rather than in kind, but without the assistance of the Jews or a similar capitalist element such payment was impossible. The Jews brought with them coin that speedily got into circulation. The king was enabled to purchase luxuries and to satisfy his military requirements; the barons were assisted to pay their dues; suitors who found it necessary to follow the king's court from one town to another, or to go to Rome to plead their causes before the Papal Curia found their course rendered easier by Jewish money. Not only were the Jews instrumental in keeping the royal treasury filled, but they also *The Jews necessary to William's policy.* *Their place in the national economy.*

managed to attract some of the odium that would otherwise have fallen upon the king and his more regularly appointed officials, and to a corresponding degree they were instrumental in relieving the latter.

A charter granted. A charter, confirmed by John, was granted, at least to individual Jews, by Henry I. By this the Jews were given freedom of movement in the country with their goods, and excused from all customs, tolls, &c., just as the king's goods were. They were given permission to reside wherever they wished. They might claim redress if molested, and hold lands in pledge until redeemed. They were permitted to buy whatever was brought to them, excepting church property and crimson cloth (? stained with blood),[1] to sell their pledges after holding them a year and a day, to be tried by their peers, and to be sworn on the Pentateuch. A Jew's oath was considered valid against the oaths of twelve Christians. To a very considerable extent the Jews' transactions consisted of loans on the security of land, and they were by law permitted to charge a very high interest. The king levied a tax on those transactions in return for the protection he extended to the Jews, and as he often accepted money from the Jews' debtors for the use of his influence on their behalf, the transactions of the Jews proved doubly remunerative to the crown.

Jews indirectly assisted by ecclesiastical law. The financial transactions of the Jews were rendered easier by the laws of the Church directed against usury. These were so stringent that an observant son of the Church was prevented from entering upon any commercial undertakings. By usury was understood not merely money-lending; the term also comprised commercial speculation, and even ordinary capitalism. Thus the field, which might otherwise have been encroached upon by the natives, was left clear for the Jews. The Church at this period was averse

---

[1] *Pannus sanguinolentus.*

to the forcible conversion of Jews lest their reversion to Judaism might create scandal. According
to its laws in force at the beginning of the twelfth The Church
century, Jews were incapable of holding Christian and the Jews.
slaves, and any of their slaves who might accept
Christianity were at once to be set at liberty. Jews
were also debarred from holding public offices, and
in common with heretics and pagans were not allowed
to accuse Christians. Converts guilty of reversion to
Judaism were to be deprived of their children and
servants lest the latter might be influenced to act
likewise. Converts from Judaism were welcomed
and well treated. An extant letter from Archbishop
Anselm recommends the Lord Prior Arnulf and the
Archdeacon William to care for one committed by
him to their charge. "Let no poverty or other
accident which we can avert cause him to regret
having left his parents and their law for Christ's
sake. . . . Do not let him and his little family suffer
any harsh want, but let him rejoice that he has passed
from perfidy to the true faith, and prove by our piety
that our faith is nearer to God than the Jewish. For
I would prefer, if necessary, that there should be
spent in this all that belongs to me from the rents
of the archdeaconry, and even much more, rather
than that he who has fled out of the hands of the
devil to the servants of God should live in misery
among us."

The Jews of necessity kept themselves distinct and
apart from the general community. Their relations
with the natives were often friendly, but on the whole
they lived an entirely different life. The many points
of agreement between the Normans and Saxons that
gradually caused the fusion of the two races were The Jews and
altogether wanting as between Jews and Christians. their neigh-bours.
Their appearance and gait at once marked the Jews
out as aliens. Instead of mixing freely with the

people they kept together in Jewries, not by compulsion, but of their free choice. None of them engaged in occupations in which they might find Christian colleagues. They took no part in the defence of the country, or in the preservation of the peace. Their seclusion from the Gilds and the Frank-Pledge deprived them of the opportunities afforded by those institutions for social intercourse with their neighbours. They took no part in the local government of the time through the Court Leet, the Court Baron, the Town-Moot or the Shire-Moot. Not only did they not worship together with their neighbours, their day of worship was even different from that of the Christians, and when death had otherwise made all men equal, Jews were buried apart from Christians. Jews were not permitted by their laws to eat food similar to that of Christians, nor to partake of food prepared by non-Jews. For them cattle had to be killed by special rites, and still more irritating was the assumption that meat, although thus killed, which might be rejected by the Jews, was considered suitable for consumption by Christians. All these differences combined to render the Jews strange, and therefore suspect in the popular eyes. The populace is always hostilely disposed to whatever it cannot understand, and there is little reason to believe that the Jews of Norman England were ever pleasing in the eyes of the lower classes. So long, however, as the people had no leader no harm could occur. The Jews were safe while they enjoyed the favour of the king, and as long as he retained his influence over his subjects.[1]

Favoured by the early Norman kings. From the first three Norman kings the Jews appear to have suffered neither exaction nor annoyance.

[1] This account of the condition of the Jews in England under the Normans is based to a considerable extent on material collected by Mr. Lionel Abrahams and published in his " The Expulsion of the Jews."

William Rufus and Henry I. exacted by violence
large sums of money from their Christian subjects;
but they spared the Jews. For instance, the ten
thousand marks needed for the purchase of Normandy from Robert were raised with great difficulty,
the abbeys, in some instances, having to melt down
their plate in order to provide their respective contributions; yet no levy appears to have been made
at the time on the Jews. On the other hand, two
circumstances arose during this period that tended to
increase, for the time at least, the prosperity of the
Jews of England. The preaching of the First Crusade
was as efficacious in England as on the Continent.
Many members of all ranks, aroused by the call of
religion, were anxious to take part in the recovery for
Christendom of the Holy Sepulchre. To equip themselves for the campaign they sold or pledged all
manner of property, and Jews, practically the only
capitalists, were in almost every instance the other
party to the transaction.

Over William Rufus, however, the Church and Rufus and the
Christianity had little influence. So far from taking Church
the cross, William II. was little better than an infidel.
He took a delight in outraging the feelings of devout
Christians, and for the double purpose of annoying
them and of filling his own coffers he was accustomed
to appropriate to himself the property of the Church.
When a bishopric fell vacant, instead of filling it, he
retained the temporalities in his own hands, farming
them out to Jews, who were free from the penalties
and fears that Christians would have suffered in a
similar position.

Rufus, however, in his cynical disregard of the His favour of
Christian properties, even went further. Whether the Jews and
out of policy, wishing to retain the Jewish colony discourage-
intact, or merely to offend the feelings of Christians, apostasy.
or solely in return for bribes, he was accustomed to

coerce converted Jews to return to their original faith. Towards the end of his reign the Jews of Rouen, being somewhat alarmed at the frequent secessions from their body, begged the king, and supported their petition by a large bribe, to compel the converts to return to Judaism. Rufus was by no means averse to the task, and by means of terrible threats forced most of the converts to return to their previous faith. On another occasion a dialogue is reported between the king and one Stephen, a convert to Christianity, whose father had promised William sixty marks if he would induce the son to return to his former spiritual allegiance. In the discussion the king was vanquished, and the convert, who did not hesitate to rebuke the ruler, remained more firm in his new faith than before the interview. The king claimed the promised payment inasmuch as, even if he had failed, he had done his utmost to succeed. The father demurred on the ground that his son was more steadfast in his new faith than before the interview, and the matter was finally compromised by the payment of half the amount originally promised. On another occasion Rufus displayed his peculiar attitude towards Christianity by arranging a public disputation in London between rabbis and bishops, on the rival claims to acceptance of Judaism and Christianity. It was on the king's own initiative that the discussion was arranged, and, perhaps to overcome anv scruples the Jews may have felt, he offered, if they prevailed in the argument, himself to accept Judaism. The avowed partiality of the king caused the chosen exponents of Christianity some misgiving, and they entered into the controversy, we are told, in trepidation, "fearing with pious solicitude for the Christian faith." As is invariably the case in such discussions both sides claimed the victory. " From this contest," the contemporary records state, "the Jews received

A public
disputation.

nothing but confusion, though they often boasted
that they had been conquered not by speech, but by
deeds." The king remained a Christian, nominally.

The favour that the Jews of England enjoyed at the
time, together with the increase in their numbers and
prosperity, seems to have aroused the attention of the
Church, and to have stimulated it to efforts calculated
to countermine any influence the Jews might have
been exerting on the Christian population. Missionary enterprises were arranged, and during the
reign of Henry I. monks were sent to all the towns of
England in which Jews had settled, for the express
purpose of preaching down Judaism. With the exception of these expeditions and one other incident,
there is absolute silence in the contemporary records
concerning the doings of and happenings to the
Anglo-Jewish community for the whole of the reign
of Henry I. and until the fifth year of that of his successor Stephen. The continued prosperity of the
Jews had meanwhile added to the feelings of suspicion and hatred that had been aroused among the
people, the additional one of envy. Not only were
the Jews still alien in race and religion, strange and
hardly comprehensible ; they were yet further separated from the people among whom they dwelt by
the acquisition of wealth, which the people must have
regarded as wrung from themselves. The debtor
generally nurses a grievance against his creditor, and
for an Englishman to see that which was formerly
his the property of another, against whom he was
already prejudiced, must have rendered him all the
more anti-Jewish in feeling. The first attack on the
rights and liberties of the Jews did not come, however, from the common people, nor from the landed
classes, nor from the Church ; the king, the constitutional protector of the Jews, doubtless considering
that he might do as he liked with his own. fined the

Jews of London in 1130 the enormous sum of £2000 (£80,000 in present day currency) on the pretence that one of their number had killed a sick man. The charge possibly amounted to one of magic, a Jewish doctor (at that day Jews almost monopolised the practice of medicine in western Europe) in all probability having without success attended a sick Christian.[1]

The general unsettlement that persisted throughout the troubled reign of Stephen reacted unfavourably on the fortunes of Anglo-Jewry. The Jew, essentially a man of peace, for he has learnt only too thoroughly the horror and miseries of war, can only flourish under a settled government. The civil wars that continued throughout the alternating governments of the Empress Maud and King Stephen

were to him fraught with misfortunes. The former, during the occupation of Oxford, compelled the Jews of that city to pay her an exchange of money.[2] On the occupation of that place by her opponent Stephen, similar but considerably increased demands were made. The Jews were then compelled to yield three and a half exchanges, together with all the property of an outlawed and apostate Jew. To dissipate any hesitation the Jews might have felt about the grant, Stephen stationed incendiaries in various parts of the city with instructions, in certain circumstances, to set fire to the houses of the Jews, and, as an earnest of his intentions and as a preliminary, the house of Aaron, the son of Isaac, possibly together with its occupants, was burnt to the ground.

---

[1] Blunt incorrectly postdates this incident by ten years.

[2] The meaning of this term is not altogether clear. The following explanation has been offered: The Jews were at the time public money-changers, changing foreign into English coin. At times Maud and Stephen, for example, imposed a rate of exchange on foreign money, which represented a considerable premium on the true market value. Thus a given quantity of bullion worth one noble might be forced to exchange for three and a half nobles (i.e. three and a half exchanges).

By this date numerous Jewish communities had sprung up throughout the country. Almost if not the first places in which the Jews settled were the towns of Oxford and Cambridge. The earliest record relating to the former is dated 1075. The first Jewish settlement in Cambridge has been fixed at two years earlier. At Oxford the Jews were early both numerous and wealthy. They held so many houses there that the students were compelled to become their tenants. At least three of the halls of learning were held by Jews, and from their occupiers were known as Moyse's Hall, Jacob's Hall, and Lumbard's Hall.[1] The Jews dwelt in the parishes of St. Martin, St. Edward, and St. Aldate; hence these became known as the Great and Little Jewries. The institutions of the Oxford Community included a school and a synagogue; and the rabbis instructed in the Hebrew language and literature not only Jews but also Christian students of the University.· The Jews of Oxford may possibly have come from Wallingford, where there was also a very early settlement.

Jews arrived at Cambridge in 1073, and dwelt at first near the Guildhall and afterwards in the neighbourhood of the Round Church. In that town also the settlement soon became one of consequence, for it was chosen as one of the chief places to which monks were sent in the reign of Henry I. to neutralise the supposed efforts of the Jews to propagate their faith. Another important Jewish centre mentioned in the same connection was Stam- ford, where monks sent in 1109 to preach against Judaism "exceedingly prospered in their Ministry, and strengthened the Christian Faith against the Jewish depravity." Jews settled in Stamford very shortly after

[1] The Guildhall also was owned a century and a half later by a Jew, Moses, the son of Isaac. From him it is supposed to have passed to the king by escheat, and by the latter it was granted by charter to the citizens.

their arrival in the country in the reign of William the Conqueror. The earliest reference to Jews in London is a mention of the Jews Street in the ward of Haco about the year 1115. The act of oppression of fifteen years later has already been mentioned, and in 1136 by the extensive fire that visited the city the Jewish quarter suffered considerably. The first settlement of the Jews in London was in the ward of Haco, in Broad Street. The Jews, however, moved westwards, closer to the great market of West Cheape, a situation similar to that almost invariably occupied by Jews throughout mediæval England. The site of their settlement is still known as Old Jewry. In this district the Jews dwelt in strong handsome mansions, worthy to house the great nobles of the land—in fact, many of the Jews' houses in the Old Jewry were purchased by contemporary barons. Others by various means came into the hands of the crown, and before the Expulsion the Jews had entirely left the Old Jewry and settled around the Guildhall. Another Jewish settlement in London of which there is some trace was farther east within the jurisdiction of the Constable of the Tower, doubtless chosen on account of the greater security. The present Jewin Street marks the cemetery that throughout the period served the Jews of London, and, until 1177, all the Jews of the kingdom. At different times the Jews possessed several synagogues within the City. St. Stephen's Church and St. Mary Colechurch were both once synagogues, until confiscated and given to the dominant faith. St. Anthony's Hospital, upon whose site the City Bank now stands, was also once a synagogue. Another Jewish place of worship at the north-east corner of Old Jewry was confiscated and granted to the newly-founded order of the Sackcloth Friars, who had been disturbed by the howling (*ululatio*) of the Jews at prayer. This building was of sufficient importance to become the residence of two lord mayors in a subsequent century. Another synagogue was defaced and partly destroyed in 1262. Finally there was the building, afterwards known as Bakewell Hall, on whose site Gresham College was ultimately built, which, although nominally a private house—for the Jews of London were forbidden by Archbishop Peckham in 1283 to have synagogues—was the chief Jewish house of prayer in London until the Expulsion.

After the university towns and London, the Jewish centre next in importance was Norwich. Other towns that sheltered Jews during the two centuries preceding the Expulsion were Gloucester, Exeter, Northampton, Leicester, Hereford, Bury St. Edmunds, Newcastle-on-Tyne, York, Tewkesbury, Winchelsea, Bristol, Southampton, Winchester, Lincoln, Nottingham, Canterbury, Lancaster, Doncaster, Beverley, Grimsby, Flint, Rhuddland, Conway, Beaumaris, Carnarvon, Newborough, Criccieth, Harlech, Bala, Derby, Bridgnorth, Coventry, Worcester, Warwick, Newport, Bedford, Huntingdon, King's Lynn, Thetford, Sudbury, Ipswich, Eye, Bungay, Colchester, Hertford, Hitchin, Dunstable, Berkhampstead, Wycombe, Cricklade, Marlborough, Devizes, Wells, Wilton, Reading, Newbury, Windsor, Guildford, Rochester, Faversham, Rye, Arundel, Chichester, Bosham, Romsey, and Dorchester.

The distribution of the Jews.

AUTHORITIES :—Joseph Jacobs, "The Jews of Angevin England," "The London Jewry, 1290" (*Publications of the Anglo-Jewish Historical Exhibition*, 1888) ; B. L. Abrahams, "The Expulsion of the Jews from England" (1895) ; W. Prynne, "A Short Demurrer to the Jews' long discontinued Remitter into England" (1655–56); D'Bloissiers Tovey, *Anglia Judaica* (1738) ; Anthony à Wood, "The History and Antiquities of the University of Oxford" (1796) ; T. Madox, "History of the Exchequer" (1769); J. E. Blunt, "The Jews in England"; E. A. Freeman, "The Norman Conquest," vol. v. (1876), "The Reign of William Rufus" (1882) ; R. Holinshed, "Chronicles" (1586); L. O. Pike, "A History of Crime in

England" (1873) ; A. Neubauer, " Notes on the Jews in Oxford " ; Francis Peck, "The Antiquarian Annals of Stamford" (1727); C. H. Cooper, "Annals of Cambridge," vol. i. (1842); Thomas Baker, " History of the College of St. John the Evangelist, Cambridge " (1869) ; Walter Rye, " The Persecutions of the Jews in England " (*Publications of the Anglo-Jewish Historical Exhibition*, 1888).

CHAPTER III

THE CRUSADES AND THE BLOOD ACCUSATION

(1146–1188)

WHILE the Normans were settling the government of the country and securing themselves in their newly-acquired possessions, the period of tranquillity that the Jews of Europe had been enjoying came to a close, and a new cycle of massacres and barbarities commenced. The eloquence and zeal of Peter the Hermit and his coadjutors in the preaching of the First Crusade succeeded in banding together men of all nations in the task of recovering the Holy Land for Christendom. They had however, another result that was hardly intended. To rouse the passions of the soldiers of the Cross lurid tales were told of all that Christians had suffered at the hands of that eastern people, estranged from God and the enemies of Christ. Christians had been massacred and their lands laid waste. Churches had been destroyed, or, even worse, devoted to anti-Christian rites. Men and women had been tortured, Christians circumcised and their blood used for superstitious purposes. By these tales of infidel barbarity Europe was aroused, and her chivalry swore eternal warfare on the savage and un-Christian race, whose atrocities had been so vividly described A huge army prepared itself to defend the honour of Christendom and to avenge the sufferings of her children. The soldiers of the Cross felt certain that they need not go so far afield as the East to find anti-

Christian maligners of Christ, the allies, as they believed, of the perpetrators of the atrocities, to whose
tale they had listened with horror. At their very doors
were colonies of Jews, and right worthily would they
open their holy mission if they rid the earth of the
blasphemers within immediate reach of their hands.
Massacres of The Crusaders in their march across Europe left
Jews on the behind them a trail of martyred Jews. Community
Continent. after community from France to Hungary was utterly
destroyed, not even the bishops having the power,
although often the will, to protect these victims of
the Crusaders' zeal.

The disasters that followed the First Crusade were
avenged on the helpless Jews of the Continent. The
Second Crusade was the signal for a recrudescence
in the anti-Jewish activity. Bernard of Clairvaux, the
spiritual leader of the movement, protested against
the barbarities. The object of the Crusade, he contended, was the honour of the Christian religion. The
reconquest of the Holy Land was itself but a means
to that end, to which massacres of Jews would in
nowise assist. But Bernard had aroused a spirit
of fanaticism that it was not in his power to quell.
A narrow-minded monk, Rudolph of Mainz, carried
the cross through the Rhine valley, calling for the
slaughter of the Jews, the enemies of Christianity.
His appeal was not uttered in vain, and among the
victims was at least one English Jew who happened
to be in the centre of disturbance at the time ; but the
efforts of Bernard were successful in narrowing the
limits of the conflagration. Bernard himself met the
monk Rudolph in open disputation, and later addressed
a letter to the peoples of Western Europe protesting
against the persecution of the Jews.

Echoes in The agitation on the Continent had its echoes in
England. England, and Bernard's letters were sent across the
Channel and the North Sea, as well as to the Con-

tinental countries. But the vague dislike of the people was quickened by the Crusades into a positive hatred of the Jews. The general crime attributed to the Mohammedans of the East of circumcising Christians and using their blood for their own anti-Christian practices was translated into a definite instance of the Blood Accusation in England, and the opening of the Second Crusade coincided with the supposed martyrdom of St. William of Norwich (1146). This martyrdom was the first of a long series of similar crimes laid to the charge of the Jews in all parts of Christendom without the slightest evidence in support. William, who at the time of his death was twelve years old, was the son of a widow, who herself was the daughter of a married priest. At the age of eight the child was apprenticed to a skinner in Norwich, and while engaged in that employment he was, according to one account, stolen, according to another, bought by the Jews, and after having undergone various tortures in imitation of the passion of Jesus, was martyred on the eve of the festival of Passover, 1144, 45 or 46. There are several accounts of the discovery of the crime, but so little worthy of credence was the evidence which could be adduced at the time that the Sheriff refused to allow the Jews to appear in the Bishop's Court to answer the charge, and took them under his protection. The legends suggest that he was bribed to take this action, and to suppress all evidence of the guilt of the Jews. The secular clergy were divided in opinion concerning the truth of the charge. Among the citizens, and even the monks of the cloister, there was also a large party of sceptics. The bishop of the diocese, Eborard, disbelieved the story whose chief supporter among the Churchmen was the Prior William Turbe, shortly afterwards Bishop of Norwich. The details of the legend are in the highest degree improbable, and

The Blood Accusation.

St. William of Norwich.

sometimes absurd. The Blood Accusation, of which this incident was the first result, was first suggested by Theobald, a onverted Jew of Cambridge, who tried to implicate the whole of Jewry in the charge of sacrificing little children in order to gratify their hatred of Christianity. According to his libellous assertions lots were cast each year to decide the town in Europe in which the next "martyrdom" was to take place. Thus the murder of William of Norwich had been decided upon at a Council of Jews held at Narbonne the previous year.

The Jews of Norwich attacked.

The immediate result of the accusation was seriously to affect the fortunes of the Jewish community in Norwich. The populace was so incensed with the Jews that, despite the protection of the Sheriff, many of the Jews of the city were killed, and others fled in all directions to escape a similar fate. The accusation once made was unfortunately repeated elsewhere. In 1168 the Jews of Gloucester were accused of a similar crime, and in 1181 it was the turn of those of Bury St. Edmunds. Other accusations were made at Winchester in 1192 and 1232, at London in 1244, and finally at Lincoln in 1255. In every instance a shrine and miracles attached themselves to the burial-place of the victim, and whoever suffered from these terrible accusations, the local abbey or cathedral invariably reaped a rich and prolonged harvest. It has also been pointed out that the Blood Accusation was as a rule made at a time at which the Royal Treasury needed replenishing. With the exception of the last-mentioned incident, that at Lincoln, in no instance was the charge submitted to judicial scrutiny. Prejudice had prepared the people to accept the accusation wherever made, and advantage seems always to have been taken of it whenever a child disappeared in the neighbourhood of a Jewish community. The story, with minor variations, was always the same.

The legendary history of St. William of Norwich was taken as the pattern, and the criminal libels of Theobald formed the basis of the general anti-Jewish accusations.

As has already been pointed out, Jews were intro- The place of duced into the country by William I. to fill a hiatus in the Jew in the national life. the social and political organisation. Their function was confined to the commercial and financial sphere, and all others were sufficiently safeguarded by the system, the interrelation of the Church and State, by which the country was governed. To every public office in the community were attached religious cere-monials of a character that rendered impossible the participation in them of a Jew by religion. The hold-ing of land by the ordinary feudal tenure was also bound up with a similar formality, in connection with the homage paid by the tenant, and thus the Jew was debarred from it. Moreover, the Gilds in which the artisan elements in the nation banded themselves to-gether were to a great extent religious confraternities, from which Jews were also necessarily excluded. In the Feudal system, as adapted in England, Jews were given a definite function, and, by the closing of all other paths, from this there was no escape. The English Jew of the early Middle Ages had either to be a capitalist, in most instances a money-lender, or to depart the country. In the early period of the Settlement the relations between the clergy and the Jews were quite friendly. The latter were regarded as a somewhat incongruous element in the population, but hopes were felt for its absorption, by means of conversion, to the dominant faith. The hopes of the clergy for such a result were, however, not realised ; while, on the other hand, it appears that the Jews were at least as successful as the Christians in making converts. The attitude of the clergy in consequence gradually changed and the anti-Jewish complexion that by degrees came over their relations was materially assisted, as has already been noticed, by the outburst of anti-Jewish activity that accompanied the Crusades, and by the result, in England, of the Blood Accusation. The votaries of mediæval Christianity were also exasperated by the critical incredulity with which the Jews received the pretended miracles and the adoration of images which to so great an extent accompanied mediæval Christian worship. The Jews were not satisfied to cast ridicule in private among themselves upon the manifestations; in several instances they interrupted religious observances with their criticisms, greatly to the indignation of the participators and also to the inconvenience and punishment of the critics.

The Church and "usury."

That Jews were left undisturbed in the practice of usury[1] was due to the Church legislation forbidding Christians to take part in that sphere of activity. Thus the whole field of finance was left free to the Jews at a time, too, when the necessity for the erection of numerous important buildings devoted to religious as well as to secular purposes became manifest. Without capital no large building scheme could be undertaken, and without the Jews the amount of available capital would have been considerably reduced. Castles and monasteries in all parts of the country were built with money borrowed from the Jews, and it was with the assistance of Jewish financiers that more than one of the stately and magnificent cathedrals that to-day grace the cities of England were raised. The fashion of using stone instead of wood for building material was also set by the Jews— the oldest existing stone house in the country is that of Aaron of Lincoln; the purpose of the Jews in erecting such dwellings was for protection as much

[1] This term should here and henceforth be interpreted in the widest sense to include capitalism, &c.

THE HOUSE OF AARON OF LINCOLN, STEEP HILL

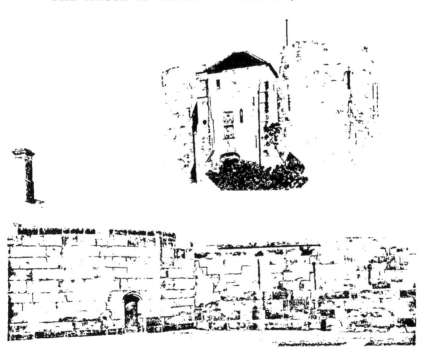

CLIFFORD'S TOWER, YORK

as for comfort—and the minor barons were only able to follow their example with Jewish financial assistance. Jewish loans created Christian debtors, and hence among these sections of the population, the clergy and the minor barons, the Jewish creditors became especially unpopular. The ecclesiastical discouragement of usury on the part of Christians, of itself of considerable influence, was reinforced by the action of the State. The king came to the assistance of the Church by decreeing that all properties of usurers should on their decease accrue to the crown, which thus became, as Dr. Joseph Jacobs has pointed out, the universal legatee of the English Jews. In practice there was a sort of partnership between the crown and the Jews of England. The king, however, seldom claimed the whole of his rights. It was more to his interest to leave the bulk of a deceased Jew's property in the hands of his natural heir, who (differing from the king, a good Christian) could use it remuneratively. In one famous instance, that of Aaron of Lincoln (c. 1125–c. 1186), the crown retained the whole of the Jew's property, which was so considerable, notwithstanding the loss after his death of his treasures at sea, that a special branch of the Exchequer, which continued active for many years, had to be created to deal with his debts. These amounted to £20,000, equal to more than half of the king's income. Aaron is first mentioned in 1166, when he appears as a creditor of the king, Henry II., to the extent of £616, 12s. 8d. Aaron was the largest English banker of the day, and was represented by his agents in all parts of the country. In fact, almost all the members of the Anglo-Jewish community appear to have been connected with his business transactions, and most of them acted as his agents. For a time he was in partnership with Isaac fil (son of) Josce, head of the London Community and officially recognised chief

(Marginal notes:)
Partnership between the king and the Jews.

Aaron of Lincoln.

Jew of the kingdom. Aaron lent large sums of money for the building of religious edifices, and it was with his assistance that at least sixteen abbeys and cathedrals, including the Abbey of St. Albans, Lincoln Minster, Peterborough Cathedral, as well as nine Cistercian abbeys were erected. At his death the owners of these edifices were indebted to him to the extent of 6400 marks (about £250,000 in the present currency). Thus, by the instrumentality of capital provided by Aaron, the Churchmen of Angevin England were enabled to raise those poems in architecture that are to-day the admiration of all beholders, as well as the headquarters of their faith. Aaron's activity was not, however, confined to financial transactions of this description. In commerce also his master-mind attained a position of eminence, and, among the records of the period still extant, are to be found references to his dealings on a considerable scale in articles of general consumption.

This tacit partnership between the crown and the Jews often made it an advantage to a debtor not to repay the capital of his debt. There was always a chance of the Jewish creditor dying, and the debtor might then, by paying a composition to the king, get quit of the debt at a relatively small cost to himself. The king's revenue derived from the Jews did not arise solely from these forfeitures. The Jews were not exempt from the usual fines levied on a variety of occasions in a man's life, such as marriage, journeys, &c., as well as the ransoms and compositions they were forced to pay in return for the king's benevolence, protection, license to trade, &c. In addition, in the purchase of justice Jews were among the king's best customers, and there were fines relating to law proceedings, amerciaments imposed on account of misdemeanours, and fines on discharge from imprisonment. Moreover, after the death of

The king's income from the Jews.

Stephen, the Jews were not overlooked when the
king was anxious to raise funds by means of gifts or
tallages. In 1168, on the conclusion of an alliance
with Frederick Barbarossa, some of the leading Jews
were seized and sent abroad, probably as hostages,
and on the remainder a tallage of 5000 marks was
levied. The same king, Henry II., twenty years later,
raised £60,000 (a quarter of their movables) by similar
means from the Jews of England, while the remainder
of the population contributed only £70,000—a tenth.
Dr. Jacobs estimates that at this period £3000, a
twelfth of the annual income of the State, was derived
from Jewish sources. The Jewish element being so
profitable a one in so far as the crown was concerned,
it can be understood there was considerable disagreement between the interests of the Church and the
king with regard to the conversion of Jews. It was
decidedly to the king's interest that the English Jews
should not be enticed away from Judaism. He did
not go so far as to forbid such change of faith or to
browbeat converts, as William II. had done, back to
their original community, but he took steps to penalise
converts, as a discouragement to the adoption of
Christianity ; the property of a Jew leaving his
ancestral faith was forfeited to the crown, which
thus compensated itself for the loss of the prospective
profits that would have accrued to it if the Jew had
remained within his community.

It is thus seen that the Jews of Angevin England by The Jews' value
their assistance enabled the Church and the barons to the State.
to erect buildings suitable for their purposes, and
that by means of Jewish money the latter were put
in a position to discharge their feudal obligations
to the king, as well as to take part in the contests for
the recovery of the Holy Land. The king, on the
other hand, by means of funds derived from Jewish
sources, was materially assisted in the government

of the kingdom, and his missions abroad, both war-like and peaceful, were rendered easier.   It was found that Jewish money could be useful in other directions also, and the results of a loan by Josce, Jew of Gloucester, in 1170 rudely awakened the king to the power of money and to the necessity for keeping the transactions of his Jews strictly under control.   In that year Richard Strongbow landed with an armed

The Jews and the conquest of Ireland. following in Ireland, and his operations ultimately led to the conquest of that island and its final annexation to the English Crown.   The expedition of Strongbow was merely a private venture conducted in defiance of the express prohibition of Henry, who feared, probably with justice, that Strongbow was anxious to carve out for himself a kingdom in the neigh-bouring island ; although in its immediate results it redounded to the advantage of the king of England. One of the direct consequences of the king's anger at this unauthorised expedition was the mulcting in fines of the Jews, who by their loans had rendered it possible.   In fact, in the absence of Jewish financiers Henry would have remained easy on that score, for without them Strongbow would have found it extremely difficult, if it had been at all possible, to translate his ambition into action.

AUTHORITIES :—Joseph Jacobs, "The Jews of Angevin Eng-land," "Little St. Hugh of Lincoln" (1895), "Aaron of Lincoln" (*Transactions, Jewish Historical Society*, vol. iii. 1899); B. L. Abrahams, "The Return of the Jews to England"; W. Prynne, "A Short Demurrer"; D'Bloissiers Tovey, *Anglia Judaica;* T. Madox, "History of the Exchequer"; J. E. Blunt, "The Jews in England"; Charles Gross, "The Exchequer of the Jews of England in the Middle Ages" (*Publications of the Anglo-Jewish Historical Exhibition*, 1888) ; A. Neubauer, "Notes on the Jews in Oxford"; A. Jessopp and M. R. James, "The Life and Miracles of St. William of Norwich" (1896) ; "Dictionary of National Biography," article "William of Norwich"; "Jewish Encyclo-pedia," article "Crusades."

CHAPTER IV

RICHARD I.'s CORONATION
(1154-1190)

DESPITE the occasional troubles and annoyances to which the Jews were subject, and the rising tide of anti-Jewish feeling on the part of most classes in the nation, the period that ended with the death of Henry II. was the Golden Age in early Anglo-Jewish history. Stephen by his protection prevented any imitation of crusading barbarities in his kingdom, and under his successor, Henry II., with the exception of occasional financial oppression, the Jews enjoyed the widest liberty. About the middle of the twelfth century an incursion of the Flemings into the south-eastern portion of the kingdom had involved the Christian population in considerable hardship, and Jews had suffered along with their fellow-Englishmen ; but the accession of Henry soon remedied this state of affairs, and within three months of the beginning of his reign the Flemings had left the country, " the disinherited get back their paternal property. . . . There is peace everywhere. . . . there come forth in safety, from the cities and castles, merchants to the fairs, Jews to seek their creditors (debtors ?)." The Jews spread still further throughout the country, and settled in many new centres. About 1164 the legal jurisdiction of the Jews was organised to their satisfaction. They were allowed their own tribunal, wherein Jewish law was enforced, and in this all disputes between Jews were settled. Of course, in cases in which Christians were involved, this court had no jurisdic-

tion ; but even in such instances, as has already
been noted, the Jews were allowed great advantages
over Christians, inasmuch as the oath of one Jew
was of as much avail as the oaths of twelve Christians.
In financial disputes the Jewish creditor had only to
prove the capital, while on the debtor lay the onus
of disproving the charges for interest.   Thirteen years
later, in 1177, a severe liability, under which the Jews
had hitherto laboured, was removed.   Until that date
they were allowed but òné cemetery in the country,
and the bodies of deceased Jews, wherever they happened to be, had to be brought to London for inter-
ment.   The removal of the limitation was accompanied
by that of the burden of which it was the cause, and
local cemeteries were established in various parts of
the country.   So satisfactory, on the whole, was the
condition of affairs in England that Jewish scholars
of European fame visited the country ; among others
Abraham ibn Ezra, the scholar and writer, in 1158,
and Isaac of Chernigov in 1181.

Relations with
the people.

On the expulsion of the Jews from France by Philip
Augustus the following year, a considerable number
of the exiles took refuge in this country.   The Jews
of England lived on fairly good terms with their
neighbours, including the clergy, and were accustomed to take refuge with their valuables in the abbeys
at times of commotion.   The community was also to
a slight extent recruited from among the natives, and
there are records of the conversion to Judaism of at
least two Cistercian monks.

An instance of the free intercourse between Jew and
Christian at this time is given by Giraldus Cambrensis.
A certain Jew, travelling towards Shrewsbury, found
himself in the company of Richard Peché, the archdeacon of Malpas, and a dean named Deville.   In the
course of conversation the archdeacon mentioned that
his jurisdiction extended from a place called Illstreet

as far as Malpas. On hearing this, the Jew, who was
of a witty disposition, replied : "Say you so, sir ?
God grant me then a good deliverance ! for it seems
I am riding in a country where Sin (Peché) is the
archbishop, and the Devil himself the dean ; where
the entrance into the archdeaconry is Ill-Street, and
the going-forth from it Bad Steps (Malpas)." A few
years later, on the occasion of a quarrel between the
archbishop and the monks of Canterbury, in which
the popular sympathies were on the side of the latter,
the Jews of the city took the same side, and sent food
and drink to feed the convent, "and likewise prayed
for the continuance of the convent in their synagogues.
The archbishop did not cease to take away nor the
Jews to present." We learn also, from both English
and Jewish sources, of the social intercourse between
the Jews and Christians of early Plantagenet England.

The satisfactory situation of the Jews of England The situation
was, however, not destined to endure, and the first changes.
sign of the coming change did not tarry long. Hitherto
the Jews, though suffering from many disabilities as
was inevitable, had at the same time enjoyed important
privileges. They were under the special protection of
the crown and had full liberty of movement ; although
debarred from many occupations, and from holding
land by feudal tenure, they were yet able to occupy
estates, and at least one entry in Domesday Book
is suspected of referring to a Jew. Moreover, the
public records of the twelfth century contain even
references to Anglo-Jewish knights. The Jews had
liberty of worship, and, from 1177, permission to
acquire cemeteries in all parts. In their liability to
fines on succession to property they were only on
an equality with Christian usurers, and there are
instances in which the property of deceased Jews
was freed from confiscation on proof that they died
innocent of the offence of usury.

C

The Assize
of Arms.

In 1181 came the first act of anti-Jewish discrimination—the opening of a century of persecution and
massacre. By the Assize of Arms of that year it was
enacted that, "No Jew shall keep with him mail or
hauberk, but let him sell or give them away, or in
some other way remove them from him."   Thus were
the Jews disarmed in preparation for the massacres
of eight years later.

The first two Crusades, it has been seen, fraught
with intense suffering for the Jewries of the Continent,
left England untouched and hardly affected. But a
distant murmur of the tragical occurrences on the
Continent reached the ears of Anglo-Jewry, and even
the English people took relatively little more than
an academic interest in the two first great efforts for
the recovery of the Holy Land. For England and

The Third
Crusade.

the Jews of England the Third Crusade differed *in toto*
from its two predecessors.   In the first place the
English contingent in the joint army of Christendom
no longer consisted of a comparatively insignificant
number of individuals, each solely concerned with
himself and his retainers. One half of the new army
had been recruited in England for its specific purpose, and at its head, the joint-leader of the expedition, was the first soldier of Christendom, who had
just ascended the English throne.

On the Jews of England the first effect of the
new Crusade was the levy of the immense tallage
of £66.000, previously mentioned. The preparations
commenced before the death of Henry II., and it was
under that monarch that this act of financial oppression was perpetrated. The following year, 1189, the
Jews of London suffered in their persons as well as

Richard I.'s
coronation.

in their property. Richard I.'s coronation was the
earliest English coronation of which there is any
detailed account, and it was conducted on a most
elaborate scale. The ceremony itself took place in

Westminster Abbey, and was followed by a banquet in the neighbouring palace. Of the disturbances that accompanied the coronation there are several accounts, which, differing slightly in details, are in agreement on all points of consequence. Among those who made their way to Westminster to take part in the important event was a deputation of the leading Jews of the kingdom, bearing costly presents for the king, from whom they hoped for a continuation of the favour that his predecessors had conferred upon them. Although the chief Jewish centres in the kingdom had sent of their leading members to take part in the deputation, they were not allowed to be present at the ceremony, either because it was considered a sacrilege for a Jew to be admitted to a Christian place of worship, or on account of the fear lest Jews (and women were excluded from the coronation for a similar reason) might exercise sorcery over the participants in the ceremony. The Jews, however, though debarred from entering the church, mingled with the crowd that assembled at its gates. Here, in the jostling of the crowd, aided probably by the eagerness of the Jews to see something of the ceremony, one or two Jews were pushed through the gates, and the keepers, on perceiving this, rudely beat them and drove them out. The populace outside, collected from all parts and to a considerable extent attendants of the nobles who were taking part in the ceremony, seeing this, and remembering the prohibition the king had issued against the intended Jewish visitors, immediately came to the conclusion that the king desired his people to celebrate the coronation by attacking the Jews. Little encouragement was needed, London Jewry and immediately a riot arose, in which the Jews were sacked. the victims and the Christians the assailants. Every Jew to be found was beaten and many killed. They were pursued to their houses, which were attacked, and if too strong to be broken into—for the Jews' houses were among the strongest in the kingdom—the straw roofs were set on fire, and in many instances the houses were burnt together with their inmates. Rapine, murder, and plunder became the order of the day. The greed for spoil grew still stronger, and Christian turned against Christian in the scramble for the plunder. The conflagration was not confined to the houses of the Jews, but spread to those of their Christian neighbours ; rioters in their rage for booty were not too careful to confine their attention to Jewish houses, and occasionally, intentionally or by accident, broke into others occupied by Christians that gave promise of being worth the trouble of attack.

Action of the King.

The king, hearing of the tumult while at his coronation banquet,[1] sent Ranulph de Glanvil, the chief justice, together with several of the nobles, to put an end to the rioting and to protect the Jews from the populace. The latter had, however, by this time become so excited and intent on outrage and plunder that the efforts of the royal messengers were ignored, and, to avoid being themselves attacked, they were compelled to withdraw. The rioting continued unabated from midday on the Sunday until two o'clock on the following afternoon, operations being conducted during the night by the light of the burning houses. When at length the movement subsided, it was not because the populace had recovered from its intoxication or repented of its outburst, but merely from exhaustion. Whether Richard was friendly disposed to the Jews or not, he was certainly very indignant that the occasion of his coronation should have been marred by such a riotous outbreak, and

---

[1] According to some accounts the outbreak occurred in consequence of he penetration of Jews into the banqueting-hall, subsequent to the coronation ceremony.

that his first command as King of England should
have been disregarded. He was perhaps more anxious
that his offended dignity, rather than that the murdered and plundered Jews, should be avenged, but
insuperable difficulties stood in the way of due punishment. If the transgressors had been nobles or prominent members of the community they could have
been dealt with, although delay might have been
expedient. The uprising was, however, a popular
one, and its participants were unknown. On the
conclusion of the coronation celebrations they had
scattered with their masters into all parts of the kingdom. Those masters could not be held responsible
for offences of which personally they were guiltless,
although there was a suspicion that some of the
barons were not altogether unconnected with the
movement, which must have appealed to many of
them as an easy method of liquidating the debts they
owed to the Jews. Richard was determined, however, that the criminals should not go altogether
unpunished. Several were apprehended, and three The punish-
ment.
hanged; one because he had stolen goods of a fellow-
Christian, and the other two because a fire they had
kindled to burn a Jew's house had, unfortunately,
spread to that of a neighbouring Christian. The
outbreak was not merely of an economic and plun-
dering description; it had also a very decided religious basis. The persecuted Jews were, in some
cases, offered by their assailants the alternatives of
death and baptism. The overwhelming majority
unhesitatingly preferred the martyr's fate. A few,
however, were cast in a less heroic mould. The
representatives of the important Jewish centre of
York in the deputation that had intended waiting
upon the king were Josce and Benedict. Both were
involved in the tumult and fled. The former escaped
from his persecutors but Benedict, less active, was

captured and beaten. His vigour impaired by age and his wounds, Benedict chose baptism in preference to death, and was immediately baptized in the Church of the Innocents by William, Prior of the Church of St. Mary of York. The following day Benedict, whose Christian name was William, was sent for by the king. When questioned he replied that, although having accepted baptism in order to escape death, he was a Jew at heart. Turning to the Archbishop of Canterbury, the king inquired how Benedict should be dealt with. The churchman, who was not over learned, and more fitted for the battlefield than for the council chamber or the altar—he was killed shortly afterwards at the walls of Acre—replied testily, " If he will not be a servant of God, let him be a servant of the Devil," and so, as Hoveden says, Benedict, "like a dog to his vomit . . . returned to the Jewish depravity." The terrible ordeal through which Benedict had passed, however, speedily effected the consummation from which the act of temporary apostasy had saved him. On the way home to York Benedict died of his wounds and sufferings at Northampton, where he held considerable property. It is related that his body was refused Jewish burial on account of his apostasy, and Christians declined to dispose of it on the ground of his relapse to Judaism. A few months later his widow and children were burnt in their house during the outbreak at York.

Despite the efforts of the king to protect the Jews, in furtherance of which he sent writs to all parts of the kingdom, forbidding any molestation to be offered to the Jews, the events in the capital found their echoes in the provinces. Exaggerated accounts spread throughout the country of the great riches the people had acquired by the plunder of the Jews, and those who heard these stories were anxious to imitate their neighbours and enrich themselves also at the

Benedict of York.

expense of the hated Jews, Anti-Jewish outbreaks arose almost simultaneously in all parts of the country. At Dunstable it is said the Jews escaped massacre by accepting Christianity in a body. Of the outbreak at Lynn the following explanation was given when the townspeople were subsequently called to account. It was said that a Jew, who had been converted to Christianity, had aroused by his apostasy the enmity of his fellow-Jews of the town. These waylaid him one day for the purpose of getting him into their power, but he fled and took refuge in a church. The Jews followed him there, and also entered the sacred building. The townspeople, although indignant at the outrage, refrained from all interference, in consequence of the writ of the king concerning the Jews, that had recently reached them; but the foreign crew of a ship lying in the harbour had, however, no such scruples. Immediately on learning of the sacrilege, they landed, bent on avenging it. The houses of the Jews were burnt, they themselves murdered, and their valuables stolen. Loaded with booty the sailors returned to their ship and sailed away, leaving the townsfolk to explain the incident to the messengers of their indignant ruler. Considerable doubt must have been thrown on this narrative by an incident that immediately succeeded this outbreak. A celebrated Jewish physician, well known and respected in Lynn, arrived in that town to find the bodies of his co-religionists lying in the streets and their property stolen. Indignant at the sight, he denounced the atrocities and threatened vengeance. Despite his popularity, his outspokenness cost him his life, although the foreign sailors were no longer in the harbour.

At Stamford, during the fair of mid-Lent, a number of young Crusaders had assembled. Anxious to emulate the exploits of their predecessors in the Wars of the Cross, and, moreover, unable for want of funds to set out on their expedition, they determined to attain both ends by one and the same means. The Jews were attacked, but for the most part took refuge in the Castle. Comparatively few were slain. Their houses, however, left unprotected, were sacked by the Crusaders. At Stamford on this occasion occurred one of the earliest recorded instances of a baron openly showing his sympathy with the perpetrators of anti-Jewish excesses. Gerard de Camville, a great baron, and at the time High Sheriff of the county, was among the abettors of the outrage. A month earlier, on February 6, the Jews of Norwich had suffered a similar attack. In that instance also the majority took refuge in the Royal Castle and thus escaped. Those however who had not the time to do so were slaughtered, and all the available property of the Jews was pillaged.

At Norwich.

AUTHORITIES :—J. Jacobs, "The Jews of Angevin England"; W. Prynne, "A Short Demurrer"; D'Bloissiers Tovey, *Anglia Judaica;* R. Holinshed, "Chronicles"; J. E. Blunt, "The Jews in England"; L. O. Pike, "A History of Crime in England"; Francis Peck, "The Antiquarian Annals of Stamford"; W. Rye, "The Persecutions of the Jews in England." The *Transactions of the Jewish Historical Society,* vol. v. (now in the press), will contain a full account of Richard I.'s coronation, by the late Rev. S. Singer.

CHAPTER V

THE MASSACRE AT YORK
(1190)

OF all the incidents in the massacres of 1189-90, the events at York, the northern capital of the kingdom, were the most terrible. The earliest reference in the records of the York Jewish community appears under the year 1130, but this is of such a nature as to render it certain that the community had then been long established, and was by that time in a position of great prosperity. The overshadowing position occupied by Aaron of Lincoln passed on his death to two Jews of York, Josce and Benedict, who, it will be remembered, were to have repre-sented the northern community at the coronation of King Richard. Both were men of great wealth, and their extensive operations and spacious and princely mansions aroused the comments of contem-porary chroniclers. So long as the king remained in England, the knowledge that any further attacks on the Jews would earn his stern disapproval, and probably lead to punishment, suppressed all active manifestations of the dislike which, for different reasons, the Jews had by now aroused among most classes in the country. With Richard, however, all other desires were subservient to the ambition to be the instrument of the recovery of the Holy Land. To this end even the Crown of England was but a means, and, at the first opportunity, Richard crossed to the Continent on his way to Jerusalem. His departure was immediately made sensible to

41

the Jews in all parts of the kingdom; the hitherto
(with few exceptions) passive hostility became active
aggression; the lowering looks and muttered curses
were rapidly translated into deeds of violence. Of
all the blows that fell in quick succession on Anglo-
Jewry during the year 1190, the most crushing was
that which annihilated the prosperous community of
York. Elsewhere pillage and murder were rampant,
and but sections of the Jewish population, frequently
minorities, escaped. At York the whole of the local
Jewry was destroyed and not an individual Jew
survived

Under cover of an outbreak of fire, whether
incendiary or accidental is not known, in the city
of York, an attack was made by a certain section
of the populace on the house of Benedict, who had
died at Northampton on his way home from London.
The house was sacked; its contents plundered;
Benedict's widow, children, and friends who, apparently fearing an outbreak, had taken refuge in
it, murdered, and the building burnt to the ground.
This, the first incident in the excesses of York, was
isolated. His friends' fate, however, alarmed Josce,
who, applying to the governor of the Royal Castle,
was invited to place his family and his valuables
there for greater security. This offer was accepted,
and Josce and his family, together with a considerable treasure, took refuge in the Castle, his house
being left with a small guard. The rabble, however,
once having tasted Jewish blood, craved for more.
Possibly they were further excited by the knowledge
of Josce's wealth. Once more they collected at
night, and Josce's house shared the fate of that of
Benedict. By this time it was manifest that great
danger threatened the Jews of York, and especially
any who might remain unprotected in the city. The
greater number of the Jewish inhabitants hastily

The Jews take refuge in the Castle.

deserted their houses, which were immediately
sacked, and joined Josce and his family in the
Royal Castle. Those who hesitated to do likewise,
or tarried too long, were slain. Possibly, as in the
cases of Norwich and Stamford, the protection of
the Royal Castle and its governor would have been
sufficient, and the orgy of lawlessness having run
its course the Jews might have returned once more
with their rescued property to their ruined homes.
Unnerved, however, by the atrocities to which they
had been witness, terrified by the rumours that had
reached them of the awful fate of kindred communities elsewhere, doubtful whom they might trust
in their extremity, and possibly also deceived by
false counsellors anxious to deprive them of their
only protection, the Jews were themselves the cause
of the next entry in the terrible catalogue of their
misfortunes. The governor, having to leave the The governor
Castle on business one day, was refused re-admission excluded.
on his return by the Jews he had sheltered there,
fearful lest he might have arranged to betray them.
Such, it had been suggested to the refugees, was
the object of the governor's business in the town.
The governor, of course, could not remain passive
while excluded from the Castle entrusted to his
charge by the king ; and, unable to recover its
custody, he appealed for assistance to the sheriff of
the county, who happened to be in the city at the
time. His application, if it needed any support,
readily obtained it from those leaders of the anti-
Jewish movement who held high positions in the
realm, and the sheriff consented to use his forces
in recovering the Royal Castle from the hands of
the Jewish rebels. His army was immediately joined
by all those who had hitherto been prevented by
the walls of the Castle from assuaging their thirst
for Jewish blood. The combined forces speedily

The Castle
attacked.

attacked the Castle, with such zeal on the part of
the irregulars that the sheriff quickly divined their
object, and, repenting of his determination, gave
orders for the attack to cease.   To foment a disturbance is, however, far easier than to suppress
one, and this the sheriff soon learnt.   His orders to
attack were carried out almost before they were
given ; those to desist passed unheeded.   The better
class of inhabitants as a whole refused to give any
countenance to the excesses, or to take part in the
attack on the Castle.   The clergy, however, had no
scruples in the matter.   They eagerly joined the
mob, and one in particular, a hermit of the *Præ-
monstratensian* Order, was especially zealous in the
cause.   Attired in his white surplice, he stood all
day in the foremost ranks, exhorting those around
him with the cry : "Destroy the enemies of Christ !
Destroy the enemies of Christ !"   So convinced
was he of the holiness of his mission, that before
going to the battle each morning this man of God
was accustomed to partake of the Eucharist.   Overcome by his zeal, he ventured one day too close
to the walls and was crushed by a stone that fell
from the battlements—the only one of the besiegers
to be killed.

Terrible plight
of the Jews.

Meanwhile the plight of the Jews within the Castle
was a terrible one.   There was huddled together a
miscellaneous crowd of men, women, and children,
old and young, rabbis and laymen.   Without arms
they could only interpose the walls and gates between
themselves and their persecutors.   Still worse, they
were without food, and, even if able to withstand the
attacks of those without, must inevitably have suc-
cumbed to starvation.   Friendless in the midst of a
hostile country there could be no hope of relief, nor
did it seem that the passions of the mob would be
assuaged in time to save their destined victims.   To

open the gates meant instant massacre ; to keep them closed, either the same fate or death by starvation. The hopeless condition of affairs was recognised by the defenders. A council was called. Up rose the learned Rabbi Yomtob of Joigny, a scholar of great renown, who had come to York from France in order to act as the spiritual head of the community, and said : "Men of Israel! the God of our fathers, to Whom none can say what doest Thou? commands us, at this time, to die for His law ; and behold, death is even before our eyes, and there is nothing left us to consider but how to undergo it in the most reputable and easy manner. If we fall into the hands of our enemies (which I think there is no possibility of escaping), our deaths will not only be cruel, but ignominious. They will not only torment us, but despitefully use us. My advice therefore is, that we voluntarily surrender those lives to our Creator, which He seems to call for, and not wait for any other executioners than ourselves. The fact is both rational and lawful ; nor do we want examples, from amongst our illustrious ancestors, to prove it so. They have frequently proceeded in the like manner, upon the same occasions."[1]

The Jews take counsel.

Such a heroic course of action did not meet with unanimous approval, and several whose courage was insufficient to enable them to take the supreme step expressed disapproval of it. Then the rabbi rose a second time and called upon those who were not of his opinion to withdraw. This they did, but the great majority remained behind and steadfastly proceeded to put into execution the advice they had received. First they burnt or otherwise destroyed all their property so that none of it should fall into the hands

The Jews destroy themselves to escape the populace.

---

[1] This speech of Rabbi Yomtob is quoted from Tovey's translation of Walter of Hemingburgh. As suggested by Dr. Joseph Jacobs, it is undoubtedly apocryphal, and appears to be based on that of Eleazar of Masada, as reported by Josephus on a similar occasion.

of their enemies. Josce with a sharp knife cut the throats of "his much loved wife, Anna" and their children. The other heads of families imitated his example, and then slew one another, until at length Rabbi Yomtob and Josce alone remained alive. Josce was put to death by his companion, who finally slew himself.

Those Jews whose courage had shrunk from the supreme ordeal were meanwhile, during that dreadful night, defending themselves from the flames that had spread from the property of the Jews to the building itself. In the morning, when the besiegers returned to their task, they were received by the wretched remnant of victims, who, from the battlements, narrated the terrible events that had happened during the night within the keep of York Castle. In confirmation of their statements they threw the bodies of the slaughtered over the battlements. The survivors begged for mercy. Any price were they willing to pay for their lives. Willingly would they accept baptism if only their lives were spared. The offer was accepted, and the terror-stricken fugitives were allowed to come out of the Castle. But the object of the besiegers was not to gain converts, but to shed still more Jewish blood. Despite the solemn promise of protection, despite the terrible occurrences that should have moved to pity the most callous of murderers, despite the harmlessness of the last insignificant remnant of what had once been the wealthy, distinguished, and prosperous Jewish community of York, the fugitives were barely without the gates before they were massacred. And then the true meaning of the whole movement became apparent. From the Castle the mob, influenced by those who knew how to profit by Jewish misfortunes, made its way to the Minster. By threats they compelled the guardians of the sacred edifice to deliver up all the

The survivors massacred.

records of debts to the Jews deposited there for greater safety. These being collected together were set on fire within the building itself, and on being consumed, the mob dispersed, and the city returned to its wonted tranquillity. The number of Jewish victims at York has been variously estimated at from 150 to 1500. From the subsequent punishment meted out by Richard, the names of some of the ringleaders in the disturbances have been preserved. Many were apparently mere citizens of York, but in addition there were several nobles of the most prominent families in the north of England. Those of Percy and Pudsey were especially represented. Of the nobles who were punished for participation in the disturbance, the following names are recorded : Richard Malebisse, Kt. (punningly translated Richard the Evil Beast), his squires Walter de Carton and Richard de Cuckney, Sir William de Percy, Picot de Percy, Roger de Ripun, Alan Malekake, Philip of Fauconbridge, Marmaduke Darell, Robert de Gant, and Robert de Turnham. From these names and further references to them in the records, still another confirmation of the real reason for the *émeute* is to be found. With few exceptions these barons were all indebted to the Jews, and to them the destruction of the records of their indebtedness must have seemed an easy method of settling their accounts. They were, however, labouring under a delusion, for duplicates of at least some of the destroyed records seem to have been in existence, and for years after the massacre the officers of the king were busy collecting the debts, forfeited to the crown, due to the martyred Jews of York.

At Bury St. Edmunds, where the monastery had got deeply into debt with the Jews, the sacristan was accustomed to shelter them and their belongings in times of commotion. But on the 18th of March, 1190, fifty-seven Jews were slain, and shortly afterwards the remainder were expelled at the instance of Abbot Samson on the ground that every man of the town had to be a vassal of St. Edmund, which no Jew, of course, could be. At Lincoln the Jews saved themselves by taking refuge in the Castle. They were befriended by the Bishop Saint Hugh, whose death ten years later was very sincerely mourned by the local community. At Colchester, Thetford, and Ospringe also, the Jews suffered massacre.

In due course tidings of the atrocities reached the ears of the king, who was enraged both that his strict injunctions not to harm the Jews had been disobeyed, and also that the evidence of the debts, which, in the natural course, would have fallen to the crown,

should have been destroyed. Geoffrey Rydel, Bishop of Ely, the Chancellor of the Kingdom, was commanded forthwith to repair to York and inflict punishment on the authors of the outrages. Collecting an army he soon arrived, but the miscreants primarily responsible had either fled into Scotland or joined the Crusade. The governor of the Castle and the sheriff were both removed from their offices on the ground that they were responsible in not preventing the disturbances, and several of the leading citizens compelled to give their recognizances that they would appear to answer for their conduct before the king on his return. The estates of Robert de Gant, Robert de Turnham, and Richard Malebisse, who had fled, were confiscated, but they were, after intervals of varying duration, restored. Notwithstanding the massacre, none of the guilty participants paid the penalty with his life.

AUTHORITIES :—J. Jacobs, " The Jews of Angevin England" ; W. Prynne, " A Short Demurrer" ; D'Bloissiers Tovey, *Anglia*

Judaica; R. Holinshed, "Chronicles"; Walter of Hemingburgh, "Chronicon" (H. C. Hamilton, editor, vol. i., 1808); J. E. Blunt, "The Jews in England"; Robert Davies, "The Mediæval Jews of York" (*The Yorkshire Archæological and Topographical Journal*, vol. iii., 1875); W. Hargrove, "History and Description of the Ancient City of York" (1818).

CHAPTER VI

THE EXCHEQUER OF THE JEWS

(1194–1216)

Richard
inquires into
the outbreaks. AT this point, however, Richard was unwilling to let
the matter rest, but until his return to England
nothing further could be done. This return was
considerably delayed by Richard's captivity, but
when at length he reached England in 1194, he
set zealously to work to have the position of the
Jews carefully investigated. Justices itinerant were
appointed to proceed to the different cities in which
anti-Jewish excesses had taken place to make inquiry
into them, and at the same time to get exact statements of the property of the Jews who had been slain,
and especially of the debts that were due to them.
In the same year ordinances were drawn up for the
registration of the estates and possessions of the
Jews. The outbreak at York had shown that the
financial interests of the Jews, and consequently also
of the king, were placed in considerable jeopardy by
the system then in force of recording debts to the
Jews. The northern barons had undoubtedly been
greatly influenced in their attack on the Jews by
the hope, justified in many instances, that in destroying the available records of their indebtedness they
would at the same time liquidate the debts. Although,
in the case of York, a few of the records were
in duplicate, many, almost certainly the majority,
had not been copied, and the incendiarism of the
rioters deprived the king of large amounts that
would in the ordinary course have reverted to

him in consequence of the murder of the Jewish creditors.

He determined, however, to profit by experience, and established in London and the other chief towns where Jews lived registries of the bonds. Officials, consisting of chirographers, copyists, and clerks, were appointed to take charge of these registries. Of the first-named officials two were Jews. All acknowledgments of debts were to be in duplicate, one copy to be retained by the Jewish creditor, and the other preserved in the archives. The chests in which these records were to be lodged were to be trebly locked, one key to be entrusted to the Jewish chirographers, a second to their Christian colleagues, and the third to the clerks. A further record was to be kept by the clerks of all payments of debts or alterations in the deeds, and no such alteration was to be made except in the presence of a majority of the officials. The acquittals of the creditors were written in Hebrew with a Latin translation, sometimes in Latin alone or in Norman French alone, occasionally in Latin written in Hebrew characters. They were known by their Hebrew name of *Shetar*, and it has been suggested that the Star Chamber, subsequently so prominent in English history, derived its name from being the depository of these *Shetars*. The regulations adopted at this time underwent some modifications at a later date, but in their essentials they remained unaltered until the Expulsion. The Ordinances of 1194 also laid down that a register should be kept of all the property of the Jews, who were also compelled to promise under oath to denounce any of their people guilty of offences against the law. While affording the Jews additional security, this arrangement also proved of still greater advantage to the crown. Henceforth, the murder of a Jewish creditor instead of releasing the debtor

The debts of the Jews to be recorded in duplicate.

Shetaroth.

merely put him directly in the power of the king;
while to destroy the record of the debt in the possession of the creditor was but a futile proceeding.
Thus the king was secured against loss by the murder
of his Jews. He was, moreover, placed in a position
to become acquainted with their exact resources, and
henceforth when in need of money could tax them
still more heavily than before, with the certainty of
his demands being satisfied.

The Exchequer of the Jews. From these registries of debts, as well as from the
branch of the exchequer that had since 1186 been
dealing with the estate of Aaron of Lincoln, grew a
new and separate institution, the Exchequer of the
Jews. The exact date of the establishment of this
institution is unknown, but in 1198 are first mentioned
the justices of the Jews who held the status of barons
of the Exchequer. Of these justices there were four,
two of the first appointed being Jews, Benedict de
Talemunt and Joseph Aaron. It does not seem,
however, that any further Jews were appointed to the
office. Jews were, however, also eligible for the minor
offices, and these were frequently held by them. The
Exchequer of the Jews exercised jurisdiction in cases
in which both Jews and Christians were concerned—
suits to which both parties were Jews were settled by
their own courts—although instances are to be found
in which such cases were heard before the ordinary
courts. The justices were assisted in their deliberations by the chief presbyter, whose participation was
probably required when questions of Jewish law arose.
By this legislation the justices of the Jews became
in fact the official protectors of Anglo-Jewry, and as
such their defenders against the encroachments of the
ecclesiastical authorities. The justices were, however, at all times subordinate to the treasurer and
barons of the Exchequer, but they were none
the less men of importance, and included among

their number a former treasurer of the Exchequer, Peter de Rivallis, chief justices such as Stephen Segrave and Hugh Bigod, royal favourites, and other influential barons. Concerning the duties and privileges of the *Presbyter Judæorum*, the chief presbyter, but little is known. He was appointed by the king, and for life, and was chosen from among the most prominent Jews in the country.[1] Whether he had any special learned or theological qualifications as his title suggests is not known.[2]

The *Presbyter Judæorum*, or Chief Presbyter.

Among the most important of the functions of the Exchequer of the Jews was the arrangement of a continual flow of money from the Jews to the royal treasury. Four different channels were available for this flow. The royal revenue derived from the Jews came in the form of reliefs, escheats. fines, and tallages. The first named were succession duties, which amounted, in the case of Jews in the thirteenth century, on an average to a third of the value of the property inherited. Escheats were estates forfeited in consequence of legal offences committed by their owners. By this means charges of ritual murder, coin-clipping, &c., were rendered profitable to the crown. Fines— the term being used in the widest sense—meant payments on a variety of occasions. They were levied on marriage, and sometimes on refusals to marry ; on the recovery of a debt, and on the opening of proceedings for the recovery of a debt. Occasionally the king levied fines on both parties to a suit, and decided in favour of the more lavish of the suitors. The fourth and most remunerative form of taxation was the tallages. These were arbitrary taxes, levied whenever

Jewish sources of income to the king.

The tallages.

---

[1] The first of these of whom there is any record was Jacob of London, confirmed in 1199.

[2] Dr. H. Adler in the "Chief Rabbis of England" suggests that this personage was in fact as well as in name *Presbyter omnium Judæorum Angliæ*, and exercised functions analogous to those of a chief rabbi of to-day.

the king was in need of money. The earliest occasions on which the English Jews suffered this form of oppression have been mentioned. They became gradually more frequent and more oppressive. It must not be thought, however, that the king always received the whole amount he demanded. The demands were sometimes so exorbitant that it was impossible to comply with them. On other occasions the amount of the tallage was accepted in instalments spread over a number of years. Dr. C. Gross estimates that the average annual income derived from this source during the century preceding the Expulsion was between £5000 and £10,000. In the money of that day this was an enormous sum, and at the lowest estimate equalled a thirteenth of the total revenue of the kingdom. The tallage was sometimes levied as a poll-tax, but more often collectively, the assessment of individuals being arranged by the Jewish community. The assessment was frequently entrusted to specially chosen Jews of prominence, who were personally held responsible for the collection of their respective amounts, and in case of distraint they were required to assist the sheriffs. By Edward I. Christians, often the heads of neighbouring religious houses, were entrusted with the collection, and a few wealthy Jews named as sureties. An ever ready means of obtaining the last available penny of the tallages was a scrutiny of the records of the debts reposing in the local registries, the seizure of a proportion of them sufficient to satisfy the demands of the Royal Exchequer, and the enforcement of payment of them. If the amount of the debt were insufficient, a further step was to imprison the wife and family of the Jew on whom pressure was to be brought, and even the Jew himself ; whereupon his property was sold, and the proceeds poured into the Exchequer. So excessive did these extortions become that the Jews were

Extent of the tallages.

Enforcement of payment.

often reduced to a state of poverty, and forced at times, it is said, to beg from door to door. Their sufferings appealed to their neighbours, and, as Matthew Paris says, " even Christians pitied and wept over their afflictions." At length, in 1254, through their spokesman, the Chief Presbyter Elias, they asked to be permitted to leave the country, for they had no more to give in response to the pressure of the tax-gatherers. But the king recognised the value of his Jews, and refused them leave to depart. Thirty-five years earlier Henry had issued orders to the Warden of the Cinque Ports not to permit Jews to leave the country. The Jews beg for permission to leave the country.

Despite this unconscionable extortion, the Exchequer of the Jews was not an unmixed evil, so far as the Jews themselves were concerned. If, on the one hand, it was merely the instrument of the rapacity of the king, on the other it preserved them from the oppression of others, and secured for the Jews, in suits with fellow-subjects, and even in criminal cases, the justice that would doubtless have often been denied them by the ordinary courts of the land. The advantages to the Jews of their Exchequer.

The terrible experiences through which the English Jews had passed during the reign of Richard had not only, by means of murder and flight, reduced the Jewish population; it had also discouraged all increase in their numbers by means of immigration. To the continental Jew, England was no longer the attractive country it had appeared to his ancestors of the eleventh and early twelfth centuries. The blood accusations, the popular anti-Jewish risings, and the royal extortions that, at the opening of the thirteenth century, were just commencing, had deprived it of its previous enviable position of a land of refuge. The consequent diminution in Jewish prosperity reacted on the prosperity of the king ; and John, immediately on his accession, recognised the necessity for more effectually protecting the Jews, and restoring the confidence that had been destroyed by the events of the previous decade. His first act was intended to flatter the religious susceptibilities of the community by the appointment of a John creates the office of chief presbyter. chief presbyter, an office apparently first created at that time. Jacob of London, the first incumbent of the office, was granted by charter absolute freedom of movement and safe conduct throughout the kingdom. He was described as our royal Jew, and removed from all other jurisdiction than that of the king or his chief justice. In his safe conduct John described Jacob as " our dear friend" (*dilectus et familiaris noster*), and directed that he, his attendants, and his property, should be guarded as if they were the king's.

The Charter of the Jews. Two years later, in 1201, a remarkable charter of liberties was granted to the Jews of England and Normandy. That of Henry I., which had been confirmed by Richard, had apparently only been granted to certain individuals. The new charter was extended to the whole of the community. All the old privileges —freedom of movement, relief from the ordinary customs, tolls, &c., permission to settle in any part of the kingdom, the grant of redress if molested, permission to hold lands in pledge, to buy whatever was offered, with the two exceptions mentioned in the previous charter ; to sell their pledges after keeping them the stipulated period, to be tried by their peers, and to be sworn on the Pentateuch—were confirmed. Moreover, the heirs of a deceased Jew were allowed to inherit his property on payment of the accustomed fines. In disputes concerning money the Jewish creditor was required only to prove the capital, while it rested with the Christian debtor to disprove the interest claimed. The Jews were exempted from all jurisdiction, excepting that of the king and his local governors. In the charter the king called upon all his loyal subjects to protect the Jews and their rights whenever necessary, and threatened with penalties any who might invade those rights. In cases of dispute between a Christian and a Jew at least two witnesses, one Christian and one Jewish, were required. At the same time, in a supplementary charter, John authorised the Jews to have all differences among themselves, that did not pertain to the pleas of the crown, settled by their own courts, according to Jewish law. Moreover, he undertook not to compel any Jew to give evidence against another Jew. The price the Jews of England paid for these charters was four thousand marks, payable in four half-yearly instalments. Such exceptional favours had their natural consequences. Confidence was restored in Anglo-Jewry, and the inflow of Jews from the Continent resumed.

The favour of the king did not, however, make the Jews more popular with the people, and despite the strict injunctions laid down in their charters the Jews were by no means exempt from attack. In consequence of such untoward events in London, the Jews appealed to the king for protection in 1204. John's action was not delayed. He immediately wrote to the mayor and barons of London pointing out that "he could not but wonder, since they well knew what special protection he had lately granted the Jews, they should so little regard his peace, as to suffer them to be evil entreated ; especially when other parts of the Nation gave them no disturbance." He commanded them to "take particular care how they were injured for the future . . . if any ill happened to the Jews through their connivance or neglect, they should be answerable for it." *John protects the Jews of London.*

For ten years, until the Jews felt assured of their permanent protection, John continued to treat them with kindness, but then his attitude towards them *John's attitude changes.*

began to change. The first signs of the altered
circumstances were the arbitrary confiscation of the
property of individual Jews and its presentation to
those of his favourites who happened to covet it. It
seems that it was only necessary for one of John's
favourites to express a desire for some article or estate
belonging to a Jew for him to receive it. The following year, 1210, the work of harrying the Jews was
resumed on a gigantic scale. The whole of the
Jewish population of both sexes was thrown into
prison, while the extent of their wealth was investigated with a view to its confiscation. The most
barbarous means were used to compel the Jews to
disclose the extent of their property. Pleas of poverty
were of no avail. Stow[1] says that most suffered the
loss of an eye. An especially terrible instance of
John's relentless cruelty was that of a Jew of Bristol,
whose property it was considered was sufficient to
justify the extortion of the enormous sum of ten
thousand marks of silver. In reply to the remonstrances that the sum exceeded his means, John gave
instructions that a tooth a day should be extracted
until the amount was forthcoming. The Jew suffered
the loss of seven teeth, and then having obtained,
either from his own means or with the assistance of
friends, the amount necessary to satisfy his torturer,
saved his eighth. The whole amount obtained by
this wholesale act of oppression was sixty-six thousand marks. Its consequences were such as to
cause so large an emigration of Jews, that a general
expulsion has been attributed by some historians to
this year.

The survivors obtained a respite of four years, at
the end of which term, the king being once more in

The whole of Anglo-Jewry imprisoned.

---

[1] He of course wrote some centuries after these events, but as " the
most accurate and business-like of English annalists or chroniclers of the
sixteenth century," his evidence is of some value.

want of money, pressure was again brought to bear upon the Jews, some of whom were committed to prison until payment had been made. A further respite from the oppression of the king was interrupted by an attack by the barons, who were then at war with their ruler. The Jewry of London was sacked, its treasures appropriated, its houses demolished, and their material used for the repair of the walls of the city. From another point of view Anglo-Jewry came into prominence in the same year (1215). The Great Charter wrung from John by his insurgent barons, in addition to taking note of a variety of other matters concerning the common weal, enacted that during the minority of heirs inheriting debts to the Jews, no interest should accrue on those debts; and that if such debts became due to the king only the amounts stated in the deeds should be claimed. In the event of the death of a debtor, his widow should have her dower, on which no part of any of his debts should be charged. In similar circumstances the children, if minors, should receive from the estate reasonable amounts for their support, "and the Jews' debt shall be paid out of the residue." These references to Jews were omitted from subsequent confirmations.

London Jewry sacked by the barons.

Jews and Magna Charta.

The peace restored by Magna Charta was but short-lived, and war soon broke out again. In the hostilities that ensued the Scotch were involved. Invading England, the king of Scotland was defeated by John and a number of prisoners taken. These were treated with extreme cruelty, and in this connection the Jews were used in a new capacity. So frightful were the tortures that John wished inflicted on his prisoners, that his ordinary free subjects refused to take any part in their execution. Denied the service of his ordinary subjects, John had recourse to his Jews, whom he compelled to act as the ministers of his barbarous designs.[1]

AUTHORITIES :—J. M. Rigg, "Select Pleas, &c.," "Calendar of the Plea Rolls of the Exchequer of the Jews" (1905); T. Madox, "History of the Exchequer"; C. Gross, "The Exchequer of the Jews of England"; M. D. Davis, "Hebrew Deeds of English Jews" (1888); W. Prynne, "A Short Demurrer"; D'Bloissiers Tovey, *Anglia Judaica;* B. L. Abrahams, "The Expulsion of the Jews from England"; J. E. Blunt, "The Jews in England"; Rymer's "Fœdera"; "Dictionary of Political Economy," article "Jews, Exchequer of the"; J. Jacobs, "The Jews of Angevin England"; P. C. Webb, "The Question whether a Jew" (1753); Matthew Paris, *Chronica Majora* (ed. Luard, 1883); L. O. Pike, "A History of Crime in England."

---

[1] Chron. de Mailross, *ad ann.* 1216.

CHAPTER VII

PROTECTION AND PERSECUTION
(1216–1241)

THE death of John meant to the Jews of England A welcome change of policy. another turn of the wheel of fortune. The unparalleled cruelties they had suffered under that ruler had impoverished them and reduced their numbers to such an extent that, compared with but a few decades earlier, they had sunk into insignificance. The statesman-like regent William Marshall, Earl of Pembroke, to whom the government of the kingdom was entrusted during the first years of the minority of the child Henry III. regarded John's policy towards the Jews during the latter part of his reign as harmful to the welfare of the state. A more liberal treatment of the Jews appeared to him to be more in the interests of the Commonwealth, and, relying on the precedents furnished by the earlier acts of John, Pembroke determined once again to encourage a Jewish settlement and to secure to the Jews of England the liberties they had previously enjoyed. His first action was to order the immediate release of all Jews to be found in the prisons of the country on the accession of Henry, no matter what charges were preferred against them. The following year, 1217, writs were issued commanding the sheriffs and other royal officers concerned to choose twenty-four burgesses for every town in which Jews dwelt, to watch over them, so that they received no injury and especiallv to guard them against ill-treatment by crusaders.

Moreover, the sheriffs were warned that the Jews were not subject to the jurisdiction of the ecclesiastical courts, or of any others, excepting those especially appointed by the king. The charter granted by John was confirmed, and those justices of the Jews who had shown themselves unworthy of their office removed. To complete their security, so that no one could plead that he had assaulted a Jew in ignorance of his race, it was ordained in The badge instituted as a means of protection. 1218 that every Jew should wear a badge consisting of two strips of white linen or parchment, on a prominent part of his dress.

This favourable treatment had its customary effect. The Jews again began to forget their past sufferings, or perhaps, with the optimism that has been the chief cause of the survival of the race through unparalleled and apparently endless sufferings and oppression, to consider that the past was a closed book, and a new era had opened for the Jews in England. A temporary dispersal of the clouds, a momentary ray of sunshine, was sufficient to attract the Jews once more, and again the flow set in from the Continent to England. But, although the crown was kindly, the people were otherwise disposed A new element had arisen in the composite hostility of the English to the Jews within the last decades, and to the other reasons for hatred, which the English people found when their thoughts turned towards the Jews, was added that of commercial jealousy, felt by the class of English merchants which had come into being since the era of the Norman kings This national antipathy to the Jews was reflected in the action of the wardens of the Cinque Ports, who, seizing many foreign Jews on their arrival in England, threw them into prison. The royal protection, however, still availed, and so soon as the king heard of this treatment, he ordered the release of the imprisoned Jews, and forbade the wardens to interfere with them or any others that might come to the country. Two conditions were placed on Jewish immigration. Newcomers had to undertake to enroll their names with the justices of the Jews, and it was stipulated that none should be allowed to leave the country without the royal license.

Soon the assistance of the crown was again needed, The Church and against a new and more formidable adversary. and the Jews. The attitude of the Church towards the Jews had gradually, and for a variety of reasons, become more hostile. The crown, at the opening of the new reign, had given several definite and tangible signs of its sympathy with the Jews, but the crown was not the only power in the land, and that other well-armed body, the Church, whose interests often clashed with those of the kingdom, had no sympathy with the new policy. In the struggle that was then in course between the civil and religious forces, neither had as yet gained an incontestable supremacy over the other. The Judeophil legislation of Henry III. was answered by a provincial synod in 1222, when, at the instance of Stephen Langton, Archbishop of Stephen Canterbury, it was decreed "That Jews do not keep Langton. Christian slaves. And let the Slaves be compelled by ecclesiastical censure to observe this; and the Jews by canonical punishment, or by some extraordinary penalty contrived by the Diocesans. Let them not be permitted to build any more synagogues, but be looked upon as debtors to the churches of the parishes wherein they reside, as to tithes and offerings. To prevent likewise the mixture of Jewish men and women with Christians of each sex, we charge, by authority of the General Council, that the Jews of both sexes wear a linen cloth, two inches broad and four fingers long, of a different

The badge as a means of isolation. colour from their own cloths, or their upper garment, before their breast; and that they be compelled to this by ecclesiastical censure. And let them not presume to enter into any church, nor for that end lodge their goods there. If they do let them be corrected by the Bishop." In addition to promulgating this decree, the Archbishop, together with the Bishops of Lincoln and of Norwich, published an injunction prohibiting all Christians within their dioceses from having any intercourse whatsoever with Jews, whom they practically placed under an interdict.[1] The crown, however, was little likely to overlook any such invasion of its authority, and the publication of the injunctions was immediately followed by a royal precept dissolving them, and directing the officers concerned to command all men to sell the Jews food and other necessaries under the pain of imprisonment, "any spiritual inhibition notwithstanding."

The anti-Jewish feeling that pervaded the ranks of the higher clerics was, however, not universal in the English church, for about the very date of these ordinances the Prior of Dunstable gave permission to the The Prior of Dunstable. Jews to reside within his lordship and to enjoy all the privileges of it, in consideration of the annual payment of two silver spoons, each of which was to weigh twelve pennyweight.

To the same period before the ordinances of Langton also belongs the interference of the papal legate Pandulf, Bishop of Norwich, with the affairs of the Jews. In a peremptory letter to Peter des Roches and Hubert de Burgh, the guardians of the realm, he complained that the well-founded complaints of the Christians against the Jews were becoming unbear-

---

[1] This outburst of ecclesiastical anti-Jewish feeling may possibly be traced to the then recent scandal caused by the adoption of Judaism by a deacon, for love of a Jewess, and the expiation of his offence at the stake.

able, and that the extortion, oppression, and usury of the perfidious people, notwithstanding the decree of the Lateran Council, had reduced the people to a condition of exhaustion. Especially had his dear sons, the abbot and monks of Westminster, been harried by one Isaac of Norwich, on account of money they had borrowed from him, and he demanded that all proceedings in the case should be stayed until he himself was at liberty to attend the Court, and consult how the evil practices of which he complained could be prevented, and the objectionable element removed from the kingdom.

This Isaac of Norwich (died *c.* 1247) was one of the richest Englishmen of the day. In addition to his purely financial transactions, he was also a great merchant, and owned a quay at Norwich for the convenience of his vessels. Isaac was one of the Jews who suffered imprisonment by John in 1210, and about the same time his house in London was seized by the king, and afterwards presented to the Earl of Derby. *Isaac of Norwich.*

So long as Hubert de Burgh, the Earl of Pembroke's successor, remained in power, the lot of the Jews remained on the whole bearable, but with the fall of that minister and the beginning of the reign of worthless court favourites, the era of persecution recommenced. A moderate tallage of 4000 marks was levied on the Jews in 1226, and followed by another of 6000, payment of which was delayed until 1230. Between 1232, the year of the beginning of the ascendency of Peter des Roches, and 1234, two tallages, amounting to a total of 18,000 marks, were enforced. Not all of this sum, however, went into the coffers of the king, nor did this represent the total of the extortions the Jews suffered during this period. To the other troubles to which the Jews were subject was added that of corrupt and oppressive officials, and before the officers *Renewal of persecution.*

E

of the Jewish Exchequer were dismissed in 1234 they had managed to enrich themselves at the expense of those whom it was their duty to protect. The year 1232 was also the occasion of a new form of oppression. Although the Jews of England had hitherto suffered a variety of torments, it appears that until this year the due observance of their religion had met with no interference. The favourable circumstances, in which the Jews found themselves in the earlier years of Henry's reign, had encouraged them to erect a magnificent and stately house of worship, to take the place of or to supplement those already in existence in London. Its erection had continued without interruption, and on its completion the general population, envious of its magnificence, petitioned the king for its confiscation. The prayer was granted, and the edifice, together with its surrounding buildings, was consecrated to the Virgin, and given to the Brethren of St. Anthony of Vienna, whence it was known as St. Anthony's Hospital. The history of Anglo-Jewry from this date becomes a long catalogue of varying forms of persecution.

A synagogue confiscated.

The towns and the Jews.

Of all the elements in the population whose policy ran contrary to the interests of the Jews, the towns were perhaps the most important. The burgesses had, by efforts spread over a long period and generally by considerable payments, gradually acquired a certain amount of autonomy and of freedom from the interference of the crown. The introduction into their midst of the Jews, an element outside their local laws, and directly under the control of the king and his officers, immediately diminished the value of their dearly won privileges, and threatened the townsfolk with a reversion to the condition from which they had freed themselves. Although the king's officers had in the ordinary course no jurisdiction within the limits of the borough, they were free to enter it whenever invited by the Jews to assist in the collection of their debts.   When the debts fell into the king's hands, his officers as a matter of course penetrated into the towns for their collection.   When the Jews were in need of protection against the violence of the towns-folk, it was in the Royal Castle that they took refuge, or the king's sheriff with his following who came to their defence.   Moreover, on many occasions the king bluntly intimated to the burgesses that they would be held personally responsible for any harm that might befall the Jews settled in their midst.   These precautions were increasingly found necessary, for attacks on the Jews became more and more frequent as the thirteenth century progressed.

The towns, however, found another method than that of brute force of relieving themselves of what they considered the undesirable burden of the Jews. In the same manner as they had obtained their charters, they found they could exclude the Jews from their midst.   the desire for the restriction of the Jewish rights of residence the king found a still further source of income, and the Jewish problem was solved, so far as many of the English towns were concerned by removal of Jews from within their boundaries,   As has already been mentioned, on the morrow of the murderous outbreak at Bury St. Edmunds in 1190, the Jews were excluded from that town.   Forty-one years later Simon de Mont-fort made a similar grant to the burgesses of Leicester. These precedents were followed at Newcastle in 1234; Wycombe, 1235; Southampton, 1236; Berkhampstead, 1242; Newbury, 1244, and Derby in 1263.   Before the last-mentioned date, organised restriction had become the general policy of the State.   In 1253 a decree was issued limiting the Jews, except in the case of special personal licenses, to the towns in which they were then settled.   By this general measure the further

The rights of residence curtailed.

expansion of Anglo-Jewry was prohibited, and, by the various local measures already enumerated, the existing limits were being continually narrowed.   During the last two generations of their settlement in the country, the limits of Jewish settlement were gradually still further restricted.   The removal of the corrupt officials in 1232 gave the Jews no respite from overwhelming taxation.   As has been mentioned, between 1232 and 1234 they were taxed at 18,000 marks.   Two years later a similar amount was levied.   In 1237 there was again a tallage.   In 1239 the Jews were forced to surrender a third of their property.   In 1241 20,000 marks were raised.   Three years later the Jews had to produce a similar amount, and in the following year the stupendous tax of 60,000 marks was levied. In 1246 the contribution was 10,000 marks; in 1247, 5525 marks, and in 1249 again 10,000.   In 1250 a great part of the property of the Jews was seized.   In 1251 they paid 5000 marks of silver and forty of gold. The following year 3500 marks were levied on them. In July 1253 the Jews gave the king 5000 marks in order that they might be exempt from further tallage until the following Easter.   In 1259 they paid 5000 marks.   In 1269 they agreed to pay £1000 a year for the three following years.   The moment that term had expired they were forced to raise the sum of 6000 marks.   Of all these tallages there are existing records. It is probable that there were still others whose records have been lost.   Contemporary with these exactions was the restriction of the Jewish rights of residence.

At the same time there was running a new series of alleged ritual offences.   In 1230, so it was stated, the Jews of Norwich abducted a child of five, Odard, the son of Benedict the physician, apparently a converted Jew,[1] and circumcised him.   The boy escaped, and

Marginal notes:

Unceasing exactions.

The Odard affair at Norwich.

---

[1] So Mr. Rye suggests with the support of probability.

finally reached his friends, from whom the Jews demanded him on the ground that he was one of them.
The Christians, however, refused to surrender the
child, and the Jews had to rest contented with warning the woman in whose care Odard was placed not to
give him pig's flesh as he was a Jew, and in reporting
to the Constable of Norwich, the royal officer, that the
Christians had taken away *their* Jew. Nothing further
is reported to have happened for four years, and then
Benedict, the father of the boy, probably urged by
the clergy, preferred an indictment against thirteen
of the leading Jews of Norwich for the alleged assault.
Of the thirteen, ten answered the summons and were
thrown into prison. The case was heard before the
local justices, twelve of the accused were found guilty
and further action referred to the king. Meanwhile
the Sheriff of Norfolk and Suffolk was enjoined to
proclaim that no Christian woman was permitted to
enter the service of a Jew. The prisoners were sent The case
to London, and tried again before the king, the Arch- transferred to
London.
bishop of Canterbury, and many of the bishops and
barons of England. It was then decided that as such
an offence was without precedent, and was a matter
that primarily concerned the Church, the case should
be referred to the ecclesiastical authorities.

This decision rendered the plight of the incriminated
Jews still worse. In the ordinary civil courts their
chance of obtaining justice was slight. Before an
ecclesiastical tribunal, with the Church itself as their
accuser, the verdict was a foregone conclusion. In
this extremity their only course was to delay the hearing, and to try to induce the king to refer the matter
to the court provided under the charter of the Jews.
By a succession of money presents this was effected.
For four years again the case slumbered, and then the
king, despite his previous decision, and his acceptance
of a further bribe, directed the local justices to try the

accused in their own way. The exact date and result of the trial are unknown, but in 1241 some at least of the prisoners were hanged, after having been dragged to the gallows at the tails of horses, and one, having fled the country, was outlawed. In the midst of the Odard affair at Norwich, the Jews of Winchester suffered persecution on account of an alleged ritual murder in that city in 1232.

AUTHORITIES :—J. M. Rigg, "Select Pleas," &c., "Calendar of the Plea Rolls of the Exchequer of the Jews," vol. i. (1905) ; T. Madox, "History of the Exchequer" ; D'Bloissiers Tovey, *Anglia Judaica;* Matthew Paris, *Chronica Majora* (Editor, Luard, 1883) ; Rymer's "Fœdera"; J. E. Blunt, "The Jews in England" ; L. O. Pike, "A History of Crime in England" ; "Jewish Encyclopedia," article, "Isaac of Norwich"; W. Prynne, "A Short Demurrer"; B. L. Abrahams, "The Expulsion of the Jews from England"; W. Rye, "The Persecutions of the Jews, on the Circumcision of a Boy at Norwich in 1230" ("Norfolk Antiquarian Miscellany," vol. i.); "Patent Rolls of the Reign ·of Henry III., 1216 to 1225" (1901), " 1225 to 1232" (1903), " 1232 to 1247" (1906) ; "Close Rolls of the Reign of Henry III., 1227 to 1231" (1902), " 1231 to 1234" (1905); "Documents illustrative of English History in the Thirteenth and Fourteenth Centuries" (ed. H. Cole, 1844).

CHAPTER VIII

TALLAGES, SPOLIATION AND IMPRISON-MENT

(1238-1251)

A REQUEST made by the Jews in 1238 is worthy of more than passing note in connection with subsequent charges of forgery, coin-clipping, &c., brought against the whole race. At their own request the king accepted from them a hundred pounds so that inquiry might be made, and evidence obtained from Jews and Christians with a view to the perpetual banishment from the kingdom of all Jews found guilty of clipping, robbery, or harbouring those guilty of such offences. In 1241 the oppression of the Jews took a new turn. The so-called Parliament of the Jews was convened by the king at Worcester. Writs were issued to the sheriffs of the counties directing them to arrange for the election of representatives of all the Jewish communities within their respective provinces. The larger communities were to send six of their worthiest members ; the smaller centres were to be represented by two. These representatives were called together "to treat with him (the king), as well concerning his own as their advantage." The summons must have come as a great surprise to the Jews of England worn by persecution and exhausted by oppression. The form of writ suggested that the Government had at length repented of its heartless oppression, and was anxious to alleviate the deplorable condition of its Jewish subjects. With hearts beating high with hope, for their existing condition could hardly have been rendered worse—expatriation, more than once ardently demanded, was recognised as preferable to the continuance of the existing condition — the elected representatives of the Jews of England repaired to Worcester on the day appointed for their gathering to consult concerning their own benefit as well as the king's. The glimmer of hope was, however, of but short duration. Immediately on their assemby the representatives of the Jews were told they had been called together to learn that they were required to raise 20,000 marks from among their people, and that the king would hold those present responsible in their persons and their properties for the raising of the amount within a stipulated time. The Parliament of the Jews was in fact only called together to consult as to the best method of taxing their constituents for the benefit of the king. Despite their efforts the appointed collectors were unable to obtain the whole of the amount required by the time appointed, and the king, in accordance with his word, had the collectors, their wives, children, and property seized in satisfaction of his demands. Two years later, by means of a charge of forgery brought against the ex-Chief Presbyter, Aaron of York, the king was enabled to force the enormous amount of 32,000 marks from that unfortunate ecclesiastic.

The Chief Presbyter Aaron was "defrauded," as Matthew Paris puts it, in 1243. The following year the discovery of an alleged case of ritual murder in London gave the king a new excuse, if one were needed, for oppression and extortion. The body of a child was exhumed, and found to bear strange marks. It being suspected that the marks amounted to an inscription in Hebrew, certain converted Jews were sent for, and under threats and penalties ordered to decipher them. Despite these outside influences

Assembly at Worcester.

An alleged ritual murder in London.

used to assist in a solution, one was reached with great difficulty. The decipherers, with the assistance of others, admitted that most of the signs were unintelligible. With persuasion, however, they managed to discover the names of the child's parents and a statement to the effect that he had been sold to the Jews. At an age at which the laws of evidence were little considered, and in the creation of martyrs and miracles the end invariably justified the means, martyrs and saints were plentiful. It is doubtful, however, whether any martyrdom was based on more slender foundation than those of this child. His sanctity being proved by the marks on his body, that body was thereupon claimed by the canons of the cathedral, who buried it near the high altar. This was the excuse for a tallage of 60,000 marks. The same year, 1244, the barons, anxious still further to limit the king's power and to increase his dependence upon them, acquired the right to nominate one of the justices of the Jews, and thus to become better acquainted with the royal resources with the view still further to control them,

The difficulties that the baronage, especially the lesser barons, attributed to the activity of the Jews were obvious. It was among them that the bulk of the debtors of the Jews were to be found, and although it was often through their instrumentality alone that the barons were enabled to perform their duties to their overlords, grievances remain in the memory long after benefits are forgotten. The barons were not allowed to forget their indebtedness to the Jews, and so long as that condition subsisted they did not fail to harbour feelings of animosity. The transfer of their debts to the crown tended to make this hostility all the more intense. For every act of harshness on the part of the royal creditor, the Jew

The barons obtain the right to nominate one of the justices of the Jews.

was made the scapegoat. The collection of every debt was a further item in the score that was gradually lengthening as it awaited the day of reckoning. The practice that had grown up of transferring the security (often the lands) for the loans of the minor barons to their overlords, from whom afterwards the debtors had great difficulty in recovering their pledges, re-acted in a still deeper feeling of hostility to the Jews. Whenever opportunities occurred, and the Civil War of the thirteenth century furnished several, the barons vented their long-stored feelings of vengeance on the Jews. Throughout the reign of Henry III., Jewry after Jewry was sacked and its inhabitants slain. Sheer love of murder and destruc-tion was however not the sole motive. Care was taken to appropriate all the property easily movable, and, when occasion offered, the registries of Jewish debts were sacked and the records of the indebted-ness of the barons destroyed. " It is impossible," says a chronicler, in describing one of these attacks, "to estimate the loss it caused to the king's exchequer."

On the part of the minor barons, the anti-Jewish feeling was almost entirely due to economic causes. On the great nobles of the country, men of great wealth, these had little if any effect. Yet, by the middle of the thirteenth century, there was practical uniformity on the subject throughout all ranks of the nobility. The great struggle between the baronage and the crown had by then commenced, and it was speedily recognised that among the weapons of the king the Jew was by no means the least useful. The easiest method for the barons to adopt, to bring pressure to bear upon the king, was to withhold supplies from him ; but so long as revenue could be wrung from the wretched Jews, this method of bring-ing pressure to bear proved insufficient. That the king understood well how valuable a weapon the

The oppression of the barons.

Economic causes.

Jews were in the struggle in which he was engaged,
is shown by the continual oppressive exactions to
which the Jews were subject throughout the second
decade of the thirteenth century, Between 1230 and
1255, on seven different occasions, the king swooped
down upon his Jews. At first he was contented with
but a third of their property. But *l'appetit vient en
mangeant*, and after the third tallage the royal officers
were instructed to wring the last possible penny from
their unfortunate victims. The king was not alone
in learning the value of the Jews in the struggle. The
barons plainly saw that, to succeed in their object,
they must control or abolish the source of revenue
the crown enjoyed in the Jews, and thus it was that
by 1244 they had exacted from the king the right to
appoint one of the justices of the Jews, so as to get
acquainted with the extent of the Jewish resources,
and to obtain some voice in their disposal.

The tax of 1245 was levied under the threat that
defaulters would be banished to Ireland, a punishment one of the most severe that could be imposed
on any subject of the king. To safeguard at least
their wives and children from the possibility of such
a terrible fate, many of the Jews secretly removed
their dependants and hid them. This action was
immediately followed by a royal proclamation to the
effect that the removal, within a year, of any wife or
child of a Jew from her or his accustomed abode,
would be the signal for the outlawry of the whole
family, and the seizure of the whole of their property
for the king's use. Thus were all means of escape
from the king's ruthless barbarity closed. At the
same time individual Jews were compelled to contribute towards the internal decoration of Westminster Abbey, then in the process of rebuilding.

Under the year 1250 a remarkable story is told of
one Abraham of Berkhampstead, who, obtaining an

Threats of banishment to Ireland.

image of the Virgin Mary, submitted it to considerable indignity, and forced his wife Flora to do likewise. The latter, however, after a time repented, and,
although she was "a very beautiful wife and faithful
to him," he did not hesitate to kill her on account of
her disobedience. The story got abroad. Abraham
was arrested and sentenced to perpetual imprisonment. At the intercession of Earl Richard of Cornwall, to whom Abraham was "very dear," the convict
was released from prison on payment of seven hundred marks. While, however, Abraham was still in
prison, it appears he was denounced by his co-
religionists as guilty of other offences, especially of
coin-clipping. Earl Richard, however, would not
withdraw his protection, in the presence of which
but little to the harm of Abraham could be effected ;
and the latter in defending himself from the new
charge, not only denied it, but expressed his ability
to prove all the Jews of England to be "most wicked
traitors." Abraham was released from prison, and
shortly afterwards, perhaps in consequence of his
disclosures or inventions, a very strict inquisition
was made into all the properties of the Jews of England. In this inquisition an unpleasant notoriety was
obtained by a renegade Jew, who rendered the
inquisition still harsher than it need have been by
threatening the persons who made the inventories,
that he would complain of them to the king for
being too mild and partial; assuring them, that if
never so strict an estimate were made of their riches,
it would fall short of truth—so many arts, he said,
they had to disguise and conceal them. His vindic-
tiveness was so intense that many Christians, we are
told, lamented and grieved at the affliction of the
Jews.

Harried and oppressed, tortured, tormented, fined,
plundered, mutilated, massacred, struck not only in

their own persons, but also in those of their loved ones, the limit was at length reached with these children of endurance, whom history has hardened on the anvil of persecution and in the fire of relentless and apparently endless oppression. Broken in spirit by the tyrants of centuries, at length in England they boldly faced their persecutors. The king, once again failing to raise money by legitimate means, turned to the Jews to wring from them their last pence. This projected levy he entrusted to his brother, Earl Richard, who in his endeavours was met by a deputation of the oppressed, with the Chief Presbyter Elias at their head. The Earl was told : "O noble Lords, we see undoubtedly that our Lord the King purposeth to destroy us from under heaven. We entreat, for God's sake, that he would give us license and safe conduct of departing out of his Kingdom, that we may seek and find a mansion in some other place, under some Prince who bears some bowels of mercy, and some stability of truth and faithfulness. And we will depart; never to return again, leaving here our household stuff, and houses behind us. How can he love or spare us, miserable Jews, who destroys his own natural English ? He hath people, yea his own merchants, I say not usurers, who by usurious contracts, heap up infinite heaps of money. Let the King rely upon them, and gape after their emoluments. Verily they have supplanted and impoverished us. Which the King howsoever dissembles to know, exacting from us those things we cannot give him, although he would pull out our eyes, or cut our throats, when he had first pulled off our skins." [1]

Earl Richard who, compared with other statesmen of the day, was considered well disposed towards the Jews, pointed out in reply that their request to be

The appeal of Chief Presbyter Elias.

---

[1] Prynne's Translation of Matthew Paris.

allowed to depart could not be granted, inasmuch as the king of France had but recently issued an edict against his Jews, and no other Christian state would receive them. For the present the king would accept as much money as they could produce. The following year a similar demand for money was made, and again leave to depart was craved. All, however, the Jews could get in reply was an impassioned declaration by the king of his financial necessities; and since it seemed impossible for him to wring anything more from his wretched Jews, he sold them for £5000 for a term of years to his brother Richard, to whom absolute control over them was assigned. Under Richard the Jews found some temporary respite, for he recognised the poverty to which they had been reduced by the grinding exactions of his royal brother.

The Jews sold to Earl Richard.

The chief Presbyter, Elias of London, otherwise Elias le Evesk, held office for twenty years until 1257. He was one of the representatives in the Parliament of the Jews, and on a subsequent occasion was the victim of royal exactions to the extent of £10,000, in addition to £100 a year for a period of four years. In 1255 he was imprisoned as a surety for a tallage levied on the Jews, and two years later was deposed, and succeeded by his brother Hagin. In 1259 he is said to have adopted Christianity, and to have confessed to having poisoned wells. Whatever truth there may be in this alleged conversion, seven years later, in 1266, Elias was again accepted in London as a Jew, and granted fifty pounds compensation for losses sustained by him in the Barons' Wars. In 1277 he was one of the few Jews to whom permission was granted to trade as merchants without entering any of the Gilds. He was also skilled as a physician, and received permission in 1280 to go abroad in order to attend to Jean d'Aresnes, Count of Hainault. At the time of the

Expulsion, in 1290, Elias was still living in London, Elias of
London. but his ultimate fate is unknown. Elias was also learned in Jewish law, and as such consulted by the king.[1]

AUTHORITIES :—J. Jacobs, " The London Jewry, 1290" ; J. M. Rigg, " Select Pleas," &c., " Calendar of the Plea Rolls," vol. i. ; W. Prynne, " A Short Demurrer"; Matthew Paris, *Chronica Majora ;* Rymer's " Fœdera " ; J. E. Blunt, " The Jews in England "; " Jewish Encyclopedia," articles, " Elyas of London" and " Aaron of York"; C. Gross, " The Exchequer of the Jews of England " ; D'Bloissiers Tovey, *Anglia Judaica ;* B. L. Abrahams, " The Expulsion of the Jews from England " ; " Patent Rolls of the Reign of Henry III., 1232 to 1247."

---

[1] This sketch of Elias is based on material furnished by Dr. Jacobs and published in " The London Jewry, 1290." Dr. H. P. Stokes takes exception, however, to several of the identifications which assist to form this sketch, and claims that there were two distinct personages of the name of Elias, who have been confused by Dr. Jacobs. The evidence he brings forward in support of this view seems conclusive.

CHAPTER IX

LITTLE ST. HUGH OF LINCOLN
(1253–1268)

THE Royal Ordinance of 1253, by refusing to the Jews all rights of territorial expansion, and by severely limiting their freedom of movement, created that which amounted practically to a Pale of Settlement. The ordinance opened with a threat that no Jew should remain in the country without doing the king some service. The synagogue accommodation under King John was laid down as the furthest limit to which such accommodation should be allowed to extend, and the Jews were forbidden to erect any new houses of worship except in place of those standing at the time of John. In the synagogues permitted, service was to be conducted in low tones, so that there should be no danger of annoyance to Christian neighbours or passers-by. No Christians were to attend these services. Every Jew was made answerable to the rector of his parish for all parochial dues chargeable on his house. Christians were forbidden to serve Jews in any capacity, to eat or stay with them. Jews were prohibited from eating or buying flesh during Lent, and from disputing concerning Christian observances. A Jew should not enter a church or chapel except quickly to pass through. Nor should any Jew deter another anxious to embrace Christianity. The penalty for transgressing any of the articles of this ordinance was forfeiture of property. This legislation was practically an adoption of the anti-Jewish decrees of the Provincial Synod of 1222, ignored at the time by the civil power, then more sympathetically disposed towards the Jews.

In 1255 the Blood Accusation underwent a revival, which, in its consequences to Jewry, proved the most terrible of all the ordeals of that nature through which Anglo-Jewry passed. The popular story of the martyrdom of Little St. Hugh of Lincoln touched the people's minds so closely that it entered deeply into the folk-songs of the nation. The ballads of the English and Scotch sing often of the child-martyr, whose story was also reproduced in Norman-French song. One of Chaucer's " Canterbury Tales," moreover, deals with the episode. The story, as told by Matthew Paris,[1] is as follows : "The Jews of Lincoln stole a boy of eight years of age, whose name was Hugh ; and having shut him up in a room quite out of the way, where they fed him on milk and other childish nourishment, they sent to almost all the cities of England where the Jews lived, and summoned some of their sect from each city to be present at a sacrifice to take place at Lincoln, for they had, as they stated, a boy hidden for the purpose of being crucified. In accordance with the summons, a great many of them came to Lincoln, and on assembling, they at once appointed a Jew of Lincoln as judge, to take the place of Pilate, by whose sentence, and with the concurrence of all, the boy was subjected to divers tortures." These included crucifixion, crowning with thorns, marking with the stigmata, and piercing in the side. Moreover, the child "was overwhelmed with reproaches and blasphemies, and was repeatedly called Jesus the false prophet by his tormentors, who surrounded him, grinding and gnashing their teeth." Meanwhile the mother, who had been seeking her son, learnt

Little St. Hugh.

---

[1] J. A. Giles' Translation (1854).

F

that he had last been seen playing with Jewish children, and, searching diligently, at length found his body at the bottom of a well in the house of a Jew. The bailiff of the city being informed had the body drawn out; and John of Lexington, who happened to be present, "a man of learning, prudent and discreet," at the time Chief Justice of the Forest, and a brother of the Bishop of Lincoln, turning to the people, said: "We have already learned that the Jews have not hesitated to attempt such proceedings as a reproach and taunt to our Lord Jesus Christ, who was crucified." He ordered the Jew, in whose house the child had been playing, to be seized, and after threatening him with mutilation and death, from which "not all the gold of England will avail to ransom you, and save you from your fate," promised to preserve his life and limbs if he would disclose all he knew about the affair. Terrified by these threats, the Jew, Cópin, confessed that the charge of the ritual murder of Hugh was true, and that "almost every year the Jews crucify a boy as an insult to the name of Jesus." Not only was Hugh crucified for such a purpose, but when his murderers attempted to bury the mutilated body, "the earth vomited it forth, and the corpse appeared unburied above ground." Such a confession naturally placed the seal of martyrdom upon the child, and the body was taken possession of by the canons of the Cathedral Church of Lincoln, and after lying in state, "it was honourably buried in the Church of Lincoln, as if it had been the corpse of a precious martyr."

As this is the most important of the Blood Accusations in England, the evidence in support of it may be noticed in some detail. First it should be noted that all other possible theories, such as accident—the child, while playing, might have fallen

John of Lexington.

down the well—are discarded, or rather not considered for a moment. John of Lexington immediately jumps to the conclusion, to which he is followed by the others, that the child was murdered by the Jews, and in order to obtain support for this theory promises the unhappy Jew he has caught, after terrifying him with threats, absolute immunity if he will make the statement Lexington desires. Copin does so, but even Matthew Paris, a contemporary chronicler, not otherwise too sympathetically inclined towards Jews, terms his statements ravings. Setting aside the miraculous embroideries of the story and the absolute incompatibility of the offence alleged, or of anything like it with the teachings or practices or spirit of Judaism, it should be noticed that the death of the boy occurred in August, at least four months later than the Passover, with which Jewish festival the Blood Accusation is as a rule, and in this case also, connected; that the child could have been concealed in a small city, while the Jews were being collected from all over the country, and not discovered by his anxious mother, who, it is said, had reason from the beginning to suspect the Jews, is hardly credible. Moreover, the occasion of a wedding in the house of an important member of the Lincoln Jewish community [1] was sufficient explanation for the gathering of the Jews in that city.

Meanwhile the king, on his return from Scotland, stopped at Lincoln to investigate the matter. He had just mortgaged the Jews to his brother, and for purposes of ordinary taxation they were out of his control. Jews found guilty of offences against the law were, however, still at his mercy, and to involve a number of prominent Jews in a crime would, he

The king investigates the charge.

---

[1] Berechiah de Nicole (Benedict fil Mosse). The identity of Benedict's daughter with the bride is conjectural.

must have seen, have been an easy manner of replenishing his treasury.   His first action was severely
to reprimand Lexington for having in any circumstances promised Copin pardon, and that wretched
demented creature was forthwith tied to a horse's tail,
dragged to the gallows, and executed.   Ninety-one of
the other prominent Jews of Lincoln were dragged from
their houses where they had taken refuge, well know-
ing what to expect, sent to London, and imprisoned.
Eighteen of them, claiming their rights to trial before
a mixed jury, were summarily condemned for their
presumption and hanged.   The remainder were confined in the Tower.   Two of these were pardoned but
the others were tried before twenty-four knights and
the same number of burgesses from Lincoln, and, as
was to have been expected from the known prejudice
from which the members of this jury suffered, convicted
and sentenced to death.

The friars
intervene on
behalf of the
Jews.

If the doubts already cast on the guilt of the Jews
had not yet sufficed, the next episode in the history
should assure to the victims of this act of judicial and
religious persecution tardy justice.   Before the execution could be carried out—according to one authority
the Franciscans, according to another the Dominicans
—appealed to the king for the pardon of the impli-
cated Jews.   The noble-hearted appeal failed of its
hoped-for effect, but the requests of the king's brother,
the Earl of Cornwall, to the same purport were
granted and the condemned Jews released.   Despite
this royal pardon, the animosity of the townspeople
seems to have been so fiercely aroused against the
Jews, that a few years later the king was compelled to
grant them a special protection.

Meanwhile the government of the kingdom was
gradually becoming more chaotic, and its condition
more disturbed.   The disputes between the king and
his barons often led to the existence of two contem-

porary governing powers, and in such circumstances, when each was fully occupied in neutralising the efforts of the other, the Church, always over-zealous to increase its influence and jealous of its assumed rights, had freer play. Thus in 1257 the prelates, assembled in Provincial Synod, complained that when any Jew was prosecuted in their courts for an offence of a spiritual nature, he was immediately removed by the king's courts from their jurisdiction, and that by their so-called proper judges the Jews were invariably acquitted whenever they could get a Christian and a Jew to affirm their innocence. It was consequently decided by the prelates that all such accused Jews should be compelled to appear before the ecclesiastical courts by "being forbidden to traffic, contract, or converse with the faithful." And so that these injunctions should be observed, all objectors should be coerced by excommunication and interdict.

Unfortunately an occurrence at Oxford, inexplicable except by the theory of insanity, materially assisted the Church in its anti-Jewish policy. The Jewry of *Sacrilege* this university centre had been much less liable to *Oxford.* disturbance than the other large Jewish communities in the country. London, York, Lincoln, Norwich, &c., had, without exception, all suffered pillage or the blood accusation. In many, devastation had visited the Jews not once but twice, and even more often. Compared with these centres the lot of Oxford had been a happy one, and the troubles of the Jews of that city of little concern. It was in 1268 that the regrettable incident, of which mention has already been made, occurred. On the occasion of a religious procession, a certain Jew of Oxford broke the ranks, seized a crucifix that was being carried and trod it under foot. Despite the heinousness of the offence, which elsewhere in England would have probably involved wholesale confiscation and imprisonment if not execution, the punishment directed by the king was remarkably moderate. The Jews were ordered to present the university with a portable silver cross, and to erect an expensive and valuable cross of marble on the spot on which the outrage was committed. It was subsequently decided that this cross should be placed outside the synagogue, but the king and council, out of consideration apparently for Jewish susceptibilities, decided that the place was inconvenient, and the cross was ultimately erected close to Merton College. The last incident in the history of the Jews of Oxford before the Expulsion was the grant, in 1286, as a favour to the scholars of the university, of jurisdiction by the chancellor in disputes between scholars and Jews.

While under the protection of the Earl Richard, the Jews of England were allowed an opportunity for recuperation. On the conclusion of his lease, however, the breathing time passed away, and once more Anglo-Jewry became the plaything of the opposing elements that were contesting for supremacy on the stage of England. The period of political contest was drawing to a close, and that of armed conflict about to open. On the eve of the hostilities between the king and the barons, the Jews of England were assigned to Prince Edward, who on his part handed them over to their rivals, the Cahorsins. These were Italian merchants, in the service of the Pope, who first appeared in England about the year 1235. Technically money-changers, they were in reality usurers, who charged higher rates of interest than did their Jewish competitors. As, however, usury was forbidden to Christians, the Cahorsins had to salve their consciences, and satisfy their superiors by a fiction. They did not lend money on interest. To a borrower who required a hundred pounds for six months, the Cahorsins were willing to lend the amount free of interest for three.

The Jews assigned to Prince Edward and by him to the Cahorsins.

For the three following months interest at the rate of The Cahorsins. 50 per cent. per mensem was charged. Thus it was contended that the transaction could not be considered usurious, for the interest depended upon a contingency that might never occur. It was against the pressure of the Cahorsins, that was gradually taking away from the Jews the means of responding to the exorbitant demands of the king, that the chief rabbi Elias complained, in his pathetic appeal to the hard-hearted ruler, to let his people depart. In 1252 Henry determined to persecute the Cahorsins, whose competition with his own Jews was certainly distasteful to him, with all the rigour of the law against usurers, but his hand was stayed by the plea that they were the servants of the Pope. The mission of the Cahorsins to England at the instigation of the Pope was probably a move in the game played by the Church during the last two generations of Pre-Expulsion Anglo-Jewry for purging England of her Jews. For the Jew the most painful stage in the competition between them and the Cahorsins was reached when the former were given as pledges into the hands of their rivals. The only mitigating circumstance was that the king resumed control of the Jews before the expiration of the lease.

AUTHORITIES :— J. Jacobs, " Little St. Hugh" (*Transactions of the Jewish Historical Society*, vol. i., 1895); W. Prynne, " A Short Demurrer"; J. M. Rigg, " Select Pleas," &c.; " The Jews of England in the Thirteenth Century" (*Jewish Quarterly Review*, vol. xv., 1903); T. Madox, " History of the Exchequer"; Matthew Paris, *Chronica Majora;* Anthony à Wood, " The History and Antiquities of the University of Oxford" (Editor, Gutch) (1792); D'Bloissiers Tovey, *Anglia Judaica;* J. E. Blunt, " The Jews in England"; L. O. Pike, " A History of Crime in England"; A. Neubauer, " Notes on the Jews in Oxford"; W. Rye, " The Persecutions of the Jews"; A. Hume, " St. Hugh of Lincoln" (1849); " The Red Book of the Exchequer," vol. iii. (ed. Hall, 1896).

CHAPTER X

THE LAST PHASE
(1262-1279)

THE opening of the Civil War was the signal for the plunder of the Jews. Even before the first blow was struck by either of the combatants, the Jews of London felt the first gusts of the coming storm. The king having broken with the barons took refuge in the Tower, and the other party, with their army, occupied the city (1262). A dispute between a Jew and a Christian inhabitant served as a spark to kindle the material to hand. The London Jewry was sacked, and seven hundred of its inhabitants slain. Similar excesses followed at Worcester (1263), London again, Northampton and Canterbury (1264), and Lincoln, and the Isle of Ely (1266). The success of the barons enabled their leader, Simon de Montfort, to take more efficacious measures than the haphazard destruction of archives for the relief of his followers from their indebtedness to the Jews. By proclamation all the remaining bonds of indebtedness were annulled, and thus at a stroke a large proportion of the property of the Jews was transferred to their erstwhile debtors. De Montfort's success was short-lived, but his downfall brought but temporary relief. Peace had repaired to some extent the inroads on the fortunes of the Jews, and many had again acquired some wealth. Dazzled by the rapid change from the oppression and cruelties of the baronial party, the Jews even aspired to attain to some degree of civil emancipation. A few slight favours had been con-

ferred on individual Jews by the king when freed
from the pressure of De Montfort, and some among
them had obtained possession of the estates of deceased or outlawed barons. An estate held by a Jew
was, however, shorn of many of its most desired
attributes. Under the existing law no Jew could, for
instance, exercise the rights of wardship, escheat, or
advowson. The Jews, blinded by an apparent sense
of security, claimed these feudal rights. As was to be
expected such an application united all the anti-
Jewish elements, lay and clerical, in the nation against
them, and instead of the request being granted, the
Jews were disqualified by Parliament in 1269 and The Jews dis-
1271 altogether from holding landed property, either qualified from
holding lands
in pledge or by purchase. Moreover, their com- in pledge.
mercial rights were very severely curtailed, and the
result of the measures was to reduce the Jews to
almost as unfavourable a situation as under De Montfort's ordinance. Immediately afterwards came a
tallage of six thousand marks to enable Prince
Edward to take the cross. The Jews were by this
time so much impoverished that they were unable
to raise the amount, and they were in consequence
again mortgaged to the Earl of Cornwall. With
the confiscation of the chief synagogue in London
because the service disturbed the neighbouring friars,
the annals of the Jews of England under Henry III.'s
tenure of the throne close.

During Henry's long reign the Jews of England
had suffered almost every possible vicissitude, and
the rapid changes in their fortunes seem at times
almost to have turned their heads. Under his son
and successor, Edward, the sun no longer broke
through the ever thickening clouds. The condition
of Jewry at the opening of Edward's reign was one of
deep affliction. So sore was the misery of the Jews
that we are told, " Nothing but weeping and wailing

was to be seen in every corner. Even the Friars who had so lately taken possession of their Synagogue, as it is said, pitied them : Nor were the Cahorsini brokers (though their rivals in extortion) without compassion. For nothing could be more rigorous and unmerciful than the King's proceedings at this time." During the eighteen years in which the Jews remained in England under Edward I. their condition became yearly more and more pitiable, so that the final act of oppression, accompanied, as it was, by individual acts of inhuman cruelty, must have come almost as a relief.

Edward, who had inspired the ordinances of 1269 and 1271, differed greatly in character from his father. First he was a statesman, not anxious to satisfy his immediate necessities at no matter what cost, but looking ahead so that his actions might redound to future benefit even more than to the relief of present needs. He was also of a religious turn of mind, and likely to be influenced by the wishes of Rome more than was his father. Already, before his accession, his sympathies and favour had been gained by the minor barons—the class most in the debt of the Jews— and the indebtedness of the ecclesiastical institutions appealed to him both as a Christian and an Englishman. He saw that the relations between the Jews and the people during the preceding reign had reacted unfavourably on both parties, and the practice that had been growing up of transferring estates to the Church in order to obtain relief from indebtedness to the Jews offended against his well-thought-out views in statecraft. Meanwhile a greater and conscientious antipathy to usury had been growing up in clerical minds both in England and on the Continent, and Edward, as a loyal son of the Church, could not be unaffected by those views. In another direction the Jewish Question had undergone a change. The

Jews were no longer of the value to the king, either absolutely or relatively, that they had been as recently as half a century earlier. The ceaseless exactions of the crown, the frequent spoliations by the people, not to speak of the competition of the Italians, had greatly impoverished a community which had once possessed considerable wealth. In financial transactions the Italians, with their wealthy continental connections, were of incomparably more use than the Jews. The greater needs of the crown had, moreover, rendered the Jewish portion of the revenue comparatively, as well as absolutely, far smaller than it had formerly been.

Edward was abroad at the time of his accession, and did not return for nearly two years. At first the attitude of the crown towards the Jews was much as heretofore. New justices were appointed, the extent of the property of the Jews carefully inquired into, individuals taxed, fined, and imprisoned, and their debtors released or transferred to the king in accordance with the royal will or whim. The opening of the reign was signalised by a tallage levied not only on adults but also on children, and failure to pay the allotted quota meant banishment as well as confiscation of property. Edward had, however, determined on dealing with the Jewish question as a whole, and accordingly, in the year after his return to England (1275), Parliament adopted the Statute *de Judaismo*, as follows :—

Tallage levied on children.

"The King having observed that, in times past, many honest men have lost their inheritances, by the usury of the Jews ; and that many sins have from thence arisen : (notwithstanding they are, and have been, very profitable to him, and his ancestors) ordains and establishes, for the honour of God, and the common benefit of the people, that no Jew, hereafter, shall in any manner practise usury. And that no usurious contracts already made, since the feast of St. Edward, last past, shall stand good, excepting covenants relating to the principal Sum. Provided also, that all those who are indebted to the Jews, upon pledges moveable, shall redeem them, before Easter next, under pain of forfeiture. And if any Jew shall practice usury against the intent of this statute, the King promises neither to give him assistance, by himself, or officers, in recovering his debts, but on the contrary, will punish him for his trespass, and assist the Christians against him, in the recovery of their pledges. And it is further enacted, that no distress for any Jew's debt, shall hereafter be so grievous, as not to leave Christians the moiety of their lands and chattels, for subsistance. And that no distress shall be made by any such Jew, upon the heir of his debtor named in the bond, or any other person in possession of the debtor's lands, before such debt shall be proved in court. And if the sheriff, or other bailiff, is commanded by the King, to give seisin or possession to any Jew, of lands or chattels, to the value of his debt, the chattels shall first be appraised by the oath of honest men, and delivered to the Jew or Jewess, to the value of the debt. And if the chattels be not found sufficient to answer it, then the lands shall be extended, by the same oath, according to their separate values, before seisin is given of them to the Jew or Jewess; to the intent, that when the debt is certainly known to be discharged, the Christian may have his lands again. Saving to the Christian, nevertheless, the moiety of his lands and chattels, and the chief house for his substinance, as is before expressed. And if anything stolen be found in the possession of a Jew, let him have his summons, if he regularly may have it: if not, he shall answer in such a manner as a Christian would be obliged to, without claiming any privilege.

Likewise all Jews shall be resident in such cities, and boroughs, as are the King's own ; where the common chest of their indentures is wont to be kept. And every one of them, that is past seven years of age, shall wear a badge, in form of two tables, of yellow taffety, six fingers long, and three fingers broad, upon his upper garment ; and every one that is past twelve years, shall also pay annually, to the King, at Easter, the sum of three pence, both men, and women. And no Jew shall have power to alienate in fee, either to Jew, or Christian, any houses, rents, or tenements, which they have already purchased, or dispose of them in any manner, or acquit any Christian of his debt, without the King's special licence, till he hath otherwise ordained. And because Holy Church, wills and permits, that they should live, and be protected, the King takes them into his protection ; and commands that they shall live guarded, and defended, by his sheriffs, bailiffs, and other liege people. And that none shall do them harm, either in their persons, or goods, moveable or immoveable, or sue, implead, or challenge them in any courts but the King's courts, wheresoever they are. And that none of them shall be obedient, respondent, or pay any rent, to any but the King, or his bailiffs, in his name, excepting for their houses which they now hold, rendering rent ; Saving, likewise, the rights of Holy Church. And the King also grants, that they may practice merchandise, or live by their labour, and for those purposes, freely converse with Christians. Excepting that upon any pretence whatever, they shall not be levant, or couchant, amongst them ; nor on account of their merchandise, be in Scots, lots, or talliage, with the other inhabitants of those cities, or boroughs, where they remain : seeing they are talliable to the King as his own vassals, and not otherwise. Moreover the King grants them free liberty to purchase

Further details of the Act.

houses, and curtilages, in the cities and boroughs where they reside; provided they are held in chief of the King. Saving to the lords their due, and accustomed services. And further, the King grants, that such as are unskilful in merchandise, and can't labour, may take lands to farm, for any term not exceeding ten years; provided no homage, fealty, or any such kind of service, or advowson to Holy Church, be belonging to them. Provided also that this power to farm lands shall continue in force for fifteen years, from the making of this Act, and no longer."

The effects of the Act. The effect of this Act was to prevent the recovery by law of interest due, and to render only half the debtor's property liable for the principal. On the other hand, Jews were permitted to trade, to purchase house property in cities, from which they were not by law excluded, and to hold farms on leases not exceeding ten years. The last concession, which was to be in force for fifteen years, was not to carry with it homage or fealty from Christians. The dependant status of the Jews was affirmed, a poll-tax of three pence per annum laid on them, and both sexes ordered to wear badges. The Church had long been striving to enforce this indignity on Jewesses, who had hitherto been free from it. The policy of the English Government for two centuries had been to exclude Jews from all occupations but finance, and to this calling they had consequently devoted almost all their talents. The Statute *de Judaismo* rendered this occupation no longer possible; and despite the concessions more apparent than real, placed the whole of Anglo-Jewry face to face with starvation. The gilds practically held the monopolies of trade and craftmanship, and from these, Jews were in many instances legally excluded, while the others it was practically impossible for them to enter. There is only one instance before the Expulsion of a Jew becoming a member of a gild. For agriculture they had had no training. The prohibition from mixing with Christians prevented them from obtaining any, and the brief tenure of their farms successfully militated against the Jews taking to agriculture in England. Peripatetic commerce was at the best a dangerous occupation in the England of that period, and to a Jew trebly so. Of all occupations the only possible one open for the Jews seemed to be the export of wool, the staple product, on a large scale. In this occupation obviously but an insignificant number could be engaged. For the remainder no avenue of earning a livelihood lay open.

Despite all enactments, however, the Jews had to live and did live. The easiest method of evading the statute was to follow the example of the Cahorsin and other Christian usurers, and lend money ostensibly without interest, but in reality at a very good profit. To assist in such evasions there were would-be borrowers without number. The poorer Jews, who had in the past either lived in the service of their richer brethren—now in many instances no longer capable of retaining them—or had eked out their existence by evasion of the anti-Jewish laws, at times and in places not too strictly enforced, had however no such opportunities. Some are said to have taken to highway robbery and burglary, lapses almost justifiable in the circumstances; a few accepted food and shelter as the price of apostasy; others again, driven to extremes by the hopelessness of their situation, tampered with the coinage in order to supply themselves with food. The coinage had long lent itself easily to clipping, and for almost half a century the offence had been prevalent in England. At an earlier period the Jews had petitioned the king for the expulsion of Jews guilty of tampering with the coinage, and an official inquiry in 1248 had decided that Jews, Cahorsins, and

Distress of the Jews.

Flemish wool-merchants were responsible for the then unsatisfactory condition of the means of exchange. The suspicions aroused on that occasion were not allowed to die away, and when Edward in 1278 proposed to reform the currency, his first step was to seize all the Jews in the country, imprison them, and have their houses searched. Similar treatment was meted out to a few goldsmiths and other non-Jews suspected of the same offence. A trial was held, and a large number of Christians and Jews found guilty. Of the former, however, only three were sentenced to death : in London alone, two hundred and ninety-three Jews were hanged and drawn. A few others escaped the same fate by accepting Christianity.

All the Jews imprisoned.

293 Jews hanged.

This new form of persecution raised up hosts of informers, who were, however, always ready to hold their peace, if sufficient blackmail were offered. When, to a Jew, accusation was almost invariably interpreted as guilt, the hunted victims were only too anxious to buy their lives at almost any price. A new and lucrative profession of Jew-blackmailing speedily sprung up, but the king, quickly recognising the state of affairs, issued writs to the effect that any Jew not accused by a certain date, might on payment of a fine to the crown be relieved of the consequences of any future accusation. Several Jews of their own accord, when in danger of false accusation, appealed to the king for inquiry. Edward recognising that his haste had endangered the success of his policy, a few years later relaxed the anti-usury laws of 1273, and by further legislation legalised money-lending at a definite rate of interest and for short periods.[1]

Edward had not only the good of the State at heart ; the advantage of religion was also his concern. Since the time of Innocent III., and in England of Stephen

---

[1] It is somewhat doubtful whether legislation to this effect was in reality adopted or only proposed.

Langton, the hostility of the Christian Church towards Jewry had grown more intense. In England the religious aspect of the persecution of the Jews had been less pronounced than on the Continent, for English rulers had always shown themselves less subservient to Papal influence than their continental fellow-monarchs. Edward, however, was more loyal in his adhesion to the Church than were his predecessors, and the wishes of Rome had consequently weight with him. So soon as the social and political status of the Jews of England had been settled, attention was directed to the condition of their souls. In 1279 a proclamation was issued directing that any Jew guilty of blaspheming the doctrines of Christianity should be put to death, or otherwise punished—one was burnt at Norwich for this offence. Writs were also issued to the sheriffs and bailiffs concerned, directing them to compel all Jews within their respective jurisdictions to attend sermons by the Dominicans, preached for the purpose of convincing them of their errors and of influencing their conversion to Christianity. The king on his part consented to forgo his right to the whole of the property of a convert, agreeing to allow him one half for his support, and to devote the other to the use of the poorer converts.

Jews compelled to attend sermons by the Dominicans.

AUTHORITIES :—J. Jacobs, London, "Jewish Encyclopedia," vol. viii. ; B. L. Abrahams, "The Expulsion of the Jews from England"; J. M. Rigg, "Select Pleas," &c., "The Jews of England in the Thirteenth Century"; D'Bloissiers Tovey, *Anglia Judaica;* J. E. Blunt, "The Jews in England"; L. O. Pike, "A History of Crime in England"; "Patent Rolls of the Reign of Edward I., 1272 to 1281" (1901) ; "Close Rolls of the Reign of Edward I., 1272 to 1279" (1900).

CHAPTER XI

THE EXPULSION
(1282–1290)

The syna-
gogues of
London
suppressed. THE last decade of the history of Pre-Expulsion
Anglo-Jewry opened with a further attack on the
religious rights of the Jews. The chief synagogues
of the Jews of London had before the close of the
reign of Henry III. been seized, and only the smaller
semi-private or private ones remained to the community. This semi-proscription of Judaism was still
insufficient to satisfy such zealous churchmen as the
primate, John of Peckham, and on his insistence,
in 1282, these smaller places of worship were also
suppressed.

Although the taxable value of the community had
gravely decreased—their impoverishment was one
of the reasons that enabled Edward to dispense with
them—the Jews had once more to suffer extortion
before they were finally released from bondage. Once
again, on this occasion in 1288, the whole of Anglo-
Jewry was suddenly seized and cast into prison. The
Commons offered a tax of a fifth of their movables if
the Jews were expelled, but the latter offered a larger
bribe, and they were released on payment of a ransom
of twelve thousand pounds of silver.

Still earlier in 1286 the Pope, Honorius IV., had
issued a bull to the Archbishops of Canterbury and
York, in which "the accursed and perfidious Jews" of
England were denounced. Their sacred writings were
condemned, and their efforts to recover persons who
may have lapsed from Judaism anathematised. The

service of Christians to Jews and the social intercourse between members of the two communities were emphasised as casting " opprobrium on the majesty of God." The English hierarchy had been often asked to remedy these evils, but had hitherto done but little in that direction. They were now told that they were " bound to rise up with ready courage against such audacity in order that it may be completely suppressed and confounded and that the dignity and glory of the Catholic Faith may increase. Therefore by this apostolic writing we give orders that, as the duty of your office demands, you shall use inhibitions, spiritual and temporal penalties, and other methods, which shall seem good to you, and which in your preaching and at other fitting times you shall set forth, to the end, that this disease may be checked by proper remedies."

These injunctions were not without effect. At the Synod of Exeter of 1287 all previous ecclesiastical enactments against the Jews of England were re-affirmed. It was decreed that Jews should not be permitted to appear in public at Easter, and that the practice of medicine by Jews should not be authorised. The bull of the Pope, beyond arousing the archbishop to this action, had also its effect on the most Christian Prince, Edward. He saw that his policy, as embodied in the Statute *de Judaismo*, of gradually assimilating the Jews with the surrounding population was distasteful to Rome, whose desires were that the Jews should be kept carefully apart from Christians. A new treatment had therefore to be meted out to Anglo-Jewry. Edward was at the time of the issue of the bull in his French possessions of Gascony, and his new policy was first put into force there by the expulsion of the Jews from that territory. *Ecclesiastical enactments.*

The Jews expelled from Gascony.

The reports of Edward's action in France preceded him to London, where, in consequence, he was re-

ceived with all the marks of popularity from every
section of the population. Parliament on its assembly
voted him a fifteenth part of their movables and the
clergy a tenth, provided that he would confer on
England the benefits he had granted his Gascon
subjects, and expel the Jews from the kingdom. On
the 18th of July 1290 the writs were issued announcing
The Expulsion. the expulsion of the Jews to take effect on the Feast
of All Saints of that year. About sixteen thousand
Jews, who had gradually been restricted to seventeen
towns, left England. The king, possessed by no
vindictive passion for persecution, took steps so that
they should be allowed to depart in peace, without
molestation. They were allowed to take their
movable property with them, as well as all pledges
that had not been redeemed. Except in the case of
one or two favourites, the houses, synagogues, cemeteries, bonds either as acknowledgments of debt or
undertakings to deliver merchandise already paid for
in part, were forfeited. The sheriffs were ordered to
make proclamation that until the appointed day of
banishment no one should harm or rob the Jews, but,
on the other hand, they should be guarded, and for
those willing to pay, safe transport out of the country
provided. The Wardens of the Cinque Ports were
commanded, under penalties, to treat the Jews civilly
and honestly, and to furnish the poorer ones with
transport to the Continent at reduced rates.

This correct attitude of the king was, however, not
shared by the people, and the last journey of the Jews
in England was pursued amid the insults and assaults
of the populace. The Jews of London departed on
St. Denis' Day. The richer ones had arranged with
a shipmaster to convey them and their belongings to
the less hostile shore of the Continent. In Holinshed's words : " A sort of the richest of them, being
shipped with their treasure in a mightie tall ship

which they had hired, when the same was under saile, and got downe the Thames towards the mouth of the river beyond Quinborowe (Queenborough), the maister mariner bethought him of a wile, and caused his men to cast anchor, and so rode at the same, till the ship by ebbing of the streame remained on the drie sands. The maister herewith enticed the Jewes to walke out with him on land for recreation. And at length when he understood the tide to be comming in, he got him backe to the ship, whither he was drawne up by a cord. The Jewes made not so much hast as he did, bicause they were not ware of the danger. But when they perceived how the matter stood, they cried to him for helpe : howbeit he told them, that they ought to crie rather unto Moses, by whose conduct their fathers passed through the red sea, and therefore, if they would call to him for helpe, he was able inough to help them out of those raging flouds, which now came in upon them : they cried indeed, but no succour appeared, and so they were swallowed up in water." The master and sailors appropriated the property of their victims and returned to London. A just retribution met them, for they were tried and hanged for their crime.

A number of the exiles sailed for France, and meeting with storms on the way were shipwrecked and drowned. The survivors were allowed by the king of France to settle temporarily in his kingdom. Such compassion, however, called forth the protests of the Papacy, and the *Parlement de la Chandeleur* accordingly decreed that all Jewish fugitives from Gascony or England should leave the kingdom. This decree appears not to have been rigidly executed, and a number of the refugees managed to conceal themselves among the comparatively considerable Jewish population of France. A body of about thirteen hundred English Jews sailed direct for

The fate of the exiles.

Flanders.[1]   Others probably reached Germany and possibly Spain, then containing a very large Jewish population.

Practically the whole of the property the Jews left behind them in England passed into the hands of the king.   It was ordered to be sold and the proceeds devoted to pious purposes.   To the king's friends rather than to pious purposes the benefit accrued.

Before leaving this part of our story, a few words may be added regarding some of the larger Jewish settlements in the provinces in the period before the Expulsion.

Lincoln.   At Lincoln, at one time the second most important town in the country, the Jews settled in comparatively large numbers ; Steep Hill, between the old Roman colony and the new Castle and Cathedral, being the Jewish centre.   The earliest mention of them occurs in 1159.   Between the attack on the Jews in 1190 and the St. Hugh incident the chief event in the history of Lincoln Jewry was another attack in 1220.   For a large portion of the thirteenth century the **Benedict fil Mosse.** leading Jew of Lincoln was Benedict fil Mosse, identified by Dr. Joseph Jacobs with Berechiah de Nicole.   Benedict, who was a son of Rabbi Moses ben Yomtob of London, was an authority, frequently quoted, on Jewish law and observance.   It was the marriage of his daughter that was the cause of the gathering of Jews in Lincoln on the occasion of the death of the boy Hugh.[2]   Benedict was one of the Jews sent to London in connection with that affair.   He was released before trial, probably in consequence of his daughter's wedding being an adequate defence against any charge of murder that might be brought against him.   Benedict died after 1256.   Another rich thir-

---

[1] Many also are said to have taken refuge in Scotland.   See Howell's " Josippon."

[2] This is a conjecture by Dr. Jacobs, but grave doubt has been thrown upon it by Dr. H. P. Stokes.

teenth-century Jew of Lincoln, who suffered severely from the exactions of the king, was Leo. In 1266, eleven years after the case of Hugh, in the midst of the Barons' Wars, the " Disinherited " made an attack on the Lincoln Jewry, and succeeded in their chief object of destroying the records of indebtedness to the Jews. Despite these troubles Lincoln continued an important Jewish centre until the Expulsion, and in addition to being, from the Jewish point of view, a place of commercial and financial importance, it was the seat of a Jewish college.[1]

After London, Oxford, and Cambridge, Norwich is Norwich. the earliest English town mentioned as being inhabited by Jews. In the interval between the so-called martyrdom of William and the charge of circumcising a Christian child in 1234, the Norwich community remained one of the most prosperous in the country. The most prominent member in the twelfth century was Jurnet of Norwich, who in 1186 was fined 6000 marks, in addition to forfeiture of his wife's lands, for marrying a Christian, Miryld, daughter of Humphrey de Havile. The massacre of 1190 has already been mentioned, as has also the great financier of the thirteenth century, Isaac of Norwich.

It was at Oxford that the deacon, who in 1222 Oxford. had embraced Judaism for the love of a Jewess, was degraded and burnt. This case of conversion was, it seems, not solitary, and to counteract the influence that the Jews were wielding over the scholars of the university and the children of the inhabitants, the Dominicans had in 1221 formed a settlement in the very heart of the Jewry. They seem to have had some success in carrying the war into the enemy's camp, for the number of converted Jews was sufficient to necessitate the establishment of a House of

[1] This is also a conjecture by Dr. Jacobs, who translates *schola* thus.

Converts. In 1235 certain Jews were imprisoned for abducting one of these converts, but released by the king, as innocent. Nine years later, however, the Jewry was attacked by the clerks who were indebted to its inhabitants. For this offence the annals of the period strangely record that forty-five of the assailants were committed to prison. In 1260 there was a dispute between the constable of Oxford Castle and the chancellor of the university as to jurisdiction over the local Jews. The decision was given by the king in favour of the chancellor.

The terrible events of 1190 had annihilated the Jewish community of the northern capital, and for a time York was devoid of Jews. After an interval the economic necessities of so important a centre compelled the re-establishment of a Jewish community, and a small number collected again within the shadow of Clifford's Tower. Of these, several were children or other relatives of victims of the massacre, and prominent among them was Aaron, a son of Josce, one of the leaders of the martyrs of York. Aaron of York, who was born before 1190 and died after 1253, was appointed Chief Presbyter in 1237, in succession to Josce of London. He held the office until 1243, when he was succeeded by Elias of London. Among the other prominent York Jews of the period were Benedict Episcopus; Samuel (*d.* 1238), brother of Aaron; Leo Episcopus (*d.* 1244); the last-named's son Samuel (*d.* 1250); Josceus of Canterbury and his sons Bonamicus and Samuel. Until the death of these, York remained an important centre of Anglo-Jewry, although it never recovered its glories of the period before the massacre. In common with those of the other Jewish centres, its fortunes, however, subsequently declined until the day on which York Jewry was overwhelmed in the catastrophe common to the whole of Anglo-Jewry.

AUTHORITIES:—B. L. Abrahams, "The Expulsion of the Jews"; R. Holinshed, "Chronicles"; J. M. Rigg, "The Jews of England in the Thirteenth Century"; D'Bloissiers Tovey, *Anglia Judaica;* J. E. Blunt, "The Jews in England"; G. H. Leonard, "The Expulsion of the Jews by Edward I." (*Transactions of the Royal Historical Society,* vol. v., 1891); W. Rye, "The Persecutions of the Jews : On the Circumcision of a Boy at Norwich in 1230" (Norfolk Antiquarian Miscellany, vol. i.); R. Davies, "On the Mediæval Jews of York"; J. Jacobs, "Little St. Hugh"; Anthony à Wood, "The History and Antiquities of the University of Oxford"; A. Neubauer, "Notes on the Jews in Oxford"; A. Hume, "St. Hugh of Lincoln"; "Jewish Encyclopedia," articles, "Berechiah de Nicole," "Lincoln," "Norwich," "Oxford," "York"; "Patent Rolls of the Reign of Edward I., 1281 to 1292" (1893); "Close Rolls of the Reign of Edward I., 1288 to 1296" (1904).

CHAPTER XII

PRE-EXPULSION JEWRY

The Chief
Presbyter and
other officials.

FEW records have remained to describe the internal organisation of the Anglo-Jewish community before the Expulsion. Of the *Presbyter Judæorum* or Chief Presbyter mention has already been made. Not only had this functionary, it appears, supervision of the spiritual affairs of the community and judicial rights in connection with the Exchequer of the Jews, but he also seems to have had some civil control over the community; and perhaps for that reason the Chief Presbyter, who was appointed by the king on the nomination of the Jews, or with his approval, was invariably chosen from among the richest Jews in the kingdom. Other officials of whom trace can be found, it has been suggested, were *Dayanim*, or Assessors in the Ecclesiastical Court. The name or title *Episcopus* that is to be found in the records has been translated as *Dayan*, but doubt has been cast on this interpretation, and Cohen or priest, a Jewish tribal name, has been suggested as more probable. References have also been found to the honorary officials usually found in Jewish communities, the *Parnassim* or presidents of the congregation, and the *Gabbayim* or treasurers. Other officers mentioned previously were the justices of the Jews, the chirographers, and the clerks.

For a long period of the sojourn of the Jews in England, there seems to have been a continual infiltration of foreign Jews, and we meet members of the community coming from France, Germany, Flanders,

Italy, Spain, and even Russia. Any computation of the numbers of the Jewish population must be little more than guess-work, for the material on which to work is almost entirely non-existent. At the time of the Expulsion the Jewish population did not exceed 10,500, and it is probable that this is the highest point it ever attained. The natural increase was always being compensated for by whole-sale executions or massacres, which involved a considerable proportion of the small number of Jews. Of course this number was relatively much greater than it would appear at present. At the close of the twelfth century, Dr. Joseph Jacobs computes that there were not more than two thousand Jews in the country, although at the same time he suggests that Jews may have formed one per cent. of the general population, amounting to about one and a half millions. Until the Jews were artificially restricted as to residence their distribution followed that of the general population. It has already been mentioned that the occupations of the Jews were necessarily almost entirely confined to finance, and to a less extent to commerce. In addition there were, as will be shown later, those who devoted themselves to Jewish literature. There seem also to have been occasional entries into other occupations. The solitary Jewish member of a gild has already been mentioned. The goldsmith's art also attracted Jews, and one Leo acted in that capacity to John. Jews throughout the Continent were especially experienced in medicine, and on repeated occasions were entrusted with the care of the health of popes and kings. In England consequently there need be no surprise at finding an occasional Jewish physician, although but few appear to have been known in the country. The suggestion has, however, been made that in the earlier period Jews taught in the English

The numbers of the Jews.

Their occupations.

hospitals. It has also been said that the Jews, when pledged to the Earl of Cornwall, were forced to work in the tin mines of his earldom, and to this apocryphal Jewish connection a portion of the nomenclature of Cornwall has been attributed.

Three classes in Anglo-Jewry.

The Jewish population of England, immediately preceding the Expulsion, has been divided by Mr. Lionel Abrahams into three classes. The first, consisting of very few members and of less families, was composed of the rich members of the community, the leading members of the various congregations, engaged formerly in financial transactions, and towards the end exporters of wool and corn. The members of the second class, more numerous, but still a minority, were money-lenders on a small scale, and pawnbrokers. Those of the third class, forming he great majority, were either in a state of poverty or bordering on that condition. Of their means of livelihood, beyond the service of their richer co-religionists, nothing whatever is known.

Their costume and social customs.

The costume of the English Jew included the horned cap, and a badge in form peculiar to this country. The language spoken by them in England was the same as that of the better classes ; French Jews fought duels just as their Christian neighbours, and one supposed reference has even been found to a Jewish knight. Until relations were embittered by outside influences, the social relations between Jews and Christians seem to have been very friendly. They visited one another, and apparently ate—or at least drank—at one another's tables. Evidence of this we find from both sides, On the one hand there are the frequent warnings by the Church against eating and other social intercourse with Jews ; on the other, a contemporary Hebrew authority states, "It is surprising that in the land of the Isle (England) they are lenient in the matter of drinking strong

drinks of the Gentiles and along with them. For
the Law is distinctly according to those Doctors who
forbid it on the ground that it leads to inter-marriage.
But, perhaps, as there would be great ill-feeling if
they were to refrain from this, one must not be
severe upon them."[1] Even as late as 1286, Bishop
Swinfeld threatened to excommunicate several of
his flock who wished to attend the wedding of the
daughter of a leading Jew of Hereford. Inter-
marriages between Jews and Christians took place,
and the balance of conversion during the periods
of prosperity seems to have tended towards Judaism
rather than Christianity.

The religious observances do not appear to have *Their religious
differed from those of the Jews of France. The *observances.*
synagogue, then the centre of the congregation, in
reality a meeting-place, was not devoted solely to
religious purposes. As in France, Jews, when "called
to the law" in the synagogue, were accustomed to
go up bareheaded. As was universal at that time
in Jewry, and still occurs where the position of the
Jews is precarious, Jews were betrothed by their
parents when quite young, for the pathetic reason
that although the father of the bride might, at the
time, be able to give his daughter a dowry, the
insecurity was so great that at any time he might
be reduced to beggary by the confiscation or looting
of his property. The frequent exactions, coupled
with the youth of the newly-married couple, were
responsible for the arrangements whereby for a time
they remained in the household of the bride's parents.
The Jews of England, as elsewhere—no matter how *Educational
bitter the persecution they suffered—never neglected *facilities.*
the education of their children, and, among the
records of Pre-Expulsion Jewry the designation
"Magister Puerorum" is to be found. Every com-

[1] See "Jews in Angevin England," p. 269.

munity had its school attached to the synagogue, and in London and the larger towns there appear to have been seminaries of Jewish learning. The knowledge of Hebrew was widespread among Jewesses as well as among Jews, and a code of education, drawn up, there is every reason to believe, for the guidance of English Jews, is still in existence. This code includes among its directions that every first-born male should be set aside for the study of the Law (*i.e.* Jewish literature). His course of studies from the age of five is carefully laid down. The teachers were to devote themselves entirely to their profession. The ritual used by the English Jews, although in the main identical with the North-French, yet had some local variations, and both differed in many details from that in use among the Jews of Germany.

Among Dr. Joseph Jacobs' many services to the study of Pre-Expulsion Anglo-Jewish history has been his piecing together of the story of Jewish literature in England during the early period. "I have come to the conclusion," he writes, "that during the last third of the twelfth century the English Jews held the lead in spiritual and literary activity among the Israelites of Northern Europe. I have discovered among them, as I think, a whole school of Massorites and grammarians, a couple of religious poets, a writer on astronomy, several exegetes of importance. . . . It should not surprise us that the Jews of England shared in the spiritual hegemony which her position as head of the Angevin Empire gave England at the end of the twelfth century over all the Romance-speaking nations of Europe."[1] This claim is too high, but the twelfth century was an illuminating period in Jewish literature, and in the general movement Anglo-Jewry took part. The literary renaissance

[1] "Angevin England," p. v.

among the English Jews came from France—the
first of the missionaries seems to have been Rabbi
Simeon Chasid of Treves, who was in England from Distinguished
1106 to 1146—but the new cult soon took root, and visitors.
flourished without outward assistance. Other prominent French scholars who visited England were
Rabbi Yomtob of Joigny, the martyr of York ; Rabbi
Samuel ben Solomon of Falaise (Sir Morell of
England); Jacob of Orleans, killed in London in 1189;
and, Dr. Jacobs believes, also Rabbi Elchanan ben
Isaac of Dampierre, and his pupil Jehuda ben Isaac
(Sir Leon of Paris) (1166-1224), one of the most important commentators on the Gemara. The most
illustrious of the foreign Jewish visitors to England
was the distinguished writer and scholar Abraham
ibn Ezra (1092 or 1093-1167).   Ibn Ezra not only
lectured during his visits to London, but also wrote
there his *Yesod Mora*, a philosophic-religious work
dedicated to his pupil Joseph ben Jacob of London,
and " The Letter of Sabbath."

In the school of Massorites (critics of the text) and Anglo-Jewish
grammarians, the first name is that of Samuel authors.
Nakdan, and prominent among his successors were
Berachyah Nakdan (Benedict le Puncteur of Oxford),
Rabbi Benjamin of Cambridge and Samuel le Pointur
of Bristol.   Other important Anglo-Jewish Massorites
and grammarians were Moses ben Yomtob of London and Moses ben Isaac.   Another Anglo-Jewish
author was Yomtob, the father of Moses Nakdan, a
writer on Jewish law.   A hymn composed by Rabbi
Yomtob of Joigny is still included in the Day of
Atonement Liturgy of the Ashkenazim or German
Jews.   Berachyah Nakdan, if Dr. Jacobs' doubtful
identification be admitted, was the famous author of
" The Fox Fables," an ethical work, *Sepher Mazref*,
and commentaries on several books of the Old Testament.   He also translated a treatise on mineralogy.

It must be added, however, that most authorities dispute the identity of the English Berachyah with the celebrated fabulist. Deodatus Episcopus was the author of an astronomical work. Anglo-Jewish authors who flourished later were Berechiah de Nicole (Lincoln), rabbi of Lincoln, and an authority on ritual matters ; Aaron of Canterbury, an exegete and dayan ; Elias of London, the chief Presbyter who bearded the Earl of Cornwall ; Jacob ben Judah of London, poet and author of *Etz Chayim*, a book on the ritual ; Meïr of Norwich, a liturgical poet. Hagin, the chief Presbyter at the time of the Expulsion, translated Ibn Ezra's astrological works into French, and *L'Image du Monde*, a French cosmographical work, into Hebrew. A large number of these Anglo-Jewish scholars were related, and a genealogical tree has been constructed by Dr. Joseph Jacobs,[1] and supplemented by Dr. D. Kauffmann.[2]

The Jews did not keep their learning to themselves ; and in the happier period they had schools at Oxford, for instance, where Christian scholars studied Hebrew and other subjects. On the Expulsion many of the Hebrew books were taken away by the fugitives, but some remained behind. These came into the hands of English scholars, among others Roger Bacon. At his death his Hebrew library passed into the possession of the Franciscan Friars.

Anglo-Jewish nomenclature.   During the period dealt with in the preceding pages, surnames, in the modern sense of the term, were of course unknown. Mere personal names were, however, insufficient to identify individuals, and explanatory additions — which in later generations chrystallised into inherited surnames—were to be found attached to the personal names. In Anglo-Jewish nomenclature representatives of four classes into which surnames may be divided are to be found.

[1] The London Jewry.   [2] *Jewish Quarterly Review*, vol. iii.

Patronymics, such as Aaron fil Isaac, Abraham fil Rabbi, Abraham fil Muriel, &c., were numerous. Other relationships were explained by such names as Aaron frater Leonis de Dunstaple, Abraham gener Elie, Avigay uxor Jacob, Anna mater Lumbardi. Of local names also a great number are to be met with ; among others, Aaron de Colcestre, Amiot de Excestre, Isaac de Joueigny, Ysaac de Russie, Deulecresse de Danemarcia (Ardennes), Josce de Domo Samson, Cok de Domo Abrahe. Occupations and offices were designated in the names Abraham Gabbai (the treasurer of a synagogue), Abraham le Vesq (Cohen), Abraham Pernas (the president of a congregation), Benjamin Magister (a schoolmaster), Isaac Medicus, Isaac Magister Puerorum, Moses Nakdan, &c. The fourth class, descriptive names and nicknames, includes Benedict Parvus, Benedict Lengus, Deudone cum pedibus tortis, Duzelina vidua Mossy cum naso, Isaac le Gros, Isaac Senex, Mosse Juvenis, &c. Early Anglo - Jewish names proper were for the most part biblical, although in many instances they were rendered by Latin or French equivalents. Of these there are, for instance, Deodatus (Nathaniel or Elchanan), Josceus and Josce (Joseph), Vivard, Vivelot, Vives and Hagin (Chajim), Deulecresse and Cresse (Deus eum crescat, Gedaliah), Bendit and Benedict (Berachyah and Baruch), Helye (Elias), Biket (a diminutive of Rebecca), Deudone (Jonathan), Deulabenie (Berach-yah), Serfdeu (Obadiah), Deulesalt (Isaiah), and many others.

Patronymics and nick-names.

AUTHORITIES :—J. Jacobs, "The Jews of Angevin England," "The London Jewry, 1290," "England" ("Jewish Encyclopedia"), "English Massorites and Berechiah Naqdan" (*Jewish Quarterly Review*, vol. ii.) ; B. L. Abrahams, "The Expulsion of the Jews from England" ; I. Abrahams, "Jewish Life in the Middle Ages" (1896) ; H. Adler, "The Chief Rabbis of England" (*Publications of the Anglo-Jewish Historical Exhibition*, 1888) ;

H

B. L. Abrahams, "The Expulsion of the Jews from England" (*Jewish Quarterly Review*, vol. ii.); M. Friedländer, "Ibn Ezra in England" (*Transactions, Jewish Historical Society*, vol. vii.); D. Kauffmann, "The Ritual of England before 1290" (*Jewish Quarterly Review*, vols. iii., iv., and vi.); S. Singer, "Early Translations and Translators of the Jewish Liturgy in England" (*Transactions, Jewish Historical Society*, vol. iii.); A. Neubauer, "English Massorites" (*Jewish Quarterly Review*, vol. ii.); J. M. Rigg, "The Jews of England in the Thirteenth Century" (*Jewish Quarterly Review*, vol. xv.); Anthony à Wood, "The History and Antiquities of the University of Oxford"; Francis Peck, "The Antiquarian Annals of Stamford"; "Jewish Encyclopedia," article, "Berechiah ben Natron ai Krespia Ha Nakdan."

"The Jews in England"

Distribution of
THE JEWS OF ENGLAND
before the Expulsion

Newcastle-on-Tyne

Lancaster

YORK
Beverley
Doncaster
Grimsby
LINCOLN
Nottingham
Derby
Stamford
KingsLynn
NORWICH
Bungay
LEICESTER
Thetford
Eye
Bridgnorth
Coventry Huntingdon
BURY St EDMUNDS
Warwick NORTHAMPTON
Worcester
CAMBRIDGE
BEDFORD
Sudbury Ipswich
Tewkesbury
HEREFORD
Dunstable Hitchin
Colchester
GLOUCESTER
Berkhamsted
Newport Cricklade OXFORD Hertford
BRISTOL Wycombe
Reading LONDON
Wells Devizes Newbury Rochester Ospringe
Marlborough Windsor
Wilton Guildford Faversham Canterbury
WINCHESTER Rye
Romsey Southampton
Dorchester Arundel Winchelsea
Chichester
EXETER Bosham

Newborough
Beaumaris
Rhuddland
Conway
Carnarvon Flint
Bala
Criccieth Harlech

Scale of Miles
0   50   100

London: Macmillan & Co. Ltd.

Stanford's Geog¹ Estab¹ London

CHAPTER XIII

THE MIDDLE PERIOD
(1290–1550)

FOR long the opinion was held, that with the expatriation of the Jews of England by Edward all
connection of the Jews with that country came to a
close, and that for the three and a half centuries
following the Expulsion no Jew touched English
ground. Such a view has, however, now been proved
incorrect. So far from the truth is it, that instead of
a total exclusion of Jewry from England, hardly a
year seems to have passed between the Expulsion
and the Resettlement in which one or more Jews,
often professing Judaism, could not be found in the
country either as wayfarers or as settlers. On the
other hand, however, until the reign of Charles I. no
organised community appears to have existed, and
interpreting the word Jewry in that sense rather than
as the haphazard gathering of individual Jews, one
is justified in saying that the history of the Jews in
England closed in 1290, not to be resumed until 1655.

Leaving the question of an organised community
aside, however, and considering merely the case of
individual Jews, the question at once arises whether
the Expulsion of 1290 included every member of
the community. Although no definite evidence can
be found of the tarrying of Jews after the bulk of
their co-religionists had departed, the English expulsion, if it had been complete, would have differed from
all similar tribulations of the Jews elsewhere. It is
beyond the limits of possibility for all the members

*Probable sur-
vivors of the
Expulsion.*

of a race without a solitary exception to be of the mould of martyrs. The great majority of the Jews of England, like, for instance, the 800,000 who followed the lead of the statesman Isaac Abravanel in the exodus from Spain two hundred and two years later, did not hesitate to prefer the loss of all temporal advantages, of the comfort that to most people means the whole of life, to resume their weary and endless pilgrimage, rather than to accept what they considered apostasy, or even as secret-Jews to render lip-service to a creed with which in their hearts they had no sympathy. To the English Jew of the thirteenth century the mere formality of baptism meant the close of all his persecutions. Despite this overwhelming temptation but few fell, and even from among those few there were continual instances of reversion to Judaism. The bulk of the Jews of England preferred exile to apostasy. As in the case of Spain, however, there can be little doubt that a minority, weaker in will and in constancy, chose baptism rather than the terrors of banishment, and as Christians, more or less sincere, remained behind and became gradually lost in the general population. The increased number of inmates of the House of Converts at this period supports the view here put forward. The eastern counties have especially been mentioned as the district in which Crypto-Jews were to be found in the succeeding centuries. At the same time there is a tradition that the Expulsion of 1290 was not complete, and that it was not until 1358 that the last vestige of Judaism was driven from the

Tradition of a remnant at Oxford.

country. Oxford had many privileges beyond the ordinary English cities, and among them, it has been suggested, was the permission to retain Jews within the limits of the city after the remainder of the country had been purged of the Semitic element. A Jewish colony, it is said, remained in Oxford for

long after 1290, but cut off from all connection with
the great body of Jewry or even any other Jewish
settlement, in the natural course the little Jewish
colony became still more attenuated, and after the
lapse of generations became lost in the surrounding
Christian population.

The generation of the Expulsion, only too sensible
of the agony of a Jewish residence in England, once
it had escaped from that purgatory was little anxious
to return. To the Jew of the close of the thirteenth
century, the name England must have appeared more
fraught with misery than did even Egypt to his
ancestors of thirty centuries earlier. Human memory
is, however, short-lived, and the second generation
after the Expulsion seems already to have forgotten
all their parents had suffered under the rule of the
early Plantagenets. 1290 was the year of the departure : only twenty years later, in 1310, six Jews
—one was a physician, of the others nothing whatever is known—came on a mission to England, if A Jewish depu-
possible to negotiate the readmission of their people England.
into the country. For the Jews to desire to return
after a short absence of twenty years seems at the
first glance surprising. The record of contemporary
Jewish history, however, helps even the casual reader
to understand how even England might appear, relatively, a land of promise. During the twenty years
that had elapsed since the Expulsion, there had been
an anti-Jewish outbreak at Colmar ; the Jews of Rome,
hastening to receive Boniface VIII. on his entry
into the city, had been scorned and threatened ; the
Jews of Germany as a whole had suffered severe
persecution, and those of Magdeburg in particular had
been plundered and slain ; and finally in 1306 the Jews
had been expelled from France. Any land in which,
for the moment, there was peace must have seemed
a harbour of refuge for these hunted victims of

expulsion, confiscation, outrage, and murder. Beyond the bare announcement of this mission of six Jews, no other mention is to be found in the surviving contemporary records. There is no reason to believe, however, that the embassy was to any extent successful, or that the hearts of the English and their rulers softened towards the helots of Christendom.[1]

Among the opportunities afforded Jews for visiting and even settling in England undetected was the presence in the country of the Italian money-changers or usurers. The Cahorsins although the first were not the only Christian financiers who acted as the bankers of mediæval England. Even before the departure of the Jews, the term Cahorsin had come to designate not merely money-changers, originating from Cahors, but those coming from Latin Europe generally. In the fourteenth century the term Lombards had become synonymous with Cahorsin and denoted the same class in the community. If the suspicions expressed by the Commons in 1376 were justifiable, these Lombards were even more heterogeneous than the widest interpretation of the term reinforced by Cahorsin would suggest. They were accused of harbouring Saracens and spies in their midst, and the Commons even went further and stated that Jews also took refuge under the cloak of Lombardism. The official control of financial and commercial operations was at the time lax, and little official difficulty would have been found by Jews in England masquerading as Lombards. So far as the king was concerned the complaints of the Commons passed unheeded, and any Jews that may have formed the basis of the suspicions remained without molestation.

Jews masquerading as Lombards.

Of the few and scanty records of Jewish visitors to

[1] MSS. Hargrave 179, fol. 295.

England during this period there exists one relating
to Solomon Levi, after his conversion Paul of Burgos, Paul of Burgos.
former rabbi, archbishop, statesman, and persecutor
of the Jews. Solomon Levi, possibly a descendant
of one of the refugees of 1290, while still a Jew visited
London, and in an extant letter of his, dated from
that city, he complained of his isolation from co-
religionists. The next reference is to one, described
as a Jew in his safe conduct to come to England,
who travelled accompanied by ten servants, the exact
number, it has been noted, required for the quorum
for service according to the Jewish rites. The king,
Henry IV., who before ascending the English throne
had come in contact with Jews on the Continent, was
well acquainted with the reputation the race had
acquired in the practice of medicine. Henry's health
declined towards the close of his life, and as he failed
to obtain relief from native practitioners, Dr. Elias
Sabot of Bologna, who had probably earned a reputa- Jewish
tion for skill in medicine, was sent for, and as a Jew physicians in England.
given a safe conduct and permission to travel or settle
in any part of the country. Sabot arrived in England
in 1410.[1] Two years later another physician, David
di Nigarellis of Lucca, strongly suspected of Judaism
by historians, followed him to this country. Nigarellis
had an annuity granted him by the king, and was also
favoured with naturalisation as an English subject.
The patent of naturalisation accorded Nigarellis full
rights, including those of holding lands and
advowsons. The last-mentioned grant suggests that
Nigarellis was not a Jew, at any rate by religion, at
that date. If he were he was certainly the first of

---

[1] Dr. Simonsen identifies this mediæval physician with Elijah Be'er ben
Shabbethai, who on account of his skill was created a Roman citizen.
Elijah was private physician to Pope Martin V., and held a similar appointment under his successor, Eugene IV. In the agreement drawn up
between the Pope and the Italian Jews in 1443, Elijah acted as one of the
representatives of the latter.

that faith to acquire English citizenship. Another Jewish doctor has been traced in England at the same period. Alice, the wife of Sir Richard Whittington, the famous Lord Mayor, having fallen ill, her husband obtained the royal permission to invite a Jewish doctor of the south of France to come to England to attend to her. Accordingly, in 1409, Maistre Sampson de Mierbeawe judeus was granted permission for one year to settle, travel, and practise his profession in any part of the kingdom.

Converts from Judaism.

Still earlier there had been some conversions from Judaism other than those to be mentioned in the next chapter in connection with the *Domus Conversorum*. In 1358 a pension was bestowed upon John de Castello on his abjuring Judaism. In similar circumstances pensions were conferred on Richard de Cicilia (1389) and William Piers (1392). In 1421 one Job, an Italian apothecary, and his son John, being found in the country, had to accept baptism before receiving naturalisation. From that date until almost the close of the fifteenth century a cloud descends on the doings of Jews in England, but from occasional oratorical attacks on Jewry during that period we may deduce that although nothing is heard of them, England was not altogether free from Jews. We are told, for instance, that in 1428 "the Jews of Abingdon" performed an interlude before Henry VI.,[1] and we hear of one Masse Salman, who was sheriff of Southampton in 1489. He might have been a member of the race. A Jewish parentage was also attributed to the pretender Perkin Warbeck, an attribution which, whether true or false, at any rate suggests that such a parentage was not rendered impossible by the entire absence of Jews from the country.

The final act of Spanish persecution, when 800,000 Jews, men, women, and children, were cast forth

[1] Mr. Sidney Lee in *The Times*, Nov. 1, 1883.

penniless and almost naked, reacted on the whole of Effects of the expulsion from Spain. the then known world. The fugitives were scattered in all directions, numbers were received into all existing Jewish communities, and stragglers founded communities here and there of their own, some only ending their pilgrimage under the protection of the government of China. There can be no doubt that some of these stragglers found their way also to England, where, however, there were none to welcome them. In 1493 Ferdinand and Isabella had already written to Henry VII. complaining that certain Jews expelled from Spain were taking proceedings in London to recover from one Diego de Soria, apparently formerly their agent, sums alleged to be due to them, and asking Henry to do them a "special service" by annulling the proceedings. From this it is seen that the Jews of Spain before their expulsion had business relations with England, and among their agents in this country it is almost certain were included relatives and co-religionists. Five years later a Spanish mission was in England to arrange a marriage between a Spanish princess and Prince Arthur. The opportunity was taken to complain of the harbouring by England of Spanish heretics and Jews. At the request of the Spanish monarchs the Sub-Prior of Santa Cruz personally brought the matter under the notice of Henry, who promised to punish soundly any Jew to be found in his dominions. Amador de los Rios[1] states definitely that on the expulsion from Spain many Jews settled in England, and in particular communities and synagogues were established at London, York, and Dover. These communities and synagogues, if they existed, must have been kept very secret, for no reference is to be found to them elsewhere. It is quite probable that small communities

---

[1] *Historia de los Judios de España*, vol. iii.

of secret Jews did collect in various towns, and that they met on the usual occasions for divine service, but it is most improbable that the privacy of these services was not most strictly guarded, or that the services were known beyond the narrow circle of the refugees.

In the following reign Judaism and the Jewish law came into very considerable prominence. Henry VIII., who had married Catherine of Aragon, his brother's widow, and lived with her for many years, in 1529 discovered doubts concerning the legitimacy of the marriage, and became anxious for a divorce. Jewish doctors The various political influences at work rendered the and Henry legitimate satisfaction of Henry's demands extremely VIII.'s divorce. difficult, if not unattainable. All the applications of Henry, fortified by the opinion of the majority of the universities of Europe, were without avail on the Pope, who supported his refusals by the Mosaic code, which positively enjoined such unions in certain circumstances. In the midst of the contention such a marriage took place among the Jews of Italy, and, having so direct an application to the state of affairs in England, it was duly reported to all the courts represented in Italy. Henry and his advisers immediately saw the value of Jewish evidence and the necessity of supporting their case by rabbinic opinions. The views of learned Jews, professing and converted, were collected from all parts of the Continent, and from several of them written opinions obtained. Of these, that of Mark Raphael of Venice attracted most attention, and the author was personally invited to come to England. The opinion of Raphael was apparently considered of great weight, for strenuous efforts were made by the other party to the controversy to gain his adhesion. Not only was an office in the service of the Pope offered to Raphael, but an attempt was made to bribe his uncle, Father Francis, also a converted Jew, with a cardinal's hat. These efforts failing, an attempt, engineered by the Spanish ambassador at Rome, was made to waylay the uncle and nephew on their journey to England. This, however, also failed, and both arrived safely in London early in 1531. The case for the divorce was then placed in all its bearings before the learned Jew, who took some time to consider his decision. Raphael's response was as follows : "That the Queen's marriage ought not to be disputed or dissolved, but, nevertheless, that the King may and can very well take another wife conjointly with his first. Although the King's marriage with the widow of his brother was a true and legitimate act, yet he does not style himself properly husband of the Queen, inasmuch as according to (Jewish) law the posterity issuing from such a union is ascribed to the first husband; and as it would be unreasonable that, in order to preserve the name and race of the deceased, the survivor should be prevented from having posterity of his own and bearing his name, the Law allows; him to take another wife." Henry was not altogether satisfied with this decision, and told Raphael that he must devise some other means of getting him out of his difficulty. Raphael thereupon set to work again, and gave the following revised response : " It is allowable for a man to take to wife the widow of his brother, provided he do it out of his own desire and will, and with the direct intention of procuring descent to his brother's line. Without such marked intention the marriage is forbidden by Divine Law. God said so by the mouth of Moses, and cast His malediction on all those who married without such an intention, for if they did so marry, no generation could spring forth from them, and if any it could not last long." Raphael deduced from the absence of any surviving male heir to Henry and Catherine that Henry could not have married with the above express intention, "and consequently his marriage is illegiti-

The views of Mark Raphael.

mate and invalid." Raphael retained the favour of Henry. He was attached to the court, and received many presents and favours.

Some ten years later, in 1542, the presence of Jews in the country was reported to the Privy Council, who directed that a list of the suspects should be drawn up. The list, unfortunately, has been lost, and no record of further action, beyond arrests, can be found. In 1547 the distinguished convert, John

Tremellius in England. Immanuel Tremellius, visited the country. At the invitation of Archbishop Cranmer, Tremellius, in company with Peter Martyr, stayed at Lambeth Palace. Two years later he was appointed " King's reader of Hebrew " at Cambridge, and in 1552 made Prebendary of Carlisle. On the death of Edward VI. Tremellius left England, but paid another visit to the country about 1565. The next reference to a Jew appears under the date 1550, when Ferdinando Lopes, a Jewish physician living in St. Helens, London, was arrested and tried before the Lord Mayor for a serious offence, and ultimately banished the country.

AUTHORITIES :—L. Wolf, " The Middle Period of Anglo-Jewish History, 1290–1656 " (*Publications of the Anglo-Jewish Historical Exhibition*, 1888), "Calendar of State Papers " ; Sir J. H. Ramsay, " Jews in England" (*Academy*, Jan. 27, 1883) ; Sidney L. Lee, " Jews in England" (*Academy*, March 18, 1882, and Feb. 3, 1883) ; I. Abrahams, " Paul of Burges in London " (*Transactions, Jewish Historical Society*, vol. iii.), " Paul of Burges in London " (*Jewish Quarterly Review*, vol. xii., 1900) ; A. Weiner, " Jewish Doctors in England in the Reign of Henry IV." (*Jewish Quarterly Review*, vol. xviii., 1906); D. Simonsen, " Dr. Elías Sabot " (*Jewish Quarterly Review*, vol. xviii., 1906); E. N. Adler, " Auto de Fé and Jew," ch. vi. (*Jewish Quarterly Review*, vol. xiv.); Nicholas Pocock, " Records of the Reformation " (1870) ; G. H. Leonard, " The Expulsion of the Jews by Edward I."; " Dictionary of National Biography," article, " J. E. Tremellius.'

CHAPTER XIV

THE DOMUS CONVERSORUM
(1213–1609)

IN the previous pages a sketch has been given of the story of the Jews in England. Attention has been solely directed to men and women practising Judaism, as distinct from those merely of Jewish birth, and but seldom has one who even subsequently accepted baptism been mentioned. The term "Jew" is, however, more than a mere religious designation. There are Jews by religion who are not Jews by birth—in the previous pages occasional reference has been made to such — and there are also many Jews by race who are not so by religion. During a long period of English history special provision was made by the State for these latter. Of the various elements in the Jewish persecution of the twelfth and thirteenth centuries, that of the Church was almost, if not altogether, entirely religious. The object of the churchmen in the successive acts of oppression directed against the Jews was to secure their conversion to Christianity. To save their souls they were anxious to sacrifice their bodies. The end justified the means. Every possible means, therefore, was used to secure converts. Bribes and threats were both pressed into the service of the Church, which in all circumstances, in the latter portion of the period, was ably supported by the State. In the latter direction, that of threats and persecution generally, the assistance of the Church was, perhaps, not the direct object of the State. In the success of the policy of bribes to which the State was an active party, however, the Church had everything to gain and the State nothing.

Earlier houses of converts. The establishment by the Dominicans, assisted by the king, of· a house for the reception of converts in the heart of Oxford Jewry about 1221 has already been noted. Three years before the death of John, in 1213, a similar institution was established in Southwark, where a relatively considerable Jewish colony was then to be found. The foundation was purely religious. It was established by Richard, Prior of Bermondsey, in honour of St. Thomas, and adjoined that monastery. The example set by this prior was followed twenty years later by the king, Henry III., Foundation of the " Domus Conversorum." who established the " Domus Conversorum," or House for Converts in the New Street now known as Chancery Lane. The house of a rich Jew, recently come into the possession of the crown, was the nucleus of the new institution. The surrounding land in the possession of the crown was added to it. The structural alterations and extensions necessary, including the erection of a chapel, were all carried out at the royal expense, and the king, moreover, promised to devote to the same purpose "all other escheats coming into our hands in London or in the suburb of London." The institution was thus from the first bountifully endowed. The House was ready for occupation early in 1233, when several converts were already awaiting admission. These, to whom grants were made for clothing, may have been the men who were engaged in preparing the building for occupation, for it appears that they were themselves also converts. A custos or warden was appointed in the person of Walter, to whose office an adequate stipend was attached. The House, when full, accommodated about forty inmates, and it was customary in addition to allow pensions to others.

The establishment of the House aroused some enthusiasm. Matthew Paris, writing at the time, records that Henry built the House and Chapel "for the ransom of his soul and that of his father, King John, and all their ancestors. To this House converted Jews retired, leaving their Jewish blindness, and had a home and a safe refuge for their whole lives, living under an honourable rule, with sufficient sustenance without servile work or the profits of usury. So it happened that in a short time a large number were collected there. And now, being baptized and instructed in the Christian law, they live a praiseworthy life under a Governor specially appointed." The higher clergy generally took a deep interest in the institution, whose endowment was supplemented by legacies besides further royal grants.

In addition to the warden, a chaplain was attached to the institution immediately on its establishment, and further chaplains appointed subsequently. In Edward I.'s reign, a new office, that of sub-warden or presbyter, was created. This appointment, which was resident, and the duties of which were connected with the financial administration, was due to the laxity that had been displayed in the administration of the "House." The inmates were not only housed and fed ; in addition they were clothed, and received allowances, and instruction in the tenets of Christianity. At a later date their children were taught trades. The converts, who bore the designation "Le Convers"—whence the modern English surnames of Convers and sometimes Conyers—were encouraged to enter the Church, and the chaplain was often himself a convert from Judaism. The House of Converts was also to some extent a house of study, in which Hebrew learning was by no means neglected. One of the inmates at a later date became the first professor of Hebrew at Oxford.

Officials of the "Domus Conversorum."

The form of
reception.
No record remains of the procedure adopted in London on the reception of a convert. In all probability it differed but slightly, if at all, from that in use on the Continent. In Rome this was as follows. Unless the circumstances were exceptional, candidates for baptism had to await the Saturday in Holy Week. Then the convert was clothed in "a mantle of white damask, having a lawn band on, and a small silver cross hanging about his neck. Then a cardinal, attended by the Canons of the Church (St. John Lateran), proceeds to bless the water: after which, the person to be baptized is presented to him, by his godfathers, and makes a public declaration that he desires baptism: whereupon the cardinal, causing him to lean his breast upon the font, pronounces the usual form of words, and pours water on his head, with a large silver spoon: which being done the proselyte proceeds with a lighted taper in his hand to one of the oratories and is there confirmed; the whole concluding with a mass." We are, moreover, told that Jewish converts as a rule wore "very rueful visages." At these baptisms distinguished personages and even the king often assisted, and occasionally the royal couple acted as god-parents to the newly baptized.

The House does not appear to have been entirely devoted to the benefit of converts, for a few years after its establishment the keeper was directed to admit the Christian widow of a convert. Some of the
The occupa-
tions of the
converts.
inmates pursued their ordinary occupations outside; for instance, in 1238, two, who were king's bowmen, had their necessaries sent to them at the Tower, where they were stationed. In 1265 the House was enlarged, but within seven years the administration had fallen into such disorder and so many abuses had sprung up, that a reorganisation became a necessity. Complaint had been made to the king that the inmates were

deprived of their due allowances, and compelled to beg from door to door. In a letter addressed to the Mayor of London and the warden of the House, the king directed an immediate investigation into the management of the institution and its reorganisation. Henry III. and "It has been shown to us on the part of our poor the converts. converts in London, that since they have nothing to maintain them and none to aid them, they are compelled to beg from door to door, and are likely to die of hunger ; and that of those revenues we caused to be assigned to their maintenance, they receive nothing. Furthermore, certain rich converts, having other incomes and property, who do not reside in the aforesaid House, receive great part of its income, which is not as we desire, because we assigned revenues to the House for the poor and needy, and not for rich converts. A reform is therefore needed, and we direct you to inquire on oath as to the property belonging to the House and the way in which it is now expended, and henceforth to apply it to the use of those who are most in want, according to their necessities, and to the support of the chapel attached to the House. We also desire that all who share the revenues of the House shall reside within the building ; and that all who resist your authority shall forfeit their proportionate allowance."

Whatever improvement may have been effected at The "Domus" the close of Henry's reign proved only temporary, and under Edward I. affairs soon relapsed into their previous unsatisfactory condition. In 1278 the inmates personally appealed to the sovereign to relieve their forlorn condition. Shortly afterwards, in another petition of a similar tenor, it was mentioned that quite a score of the inmates had died of destitution. These piteous appeals bore fruit in 1280, when the king consented to forgo for seven years his right to the property of all converts, to whom half of their means was left, the

Sufferings of
the converts.

remainder going to the Home, and to devote the proceeds of the poll-tax levied on professing Jews to the upkeep of the House. The good intentions of the king were, however, to some extent defeated by the warden, who, relying on precedent, refused to submit his accounts for audit, from which refusal may be deduced the channel into which a portion of the funds disappeared. In 1290 another crisis arrived in the affairs of the House. Again the inmates were starving. The ordinary income, it was contended, was insufficient. This was increased in response to the appeal, and a regular payment ordered. The inmates asked that a keeper, who would pay due heed to their affairs, spiritual and temporal, should be appointed. The king directed the chancellor to find a person suitable for the office.

The "Domus"
after the
Expulsion.

With the expulsion of the Jews from England, it might reasonably have been expected that the days of the institution's usefulness would be numbered, and that it could not long survive the expatriation of the Jews of England. The surmise was, however, unfulfilled. The House remained in existence until the eighteenth century with a varying number of inmates, but until 1552 never totally devoid of some of Jewish birth. As the supply of Jewish recruits became weaker, applicants for admission, otherwise qualified than by birth, were received. Arthur Antoe, "a Pagan born, but converted to the fayth of Christe Jesus," presumably an American Indian, who was

The distribution of the
candidates for
admission.

admitted in 1605 was in all probability one of these. From the designations of the Jewish converts we may perhaps receive some hints of the relics of the Expulsion, and of the places in which they were to be found. During the centuries subsequent to 1290 converts were received at Chancery Lane, originating from London, Exeter, Oxford, Woodstock, Northampton, Leicester, Canterbury, Merton, Winchester, Stamford,

Lincoln, Bury, Arundel, Norwich, Bristol, Nottingham, and Cricklade, all Jewish centres before the Expulsion. In 1377 the office of Warden was united to that of Master of the Rolls. The two offices had for some years previously been held jointly by the same person. The first layman to hold the office was Thomas Cromwell, appointed in 1534. The inmates during the period subsequent to 1290 included Elizabeth, daughter of Rabbi Moses, *episcopus Judæorum*, otherwise described as *levesque des Jues de France et dalmaigne* (the Bishop of the Jews of France and Germany), who entered the House in 1399, ten years later married David Pole, a citizen and tailor of the city of London, but remained a pensioner and inmate of the House for another seven years. In 1409 Johanna and her daughter Alice, lately Jewish "miscreants," of the royal city of Dartmouth, where they had apparently been engaged in business, were admitted. In 1578, after the House had been devoid of converts for twenty-six years, Jehuda (Nathanael) Menda was admitted. He came from the Barbary States, and had been resident six years in London before his conversion. The scene attending this event in 1577 was remarkable. In the Church of All-Hallows, Lombard Street, Menda, who was both a Hebraist and a biblical scholar, read a long statement in Spanish explaining his conversion. The statement was followed by a famous sermon by John Foxe, the martyrologist, *De Oliva Evangelica*, which took four hours in delivery. Sir Francis Walsingham, the Secretary of State, who had been anxious to be present, was prevented by illness, and Foxe immediately repaired to his house and repeated the sermon for his benefit. Menda's statement was translated into English and published, and, together with the sermon, circulated widely, thus serving to attract public attention to Jewish matters, and indirectly causing the many Jewish references

Master of the Rolls as Warden of the "Domus."

Foxe and Menda.

that from that time began to appear in English literature. The presence of Menda and a colleague, Fortunati (Cooba) Massa, in the House may very well have been one of the elements that combined with others to suggest to Marlowe and to Shakespeare the treatment of Jewish topics.

In 1598 the most distinguished of the inmates of the House joined the small circle of converts. Philip Ferdinandus was born in Poland about 1555. He was first converted to Catholicism, but afterwards adopted Protestantism. A poor student at Oxford University, his knowledge of Hebrew soon attracted attention, and he lectured in several colleges. In 1596 he entered Cambridge University, where also he taught Hebrew, and counted most of the professors among his pupils. Shortly afterwards, by the introduction of his friend, the noted Hebraist, Joseph Scaliger, Ferdinandus was appointed Professor of Hebrew at Leyden University. In 1599 he was an inmate of the " Domus Conversorum." While at Cambridge Ferdinandus published a Latin volume containing the 613 precepts of the Mosaic Law, together with extracts from rabbinical literature. A later inmate, Jacob Wolfgang (admitted 1606), was one of the earliest readers in the then newly-established Bodleian Library at Oxford. The last reference to an inmate of the House appears under the date 1609. In subsequent years occasional applications were made for pensions by converted Jews, the last of them by Henry Cotigno in 1717.

A large proportion of the converts from Judaism who found refuge in the House during the three hundred and fifty years of its activity came from abroad, many from Spain, where the lot of Jewry was especially fraught with trouble throughout the whole of the period. On the other hand, a number of the inmates, as has been pointed out, came from different parts of

Philip Ferdinandus.

The last inmate.

England.   This fact proves definitely the existence of English and
unconverted Jews in the country.   Many of the con- foreign
verts were known to have lived in England as observant converts.
Jews before their conversion, and the existence of
such points conclusively to others who remained loyal
to their ancestral faith.   The foreign converts, it has
been suggested, in many instances came to this country
for the definite purpose of entering the House, but
except in the case of one from Flanders, who obtained
admission while still on the Continent, but who never
seems to have entered the House, this can only be
surmise.   In fact, the view is altogether improbable,
for it would have been as profitable to have adopted
Christianity abroad as to have come to London for
the purpose.   The foreign inmates of the House were
in all probability a proportion of the Jewish wayfarers, who from time to time found themselves on
these shores.

AUTHORITIES : — M. Adler, "The Domus Conversorum"
(*Transactions, Jewish Historical Society*, vol. iv., 1903) ; C. Trice
Martin, "The Domus Conversorum" (*Transactions, Jewish His-
torical Society*, vol. i.) ; S. L. Lee, "The House of Converts"
(*Jewish Chronicle*, January 26, February 16, April 27, and June 15,
1883) ; W. J. Hardy, "A History of the Rolls House and Chapel" ;
D'Bloissiers Tovey, *Anglia Judaica*.

CHAPTER XV

QUEEN ELIZABETH'S JEWISH PHYSICIAN
(1581–1650)

The English discover an interest in the Jews. AMONG the consequences of the Reformation and the Revival of Learning in England was a new interest, both literary and popular, in Jews. From the middle of the sixteenth century repeated editions of an English translation of Joseph ben Gorion (Josippon), the pseudo-Josephus—whose history was currently believed to have been written for the Jews, that known as Josephus being intended for the Romans—were called for and eagerly read. The people newly introduced to the Bible were anxious to learn more of those to whom that literature is devoted. This popular interest in Jews was reflected by the drama of the day. As early as 1579 mention is made of a play, "The Jew," **The Jew in English drama.** then being performed in London, and during the succeeding generation hardly a year passed without the Jew being depicted on the English stage. The contributions of Marlowe (*c.* 1590) and Shakespeare (1596) are well known. In addition there were Jewish characters in "The Three Ladies of London" by Robert Wilson (1584), an anonymous play entitled "Selimus," "Machiavellus" (1597), "Jacke Drum's Entertainement" (1601), "The Travels of the Three English Brothers," dramatised by John Day (1607), "The Jew of Venice" by Dekker, "The Jewish Gentleman" by Richard Brome, and "Customs of the Country" (1622) by Beaumont and Fletcher. Miscellaneous references to Jews and Jewish customs are also to be found in many other contemporary dramas.[1] This interest in Jewish matters was not confined to the common people. The study of Hebrew occasionally, as has been pointed out, with the assistance of Jewish professors, was pursued at the universities, and among the students of that language were the ill-fated Lady Jane Grey and Queen Elizabeth. The latter before her accession had shown great favour to Tremellius, and on his second visit to England had endeavoured to induce him to remain in the country. *English students of Hebrew.*

The sixteenth century in England saw revivals other than those of learning and religion. New energy and life were also introduced into industry, and one branch, that of mining, which had entirely fallen into disuse, was revived and reinvigorated with the assistance of foreign skill and foreign experience. By Henry VIII. Joachim Hochstetter was invited to England to undertake the development of its mineral resources. His operations were continued for many years. In 1581 Joachim Gaunse of Prague was conducting mining operations in Cumberland, where he seems to have taken the place of Hochstetter, who had lost favour. *A Jew develops mining in England;* Gaunse's success at Keswick appears to have been such as to induce the government to entrust to him similar work in South Wales, where the mining industry was then being founded. For several years Gaunse was in control of operations in both districts. In 1589 he was at Bristol, and it is through his connection with that city that his value to our story becomes apparent. According to the affidavit of Richard Curteys, minister, the latter met Gaunse there for the purpose of a " conference in the Hebrew tongue." In the course of the conversation Gaunse denied the divinity of Jesus. For this blasphemy

---

[1] Particulars of these Jewish references in the dramatic literature have been obtained from Mr. Sidney Lee's " Elizabethan England and the Jews."

Gaunse was summoned before the mayor and alder-
and is accused
of heresy. men, to whom he declared himself to be a Jew born
at Prague, who did not "beleeve any Article of our
Christian faithe for that he was not broughte uppe
therein." The case was too important for the local
justices to decide, and Gaunse was sent to London
to appear before the Privy Council. Of the next
scene in London, however, no record exists, and it
is unknown whether Gaunse was punished for his
avowal of Judaism, or whether the influence of Walsingham, who was well acquainted with Gaunse's
services, was exercised to secure his liberation.

In Elizabethan England the neighbourhood of
Houndsditch was still, as in the days of the Plantagenets, the foreign quarter of the capital. Aliens of
all descriptions congregated there, and there is evidence that among the inhabitants were Jews, either
converted or secret, engaged in the second-hand clothing and the pawnbroking businesses. Jews were also
associated with Englishmen in the Levant trade, and
among the fashionable doctors of the country, mostly
foreign, seem to have been members of that race.
One, Jacob, was at the request of the queen admitted
to the College of Physicians in 1585, and subsequently
sent by her to Russia to attend the Tzar. Another
Jewish doctor, Ferdinando Lopes, as has already been
mentioned, had found himself in trouble in 1550. The
most interesting of all the Anglo-Jewish doctors of
the period was, however, undoubtedly Roderigo
Lopez.

Roderigo
Lopez.
Roderigo Lopez, a Portuguese Jew, settled in England in 1559. He is said to have been captured by
Drake during one of his anti-Spanish forays, and to
have been brought a prisoner to England. In the
practice of the profession of medicine Lopez speedily
attained fame. He was the first house physician at
St. Bartholomew's Hospital, where a very high opinion

was held of his skill and learning. Before 1569 he was a member of the College of Physicians, and in that year invited to deliver the anatomy lecture there. In 1571 he was acting as physician to Sir Francis Walsingham. Four years later he was acknowledged as one of the leading physicians of the metropolis, and shortly afterwards was appointed chief physician to the Earl of Leicester. Lopez maintained a correspondence with many friends and relatives on the Continent, some of whom, among them his brother Lewis Lopez, at his invitation, settled in London. He married Sarah, a Jewess of Antwerp, the founders of which Jewish community had come from Spain and Portugal *viâ* England.

In 1586 Lopez was appointed chief physician to the queen, who three years later granted him the monopoly of the importation of aniseed and sumach. At court Lopez rapidly became acquainted with the leading statesmen and courtiers of the day. The death of Leicester had elevated the Earl of Essex to the position of chief favourite of the queen, and with Essex Lopez became intimate. The ambitious young favourite, not content with his success as a courtier, was anxious also to shine as a statesman. In order to give his talents in this direction opportunity for display, he thought it advisable to obtain a private supply of secret information, especially with regard to Spanish affairs. In pursuance of this policy, Lopez and his continental agents must have appeared extremely useful, and Essex accordingly applied to him for assistance. Lopez was, however, unwilling to take any part in the business, and disclosed Essex's communications to the queen, much to that nobleman's chagrin. In another matter, however, Essex found Lopez more amenable. Essex, whose policy was to fan the flame of English hostility to Spain, received with an enthusiastic welcome Don Antonio Perez,

Chief physician to the queen.

pretender to the throne of Portugal, and a fugitive from Spanish persecution. Antonio became the popular idol, but as he was unacquainted with any language but Portuguese, his stay in England would have been attended by serious discomfort if Lopez had not consented to act as interpreter. For a time Lopez became very closely connected with the household of Essex and Antonio. Causes of dispute, however, arose between them, and the atmosphere was not cleared by a disclosure on the part of Lopez to Antonio and others, of some professional secrets concerning Essex "which did disparage to his honour." Of Antonio's attendants, who also were dissatisfied with their master's behaviour, many were very friendly with Lopez, even staying at his house. These had been approached by emissaries of the king of Spain with inducements to get rid of Antonio, who was still a claimant to the kingdom of which Philip had taken possession. The plot was disclosed to Lopez, who seems to have entered into it so far as to state that Antonio would not recover from his next illness. This was the most important piece of evidence incriminating Lopez that was elicited at the subsequent trial. At the same time a suggestion was made that the death of Elizabeth would also cause considerable pleasure to the Spanish king. This suggestion Lopez refused altogether to entertain, and although he did not directly communicate it to the queen or her advisers, Lopez let hints of the movement drop in Elizabeth's presence.

Lopez accused of high treason.

Meanwhile the conspiracy was discovered by the Council, through the instrumentality of Essex. Two of Antonio's attendants, one of them staying at the time with Lopez, were arrested. From them the physician's connection with the plot was learnt, and he also was committed to the Tower. Essex, anxious to implicate him, personally searched his papers, but with no satisfactory results, and on his failure to find any incriminating documents, he was reprimanded by the queen as a "rash and temerarious youth to enter into a matter against the poor man which he could not prove." This reproof made Essex all the more eager to involve Lopez in the charge of treason. That which the search failed to secure was obtained with difficulty by the threat of torture. To save himself immediate suffering, the old man made some sort of confession, afterwards withdrawn. The trial was held Trial of Lopez. without delay. A special bench was appointed in place of the ordinary judges. Essex himself presided, and his colleagues were equally prejudiced against "the Jew," as he was frequently described during the proceedings. Charges of Spanish machination were always pleasing to the populace, who were thus both politically and religiously prejudiced against the prisoner. The prosecution was led by Coke, then Solicitor-General, who referred to the accused as "that vile Jew," "wily and covetous," "mercenary," "corrupt," &c. As a matter of course Lopez was found guilty, and sentenced to be hanged and drawn.

Before this sentence could be carried out, however, an unexpected difficulty arose. For some months the queen could not be induced to sign the death-warrant. Very probably she felt considerable doubts concerning the justice of the whole proceedings. In the meanwhile one of Essex's partisans was appointed Chief Justice, and by his persuasion the signature was given. Lopez was hanged at Tyburn on the 7th of His fate. June 1594. The whole affair created so much excitement that no less than five official accounts, one by Bacon, then in the service of Essex, in addition to numerous private ones, were published. Although Elizabeth had at length been induced to consent to the execution, she did not claim her right to the con-

demned man's property. With the exception of a
ring, said to have been given to Lopez by the king of
Spain, which Elizabeth wore until her death, she
allowed the widow to retain the whole of her husband's estate.

Three years before the execution of Lopez, Elizabeth gave a very definite proof of her sympathies
with Jews. A ship-load of Marranos or Crypto-Jews,
fleeing from Spain, was captured by the English, and
the passengers brought to London. Among those on
board was Maria Nuñes, a lady of such beauty that
her charms immediately attracted the English captain,
a nobleman, who offered to marry her. Maria and
her companions, however, had set sail for the purpose
of openly confessing Judaism, and she was unwilling
even for the love of an English noble any longer to
remain a nominal Christian. Maria's beauty and
story created a great sensation in London, and the
queen was anxious to meet the heroine. She was
invited to an audience, was befriended by Elizabeth,
who drove with her through the streets of the capital,
and by her was, together with her companions, permitted to sail for Holland, there to join others who
had already thrown off the cloak of Christianity. The
same year Elizabeth, through her ambassador at Constantinople, successfully used her influence to obtain
the appointment of a Jew as Viceroy of Wallachia,
and in 1599 she was in correspondence with Esper-
anza Malchi, the Jewish secretary of the Sultana of
Turkey. Further evidence of the existence of Jews
in London during the sixteenth century is afforded by
Thomas Coryat, who, when in Constantinople in 1612,
visited "the house of a certaine English Iewe called
Amis, borne in the Crootched Friars in London, who
hath two sisters more of his owne Iewish Religion,
commorant in Galata, who were likewise borne in the
same place."

There is one other item of Jewish interest before Jews and the reign of Elizabeth is brought to a close. In the geographical discovery. series of geographical discoveries by which the sixteenth century is marked, Jews took a not inconsiderable part. A Jew, Jehuda Cresques, was the director of Prince Henry the Navigator's School of Navigation at Sagres. Another, Abraham Zacuto, compiled the astronomical tables that were constantly used by Columbus, and which, on one occasion, saved the life of the navigator. Columbus also on his first voyage to America had a Jew as his interpreter. The money that enabled him to make his first voyage was lent by a Jew, Luis de Santangel. His map was drawn by Ribes, the "Map Jew"; his ship's doctor was Bernal, also a Jew; his superintendent, Rodrigo Sanchez the Jew. The Jewish sailor Rodrigo de Triana was the first to see land, and the interpreter, Luis de Torres, the first to set foot on shore. Vasco da Gama owed much to Zacuto, as well as to his Jewish pilot, Gaspar da Gama. More than one Jewish interpreter was of service to D'Albuquerque. English seamen and explorers relied to a less extent on Jewish assistance. In the first voyage of the East India The East Company in 1601, however, a Jew acted as interpreter. India Company. Captain James Lancaster, who was in charge, had as his servant a Moroccan Jew who had been brought a prisoner to England. His knowledge of Arabic, it was thought, would prove of service in negotiations with the ruler of Achin, to whom the expedition was sent. In the sequel this view proved correct, and the Jewish interpreter succeeded in negotiating a treaty satisfactory both to the English and to the Sultan.

The question of the conversion of the Jews began to agitate the minds of English thinkers early in the reign of Elizabeth, and among other books on the subject was one by Finch, the lawyer, which, on account of its Judaical tendencies, caused the imprisonment of its author by the Court of High Com-

mission. At this epoch the commerce of Spain was
almost entirely in the hands of Marranos,[1] and business relations with England attracted many secret
Jews to these shores. It is a curious fact that the
charter and list of freemen of the Anglo-Spanish
Trading Company in London, dated 1605, has its
pages numbered with Hebrew characters. In the
lists of foreigners resident in London at the beginning
of the sixteenth century such names as Da Costa,
Lopez, Alvarez, Mendez, Meza, Casseres, afterwards
well known in Anglo-Jewish annals, continually recur.
It was not until 1618 that the English version of the
Statutum de Pistoribus contained the clause prohibiting Christians from buying meat of Jews, and from
this it has been deduced that about that time the
presence of Jews in the country became generally
known. A few years later it is stated in a tract, "The
Wandering Jew Telling Fortunes to Englishmen,"
that "A Store of Jews we have in England ; a few in
Court ; many i' the citty ; more in the country." It
is also noteworthy that the author did not hesitate
to claim Judaism openly, the better to succeed
in his profession of fortune-teller. A somewhat
similar incident some years later was the pretended
adoption of Judaism by a Jesuit, in order that by
being baptized he might obtain the public sympathy
necessary to him in the furtherance of his designs.
Outside of London it is in the university towns that
traces of Jews are to be found at this period. In 1608
Jacob Barnett was teaching Hebrew at Oxford, where
he became acquainted with Casaubon, who was among
his pupils. Developing a friendship for the young

---

[1] A term applied to the Crypto-Jews of Spain and Portugal, who, while
outwardly conforming to Christianity, in secret continued the practices
of Judaism. These Marranos were not always themselves converts from
Christianity ; they were often the children or even more remote descendants
of baptized Jews.

Jew, Casaubon induced Barnett to live in his house in London. After a time Barnett seemed to show a tendency towards Christianity, and Casaubon, hoping for his conversion, sent him back to Oxford. There, after a further interval, Barnett consented to accept baptism, and great preparations, in which the archbishop and the king were interested, were made for the public acceptance of Christianity by the proselyte. The conversion and the arrangements became a leading topic of conversation, and as the appointed day drew nigh the excitement increased. All was ready, the special preacher appointed and the sermon prepared, but the intended convert could not be found. All search within the city proved in vain, and the intended participants in the event had to disperse unsatisfied. Enraged at their disappointment, the university authorities sent messengers in all directions to seek the fugitive. Barnett was overtaken on the way to London, and brought back to Oxford. There he was imprisoned, but on the intervention of Casaubon, released and expelled the university. He was subsequently, by order of the Privy Council, expelled the kingdom. *Casaubon and Barnett.*

The conversions, or attempted conversions, were not all, however, in favour of Christianity. In 1624 James Whitehall of Christ Church, Oxford, was prosecuted for preaching Judaism. About the same time several English converts to Judaism were living in Holland, and in 1635 a woman, described as a Jewess, was imprisoned by the Court of High Commission for adhering to Jewish customs, and refusing to eat meat not killed in the Jewish fashion. On the other hand, in 1623 Paul Jacob, a converted Jew, petitioned the king for a pension, and two years later Charles I. granted an allowance of forty pounds a year to a Jew at Cambridge, presumably on conversion. *Converts to Judaism.*

In 1614 and 1615 two attempts were made by the

Attempts by
Spain to pro-
secute Jews in
the English
courts.

Spanish ambassador to prosecute Jews in the English courts. The first was a charge of piracy against Samuel Palache, the envoy of the Sultan of Morocco to the States General, who had brought three prizes into Plymouth. His successful defence was that he was a Moroccan subject and in the service of the Sultan, then at war with Spain. In the second case the ambassador attempted, also without success, to obtain the assistance of the Privy Council in proceedings against a Jew regarding a cargo of sugar. In 1620 David Sollom, a "Jewish Merchant," bought an estate in Meath, Ireland. Shortly afterwards Antonio de Verona was at both universities, and for the earlier portion of his visit at any rate was a professing Jew. He was described by Queen Henrietta Maria as in her service. Somewhat later another Jew, Alessandro Amidei, taught Hebrew at Oxford. In 1627 Charles I. borrowed several amounts from Abraham Jacob, and at a subsequent date 20,000 ducats from a Jew of Amsterdam. Finally, in 1650 another Jew, Jacob, opened a coffee-house at Oxford, the introduction of the beverage into the country being due to him.

AUTHORITIES :—L. Wolf, "The Middle Period of Anglo-Jewish History"; S. L. Lee, "Jews in England before 1643" (*Academy*, March 18, 1882), "Elizabethan England and the Jews" (*Transactions, New Shakespeare Society*, 1888), "The Original of Shylock" (*Gentleman's Magazine*, 1880); H. Graetz, "History of the Jews," vol. iv. (1892); I. Abrahams, "Joachim Gaunz" (*Transactions, Jewish Historical Society*, vol. iv.); "Queen Elizabeth's Jewish Physician" (*Jewish World*, Jan. 23 and 30, 1880); E. N. Adler, "Auto de Fé and Jew," ch. vi.; B. L. Abrahams, "A Jew in the Service of the East India Company in 1601" (*Jewish Quarterly Review*, vol. ix., 1897), "Two Jews before the Privy Council and an English Law Court in 1614-15" (*Jewish Quarterly Review*, vol. xiv., 1902); "Dictionary of National Biography," article, "Roderigo Lopez."

CHAPTER XVI

THE TRANSLATION OF THE BIBLE

IN a history of the Jews in England place may, Influences of the Bible upon the English. without excuse, be found for some mention of the translation of the Hebrew Bible into English. Not the least of the influences that have combined to mould the character and to form the language of the English nation is that of the Bible, and in an especial degree the earlier portion thereof, that in which the Jews are particularly interested. From the Puritans, whose spiritual nurture consisted of the Jewish scriptures, are descended the Nonconformists of to-day, who are, if not the backbone of the English nation, as they have been termed, at least an integral portion of it. The English of the first important Bible translation, originally hardly more than a local dialect, has become the English of the whole people, and, in the words of Dr. Westcott, "He (Tyndale) felt by a happy instinct the potential affinity between Hebrew and English idioms, and enriched our language and thought for ever with the characteristics of the Semitic mind."

One of the earliest of the distinguished Hebraists among the English Churchmen was the great bishop, scholar, and patriot, Robert Grosseteste (*d.* 1253), whose influence survived his death by two centuries. It was at this great bishop's instance, in 1244, that it was decided that the jurisdiction in disputes between Jews and scholars at Oxford should rest with the Chancellor of the University. He was also consulted very widely on the correct attitude to be adopted towards Jews.

The earliest translations into English.

Before the first complete English edition of the Bible, that of John Wycliffe, portions, especially the Psalms, had already been rendered into Anglo-Saxon and English. These early translations, so far as is known, had in no instance any Hebrew or Jewish connection. The · same may be said of Wycliffe's translation, or, to be more exact, Nicholas Hereford's rendering of the Old Testament as far as Baruch, which Wycliffe incorporated in his Bible. Nicholas and Wycliffe by whom the Old Testament was completed, both used the ·Vulgate as their text. The work of Wycliffe was soon revised by his disciple and curate, John Purvey, whose edition was completed about 1388. Purvey in his work relied to a considerable extent on the writings and researches of Nicolas de Lyra, and the translator himself states in his Prologue : "And where the Ebru (Hebrew), by witnesse of Jerome, of Lire (de Lyra), and other expositouris discordith from our Latyn biblis, I haue set in the margyn, bi maner of a glose, what the Ebru hath, and how it is vnderstondun in the same place; and I dide this most in the Sauter (Psalter), that of all oure bokis discordith most fro Ebru."

Nicolas de Lyra.

Nicolas de Lyra (c. 1270–1340) was born at Lyre, near Evreux, it is said of Jewish descent. He entered the Franciscan Order in 1291, and became renowned both as a biblical scholar and as a controversialist. In the latter capacity he wrote his anti-Jewish *De Messia, ejusque adventu præterito;* in the former his best known work is *Postillæ perpetuæ, sive brevia commentaria in universa biblia.* De Lyra, who possessed a good knowledge of Hebrew, may almost be considered the founder of natural exegesis. His influence on all subsequent translators of the Bible was considerable. To such an extent was Luther indebted to him that the saying, "Si Lyra non lyrasset, Lutherus non saltasset," became prevalent. The many traces in Luther's work of the influence of the great Jewish commentator Rashi all come through De Lyra.

The interest in the study of Hebrew throughout Christendom dates from the opening of the four- teenth century. In 1310, at a General Council con- vened by Clement V. at Vienna, it was decided that Hebrew should be taught at the principal universities. So far as Oxford was concerned, this decision was put into force ten years later, when, at a synod convened by Archbishop Reynold at Lambeth, a Hebrew lectureship was established and endowed by a tax of a farthing in the pound on all the livings within the province of Canterbury. John of Bristol, a converted Jew, was appointed lecturer. The study of Hebrew appears to have declined somewhat after a time, but two centuries later it seems to have been flourishing at both universities. Robert Wakefield (*d.* 1537) was Professor of Hebrew at Louvain in 1519, and was succeeded there by another English- man, Robert Shirwood, when he removed to Tübin- gen. There he continued to teach until 1523, when he was summoned back to England. So valuable were his services considered at Tübingen, that both the Archduke of Austria and the heads of the uni- versity wrote—the former to Henry VIII., the latter to the Chancellor of Cambridge—asking that Wake- field might be permitted to remain somewhat longer at Tübingen. In England Wakefield lectured on Hebrew at Cambridge in 1524 and at Oxford in 1530. His brother, Thomas Wakefield (*d.* 1575), was the first Regius Professor of Hebrew at Cambridge (1540). In 1549 the same office was filled by Paul Fagius (1504–49), a German refugee. Fagius, who was a Hebraist of renown, had been a pupil of

The study of Hebrew in England.

Wolfgang Capito and the celebrated rabbi, Elias Levita, whom he had induced to come from Venice in order to instruct him. Fagius established a Hebrew printing-press at Strassburg, whence he issued many books of great value to scholars. On the death of Capito, Fagius was invited to take his place as Professor of Hebrew, but preferred another appointment that happened to be offered him at the same time.

William Tyndale.

The knowledge of Hebrew that William Tyndale used in his translation was, nevertheless, for the most part not acquired in England. While still engaged on the New Testament he was compelled to settle on the Continent. He chose Hamburg for his resting-place, and while in residence there visited Luther at Wittenberg. He subsequently settled at Marburg, where he commenced his translation of the Old Testament, visiting the Low Countries and Hamburg, where again he took up his residence. Ultimately Tyndale returned to Antwerp in 1533, and there occupied himself with the revision of his translations. Three years later he was burnt at the stake as a heretic at Vilvorde. Tyndale's published translations include the Pentateuch and the Book of Jonah. There is reason to believe that he also translated Joshua, Judges, Ruth, Samuel, Kings, and Chronicles. His translation was made direct from the Hebrew, with the assistance of the Vulgate and Luther's translation. It is possible also that John Frith (1503–33), who helped Tyndale, was a Hebrew scholar.

Miles Coverdale.

Miles Coverdale appears to have been quite unacquainted with the Hebrew language ; the material on which he worked consisted of German and Latin translations. Tyndale's translations of the Pentateuch and the New Testament were incorporated in the new edition. Coverdale was also indebted to

Luther's Bible, the Vulgate, the Zurich or Swiss German Bible, and the Latin version of Pagninus. The Zurich Bible was, to a great extent, a revision of Luther's. Among others engaged on it were Leo Juda, who, despite his name, was not of Jewish origin, and Pellicanus, the Professor of Hebrew at Zurich. Sanctes Pagninus was a Dominican monk and pupil of Savonarola. Although Coverdale had no recourse to the Hebrew text in his translation, he used Hebrew characters to a very slight extent in his edition. The name of the Deity appears in that language on the title-page, and Hebrew characters are used to mark the divisions of the Book of Lamentations. In 1536, the year after Coverdale's publication, Matthew's Bible appeared. Despite unrelenting research, not a glimpse can be obtained of the personality of Thomas Matthew, and it is now generally accepted that this name was a disguise for John Rogers, a friend of Tyndale, whose fate he was anxious to avoid. Matthew's Bible is a combination of Tyndale's and Coverdale's work. The only original contribution of Rogers was the translation of the Prayer of Manasses, and that he merely rendered from the French. Rogers was subsequently the first martyr in the Marian persecution.

The next important English translation of the Bible was that known as the Geneva or "Breeches" Bible. It took the former name from the city of refuge of the English Protestants, and on reaching England speedily became the popular Bible of the English people. In the earlier stages of its preparation Coverdale was engaged upon it. The work was not a translation so much as a revision of the former translation, by scholars acquainted with the languages in which the books of the Bible were originally written. The responsible editors were William Whittingham, Anthony Gilby, and Thomas

The Geneva or "Breeches" Bible.

Sampson. Whittingham, afterwards Dean of Durham, took the leading part in the translation, and assisted materially in giving the Bible a Calvinist tinge. Among the other works of Whittingham, who was a Hebrew scholar, were included metrical translations of the Psalms and the Decalogue. Gilby, another extreme Puritan, afterwards Dean of Christ Church, was also a Hebrew scholar. Gilby's writings included commentaries on Micah and Malachi, and translations of "The Testamentes of the Twelve Patriarches" from the Latin of Robert Grosseteste, Calvin's Commentaries on Daniel, and Beza's Paraphrase of the Psalms and Paraphrase of the Fourteen Holy Psalms. Sampson was Dean of Chichester under Edward VI., and, after the accession of Elizabeth, Dean of Christ Church after refusing the bishopric of Norwich. At Strassburg Sampson met Tremellius, and profited much by his companionship.

The Bishops' Bible.   The definite adoption of Protestantism after the accession of Elizabeth presented the opportunity for still another translation. This was known as the Bishops' Bible or Parker's Bible, since Archbishop Matthew Parker was the leading spirit in the translation. His assistants were Edwin Sandys, Bishop of Worcester ; Edmund Guest, Bishop of Rochester ; and Richard Cox, Bishop of Ely. The other ecclesiastics engaged in the work were Andrew Pierson, Prebendary of Canterbury ; William Alley, Bishop of Exeter ; Richard Davies, Bishop of St. David's ; Andrew Perne, Dean of Ely ; John Parkhurst, Bishop of Norwich ; William Barlow, Bishop of Chichester ; Robert Horne, Bishop of Winchester ; Thomas Bentham, Bishop of Lichfield and Coventry ; Edward Grindal, Bishop of London. Additional scholars were engaged on the New Testament.

Archbishop Parker, the editor in chief, dealt himself with Genesis and Exodus. Sandys, afterwards Bishop of London and Archbishop of York, was in charge of the Second Book of Kings and Chronicles. In a subsequent translation, that of 1572, his share was Hosea, Joel, and Amos to Malachi inclusive. Guest or Gheast was in charge of the Psalms. Cox was engaged on a portion of the New Testament. Pierson revised the translation of Leviticus, Numbers, Job, and Proverbs, and possibly Ezra, Nehemiah, and Esther in addition. Alley, according to John Vowell, "was verie well learned universalli, but his cheefe studie was in divinitie and in the tongs." Among his writings was a Hebrew grammar, never published. Deuteronomy was assigned to him for revision. Davies dealt with Joshua, Judges, Ruth, and the First Book of Kings. Perne, who was Master of Peterhouse as well as Prebendary of Canterbury, revised Ecclesiastes and the Song of Songs. Parkhurst's share was Ecclesiasticus, Susanna, Baruch, and the Maccabees. Barlow was successively Bishop of St. Asaph, St. David's, Bath and Wells, and Chichester. He also was engaged on the Apocrypha, having Esdras, Judith, Tobit, and Wisdom assigned to him. Horne, who dealt with Isaiah, Jeremiah, and Lamentations, had, while in exile on the Continent during Mary's reign, acted as reader in Hebrew at Frankfurt. Bentham had while at Oxford attracted considerable attention by his knowledge of Hebrew. He translated Ezekiel and Daniel for the Bishops' Bible. Edmund Grindal (? 1519-1583) was ultimately Archbishop of Canterbury, from which office he was suspended in consequence of differences with Queen Elizabeth. Parker's Bible was based, in so far as the Hebrew portion is concerned, on the translation of Münster and Pagninus. Of Pagninus mention has already been made. The famous Hebraist Sebastian Münster, who, in addition to his translation of the

Bible into German and other contributions to Hebrew literature, was the author of the first translation of the New Testament into Hebrew, owed his knowledge of that tongue almost entirely to Elias Levita, whose grammatical works he edited and translated.

Other Versions.

Between the date of the Bishops' translation and the close of the sixteenth century, further material became available for translators of the Hebrew Bible. In 1553 the famous Jews' Bible in Spanish was published at Ferrara for the use of Marranos, by Usque, and with slight modifications for Christians by Vargas and Pinel. In 1572 the Latin translation of Arias Montanus was published, and in 1579 came the version of Tremellius, together with a commentary. Other translations by Hebraists of repute that followed were those of C. B. Bertram, assisted by Beza, Goulart, and others, into French (1587–88), by J. Diodati, Professor of Hebrew at Geneva, into Italian (1607), and by Cassiodoro de Reyna (1569) and Cipriano de Valera (1602) into Spanish. This additional supply of material smoothed the path of the translators who, at the instance of James I., undertook the task that resulted in what has since been known as the Authorised Version, a translation that has practically held the field from that day to this.

James I. and Hebrew.

James himself among his many other interests included that of the study of the Bible. He wrote a commentary on a portion of the First Book of Chronicles, and translated or collaborated in the translation of some of the Psalms. In conversation his references to and quotations from the Bible were continuous, and it is related that during a visit to Edinburgh in 1617 one of the addresses presented to the king was in Hebrew. The considerable interest the king took in the Hampton Court Conference and its deliberations is therefore not remarkable. Almost the only definite result of that Conference was a new translation of the Bible. For the work Hebrew scholars were especially sought. In a communication to Bancroft, then acting as the head of the Church, the king wrote : " Furthermore, we require you to move all our bishops to inform themselves of all such learned men within their several dioceses, as having special skill in the Hebrew and Greek tongues, have taken pains in their private studies of the Scriptures, for the clearing of any obscurities either in the Hebrew or in the Greek, or touching any difficulties or mistaking in the former English translation, which we have now commanded to be thoroughly viewed and amended ; and, thereupon, to write unto them, earnestly charging them, and signifying our pleasure therein, that they send such their observations either to Mr. Lively, our Hebrew reader in Oxford, or to Dr. Andrewes, Dean of Westminster, to be imparted to the rest of their several companies."

Edward Lively (? 1545–1605) was Regius Professor The Authorised of Hebrew at Cambridge, being unanimously elected Version. to that office despite the competition of a protegé of the chancellor, Lord Burghley. Lively obtained his knowledge of Hebrew from John Drusius (Johannes Driesche), the Dutch linguist and writer. Drusius, who himself taught Hebrew at Oxford, acquired his knowledge of the language at Cambridge from Anthony Cevellier or Chevalier. Next to Pococke, according to Dr. Pusey, "Lively was the greatest of Hebraists." Dying in 1605, Lively was, however, unable to take any part in the translation of the Authorised Version. Lancelot Andrewes (1555–1626), afterwards successively Bishop of Chichester, Ely, and Winchester, was the first on the list of divines appointed to make the Authorised Version. His department of the translation comprised the Books ranging from the Pentateuch until

First Chronicles.   Andrewes was renowned for his patristic learning.   He was acquainted with fifteen languages, including Hebrew, Chaldee, and Syriac.

The revisers of the Old Testament were all excellent Hebrew scholars.   The first portion, Genesis to First Kings, was entrusted to the Westminster Committee. This was formed of Andrewes (President); Overall, Bishop of Norwich; Saravia, Prebendary of Westminster; Clerke, one of the six preachers of Christ Church, Canterbury; Layfield, Rector of St. Clement Danes; Teigh, Archdeacon of Middlesex; Burleigh, Fellow of Chelsea College; King, Bishop of London; Thomson, of Clare Hall, Cambridge; and Bedwell, Vicar of Tottenham.   John Overall (1560–1619) had been Regius Professor of Theology, at Cambridge. Among his correspondents were Gerard Voss and Hugo Grotius.   Hadrian à Saravia (1531–1613) was of French birth and of mixed Spanish and Flemish ancestry.   For a time he was Professor of Divinity in the university.   Removing to Holland he was compelled, for political reasons, to leave that country and came to England, where he had already previously lived.   Saravia, who was especially noted for his Hebrew learning, included Isaac Casaubon among his friends.   Richard Clerke (*d.* 1634) was Vicar of Minster and also of Monkton.

John Layfield (*d.* 1617) "being skilled in architecture, his judgment was much relied on for the fabric of the Tabernacle and Temple."   John King (? 1559–1621) was Regius Professor of Hebrew at Cambridge.   His publications included lectures upon Jonah.   Richard Thomson (*d.* 1613) was "a most admirable philologer."   William Bedwell (1561 or 62–1632), the greatest Arabic scholar of Europe and the father of Arabic studies in England, was also a diligent student of other oriental languages.   He left the manuscript of a lexicon of Hebrew, Syriac, Chaldee, and Arabic.

The Cambridge Committee, which dealt with First Chronicles to Ecclesiastes, was to have been under the presidency of Lively. At his death his place was taken by Spalding, Fellow of St. John's. The other members of the Committee were Richardson, Master of Trinity; Chaderton, Master of Emmanuel; Dillingham, Rector of Dean, Beds.; Harrison, Vice-Master of Trinity; Andrewes, Master of Jesus College; and Byng, Archdeacon of Norwich. Spalding was King's predecessor as Regius Professor of Hebrew at Cambridge. John Richardson (*d.* 1625), Regius Professor of Divinity at Cambridge, was also an excellent Hebraist. William Chaderton or Chatterton (? 1540–1608) was successively Lady Margaret Professor of Divinity, Regius Professor of Divinity, Bishop of Chester, and Bishop of Lincoln, besides filling other offices. He was familiar with Hebrew, and also the Rabbinical writings. Francis Dillingham "was an excellent linguist and subtle disputant." Thomas Harrison (1555–1631) had "exquisite skill in Hebrew." Andrew Byng (1574–1651) was also Regius Professor of Hebrew. *The Cambridge Committee.*

The third Committee, that of Oxford, consisted of Harding, Regius Professor of Hebrew and President of Magdalen (President); Reynolds, President of Corpus Christi; Holland, Rector of Exeter College and Regius Professor of Divinity; Kilbye, Rector of Lincoln College; Smith, Bishop of Gloucester; Brett, Fellow of Chelsea College; and Fareclowe, Provost of Chelsea College. Of John Reynolds or Rainolds, who died in 1607, Bishop Hall said: "His memory and reading were near to a miracle, for he was himself a well-furnished library, full of all faculties, all studies, and all learning." He was one of the moving spirits in the translation. Thomas Holland (*d.* 1612) was Regius Professor of Divinity at Oxford, and "mighty in scriptures." Richard Kilbye (? 1561–1620) was Regius Professor of *The Oxford Committee.*

Hebrew. His works included a Latin commentary on Exodus, based to a considerable extent on Rabbinical sources, and a continuation of Jean Mercier's commentaries on Genesis. Kilbye was one of the chief English students of Hebrew of his day. Miles Smith (*d.* 1624), a distinguished oriental scholar, "had Hebrew at his fingers' ends." "Chaldiac, Syriac, and Arabic," says Wood, were "as familiar to him almost as his own native tongue." Smith was one of the final revisers of the translation. Richard Brett (? 1560–1637) was famous for learning as well as piety, and "skill'd and versed to a criticism in the Latin, Greek, Hebrew, Chaldaic, Arabic, and Ethiopic tongues." Daniel Fareclowe (otherwise Fairclough or Featley) (1582–1645) was a well-known controversialist and the godson of John Rainolds.

Character of the Authorised Version. Although this long array of scholars was impressed in the work, the result was rather a revision of the Bishops' Bible than a new translation. The translators or revisers, who had the choice of several texts, and made special use of the Complutensian Polyglott and the Antwerp Polyglott, consulted Hebrew authorities. In addition to profiting by the work of Luther, Pagninus, Arias Montanus, Münster, Tremellius, and Junius, the translators had recourse to the Targum of Onkelos and that of Jonathan ben Uzziel and also the Peshito. They also made much use of the mediæval Jewish commentators, in particular of David Kimchi. The result of the combined labours was a masterpiece. "It is homely but not vulgar, and musical without the aid of tawdry expletives. Having kept its place for more than two centuries and a half, it has 'waxed old,' but it has not 'decayed' . . . Though it may vary with the themes of the original, it never loses its identity. So quiet and clear in narrative, so direct and urgent in precept, so fervid and spiritual in the psalter, so impressive and magnificent

in the prophets, it bears upon it the imagery of the Its style.
Hebrew lyrics without being overborne by it, and
gives earnest and impressive utterance to apostolical
argument and appeal."[1]

AUTHORITIES:—B. F. Westcott, "A General View of the History
of the English Bible" (1905); John Eadie, "The English Bible"
(1876); F. H. Scrivener, "The Cambridge Paragraph Bible" (In-
troduction) (1873); Anthony Johnson, "An Historical Account of
the Several English Translations of the Bible" (1730); William
Newcome, "An Historical View of the English Bible Translations"
(1792); John Lewis, "History of the English Translations of the
Bible" (1818); W. F. Moulton, "The History of the English
Bible" (1878); John Stoughton, "Our English Bible" (1878);
A. Edgar, "The Bibles of England" (1889); Dr. Mombert,
"English Versions of the Bible" (1890); H. W. Hoare, "The
Evolution of the English Bible" (1901); C. Anderson, "Annals of
the British Bible" (1845); "Dictionary of National Biography";
"Encyclopedia Britannica," articles, "The English Bible" and
"Hebrew."

---

[1] Dr. John Eadie, "The English Bible," vol. ii. p. 228.

CHAPTER XVII

ENGLISH ELEMENTS IN THE RE-SETTLEMENT

(1630–1649)

Changes in England since the Expulsion. MEANWHILE the economical and intellectual condition of the country had changed considerably since the time of the Plantagenets and the Expulsion. The Renaissance and the Reformation, twin-workers in intellectual emancipation, had combined to awaken the minds and the souls of the people. The old beliefs in both the religious and political spheres had undergone re-examination, and the amendments that had in consequence been found necessary had altered the political and religious systems of the country almost beyond recognition. With the religious and political awakening had also come industrial and commercial developments. At the time of the Expulsion England was a pastoral country. The average Englishman devoted himself to the care of flocks and herds, and their surplus produce, after providing for his own personal needs, was sent to the Continent to be turned into manufactured goods. In the era of the Commonwealth, however, agriculture and stock-raising were no longer the sole occupations of the people. The sailors of Elizabeth had forced introductions to other climes, and England, taking advantage of her unique situation, was hastening towards the position of clearing-house of the commerce of the world. To other points of the industrial world, also, attention was directed. The nether-world was pierced and forced to surrender its secret hoards. It was at this period that mining found its inception, and in this branch of industry, as has already been shown, the Jew was not wanting. In other industrial departments of English life isolated Jews also took part. In those of politics and religion, however, none of them could as yet have place. Under the old political and religious systems, as they developed, no room for the Jews could be found in England. Changes and developments had come over English life, however, and the anti-Jewish aspects of the systems had apparently to a considerable extent passed away.

Under the Feudal System Jews had been tolerated in the country, but their position had always been anomalous. Neither tenants of the crown nor of the tenants-in-chief, nor exactly villeins, not citizens, not clerics, under the Normans and the Plantagenets the position of the Jews resembled that of the villeins more than of any other class, but with the passing of the Feudal System the status of villenage also passed away. *Jews under the Feudal System.*

The Reformation, although it unsettled the religious foundations of the State, did not, in its legal consequences, immediately render nonconformity easier. From the opening of the fifteenth century two series of legislative enactments directed against critics of and seceders from the national Church were gradually adopted. All would-be propagators of any faith but the official one were liable to severe penalties under the Heresy Acts. Mere passive dissenters, on the other hand, those who were satisfied to abstain from attendance at divine service, were aimed at by the Uniformity legislation.

By the laws of the Church heresy had always been an offence meriting the severest punishment. The ecclesiastical party, whenever it had the power, did not hesitate to punish heretics with death, and clerics *Legislation against heresy.*

claimed that the Common Law of England provided the punishment of burning for heretics. In 1222, as has already been noticed, a deacon was burnt for embracing Judaism. The punishment was carried out by the civil power, to which the deacon, after having been degraded, was handed by the Church. At the same time a youth and an old woman were condemned to lifelong imprisonment for posing as Jesus and Mary. In 1210 an Albigensian was burnt in London, also apparently under the Common Law, for the ecclesiastical law forbade clerics to pass sentence of death. Very probably there were other similar instances.

The Statute *de Hæretico.*   In 1401 the Statute Law came to the reinforcement of the Common Law. By the Statute *de Hæretico* of that year it was enacted that none "presume to preach openly or privily without the license of the Diocesan . . . that none from henceforth any Thing preach, hold, teach or instruct openly or privily, or make or write any Book contrary to the Catholic Faith or Determination of the Holy Church, nor of such Sect or wicked Doctrines or Opinions shall make any Conventicles, or in any wise hold or exercise Schools; and also that none from henceforth in any wise favour such Preacher, or Maker of any such or like Conventicles, or holding or exercising schools, or making or writing such Books, or so teaching, informing or exciting the People, nor any of them maintain or otherwise sustain; and that all and singular having such books or any Writings of such wicked Doctrine and Opinions, shall really with effect deliver or cause to be delivered all such Books and Writings to the Diocesan of the same Place within XL Days from the Time of the Proclamation of this Ordinance and Statute." Persons guilty of offences under the Statute were to be punished by the ecclesiastical power. If they refused to abjure their erroneous doctrines, or after abjuration relapsed into their former heresies, they were to be handed over to the civil power and publicly burnt. This Act was especially directed against the Lollards.

By earlier legislation, in 1382, commissions were issued for the arrest of preachers of the Lollard heresy. They were, however, only to be retained in custody and not otherwise punished.

Thirteen years after the enactment *De Hæretico Comburendo*, the laws against heretics were further strengthened. The chancellor, judges, and others were sworn to make every effort to discover all heresy and to uproot it, and specially to assist in the arrest of Lollards and other heretics. The Statute further decreed the forfeiture of the property of persons convicted of heresy. Since the cognizance of heresy belonged to the spiritual judges, those charged with the offence were to be tried by them. Alterations in the law took place under Henry VIII. and Edward VI., but there was no relaxation in its severity; while under Mary the lot of the critic of the Church as by law established became even harsher. A predecessor of Henry VIII.'s—Edward V.—had repealed all previous legislation on the subject, and thus for a brief period no anti-heresy enactments appeared on the statute book.

In the first year of Elizabeth's reign, in a series of enactments relating to religious matters, the sixth repealed the heresy legislation of Philip and Mary as well as all previous legislation that might then be in force. The same Act provided for the first time a legal definition of heresy, or rather stated definitely what should not be considered heresy. It was laid down that the ecclesiastical commissioners should not adjudge matters to be heresy unless they had been so declared according to Scripture or by any one of the General Councils, or should in the future be declared heresy by Parliament in agreement with Convocation.

Heretics were, however, still occasionally burnt, and one suffered this punishment, so late as 1612, for holding beliefs to which every professing Jew would subscribe without hesitation.[1]

In 1640 the Court of High Commission was abolished; and although heresy remained an offence, there was no longer any penalty available beyond a purely ecclesiastical one. By such, Jews would, of course, be unaffected.

The Uniformity legislation commences at a date much later than the first of the Heresy Acts. Before the Reformation such legislation was quite unknown, and its object when once it came into existence was as much to compel attendance at church as to create a uniformity in church services. It is from the former aspect that the legislation is for the present purpose of interest. The Act of Uniformity of the first year of Elizabeth's reign enacted that all persons should diligently and faithfully attend church unless they absented themselves for reasonable excuse. Otherwise every absentee was liable to suffer spiritual censure and to be fined a shilling, the proceeds of the fines to be devoted to the benefit of the poor. In 1580 an additional penalty of £20 a month for failing to attend church was enacted, and by legislation of six years later the property of the recusant, with the exception of a third of his lands, was forfeited in the case of future convictions.

In 1592 still more stringent steps were taken. All persons above sixteen years old, who should obstinately refuse to attend divine service according to law, and should persuade others to dispute the Queen's authority in ecclesiastical cases, &c., or

The Uniformity legislation.

---

[1] "2 State Trials," p. 729. See also H. S. Q. Henriques, "The Return of the Jews to England."

should attend unlawful conventicles, were to be imprisoned until willing to conform and submit. Those who refused to do so within three months were to abjure the realm. On refusing to depart or on returning after having once left the country, they were to be deemed felons without benefit of clergy.

The opening of the following reign saw further legislation of a similar tendency. The Act of 1606 was specially directed against Popish recusants. Among other enactments it laid down that any person indicted of recusancy, or who had not taken the sacrament within the year, might be compelled to take the oath of Allegiance. This oath, then newly adopted, included the form of words "upon the true faith of a Christian." With the omission of this phrase the oath would have been quite unobjectionable to any Jew. It however introduced a phrase that proved for centuries a bar to Jewish emancipation, for although the Act of 1606 was repealed by the Bill of Rights in 1688, the objectionable form of oath survived to be the centre of the struggle for Jewish emancipation during the first half of the nineteenth century.[1]

Popish Recusants.

A breach was made in this high wall of anti-nonconformist legislation in 1630, when in a treaty with Spain a clause was inserted exempting all Spanish subjects from the Recusancy Laws. By this clause, as will be seen later, Jews were directly affected. From the combination of all these political, social, religious, industrial, and legal changes, it resulted that a Jewish settlement would no longer interfere with the English scheme of government or life. England seemed ready to receive the Jews so long as their return would do no violence to established institutions.

Spanish subjects exempted from the Recusancy Laws.

[1] The references to the various statutes affecting heresy and uniformity are given by Mr. H. S. Q. Henriques in his "Return of the Jews to England," and also appear in Renton's "Encyclopedia of the Laws of England."

England however required the scourge of the Civil
War before the last vestiges of the old system could
be finally cleared away.   The principle of toleration
Nonconformist of Nonconformity could only be officially accepted
sects. after its advocates had won it on the battlefield.   And
with the victory of Puritanism and its ideals came
the growth of innumerable Protestant sects with
strange doctrines and peculiar beliefs.   Yet the very
diversity of these sects—which in many cases being so
insignificant in numbers had necessarily to be tolerant
of other opinions—formed in itself an element in
the campaign for the Return.   Many of these sects
were silent agents.   Others, however, placed religious
toleration, even of Jews, among their declared teachings.   The Old Testament and its Hebraism were
taking possession of the minds of the people.   The
Hebrew Scriptures were studied and expounded with
increasing intensity.   A desire to see God's chosen
people in the flesh found frequent expression.   The
The Puritan Hebrew spirit spread to such an extent among the
and the
Hebrew spirit. extreme Republicans that it was even suggested in
1649 that the Lord's Day should be altered from
the first to the seventh day of the week.   This suggestion was at the least premature.   The work that
contained the proposal was declared heretical, scandalous and profane.   It was ordered to be burnt, and
the author and printer were punished.   Barebone's
Parliament suggested seventy as the number of
the Council of State, in imitation of the Sanhedrin.
Hebrew personal names were adopted in place of
the Anglo-Saxon ones received at baptism.   Biblical
idioms were used in ordinary conversation.   The
" Levellers " even called themselves " Jews," while
denouncing their opponents as " Amalekites," and
the government of the Stuarts was termed " the
Egyptian Bondage."   " The Lion of Judah " was in-
scribed on the banners of the victorious Puritans,

and the pass-word "The Lord of Hosts" taken and given. Some advocated the adoption in England of the Levitical legislation. Others even went to the extreme of travelling to the Continent in order to be received into the fold of Judaism. The Fifth Monarchy men—millenarian extremists—believed that Cromwell's government was the fifth empire that betokened the millennium. Their views were by a coincidence in agreement with those of the Jewish Cabbalists to whom the Messianic year, foretold by the Zohar, appeared almost in sight. These Fifth Monarchy and Cabbalistic beliefs, mingling and giving one another mutual support, were fed by the strange and exaggerated stories, that found their way from the Levant by various indirect means, of the earlier exploits of the notorious pseudo-Messiah, Sabbathai Zevi, who a few years later flashed like a meteor across the page of Jewish history.

Fifth Monarchy men.

Another element in the philo-Jewish attitude of a large portion of the English nation was the desire for the conversion of the Jews to Christianity. The millennium, it was thought by one party, only delayed until this conversion was effected, and so long as Jews were excluded from the country they must perforce continue the error of their ways. Thus even the opponents of Judaism and its would-be eradicators joined with more tolerant classes in their advocacy of the Re-Settlement. It was one of these writers, Sir E. Spencer, who at a later date, in reply to Menasseh ben Israel's address to Parliament, proposed the admission of the Jews, in order that they might be available for conversion, on the following conditions: 1. Circumcision should be abandoned. 2. Conversion should not be forced, but reversion to Judaism severely punished. 3. The confiscation of two-thirds of the estates of Jews dying in the country. 4. Compulsory attendance at conversion

Conversionist influences.

sermons on Good Fridays. 5. The payment of double custom duties until conversion. 6. Freedom of movement and trade in the country, but exclusion from gilds and corporations and the necessity to maintain their own poor. 7. Prohibition, while unconverted, of marriage with Christians. 8. The election of their own king, or combination with the Levellers or Anabaptists for a similar purpose, should be made a capital offence. The clerics did not tarry behind the laymen in the advancement of this portion of the argument, and from hundreds of pulpits was preached the Christian duty of admitting the Jews into England so that they might be brought to see the truth.

The pamphleteers. Accompanying, and to some extent in consequence of the activity and multiplication of these sects, was the activity of the pamphleteers. At an epoch at which events, both interesting to the observer and of deep consequence to his welfare, followed one another in quick succession, there was always a large public ready to read of current occurrences and living controversies. The age of the newspaper was at its very opening, and the pamphlet for the time occupied to some extent the place it was afterwards to fill. The Jewish Question, no less than the other questions of the day, failed not to attract the attention of the pamphleteer, and among the elements that prepared the ground for the Re-Settlement of the Jews in England, the pamphlets and their writers occupy no mean place. The first published advocacy of Jewish claims was the Brownist, Leonard Busher's "Religious Peace," which pointed out that by the exclusion of the Jews their conversion was prevented. Seven years later, in 1621, Mr. Sergeant Finch published anonymously "The Calling of the Jewes," with a prefatory epistle in Hebrew, wherein on the one hand he invited the Jews to reassert their national independence in Palestine, and on the other called upon all Christian princes to do homage to the Jewish nation. Roger Williams (1604-83), the colonist, in his "Bloody Tenent," published in 1644, pointed out that Jews, even though heretics, might make good citizens, and in subsequent pamphlets he put forward similar arguments. In 1646, Leonard Busher's "Religious Peace" was re-issued. The same side was taken by the Independent divine, military historian and chaplain to the Council of State, Hugh Peters (1598-1660), afterwards executed for his complicity in the punishment of Charles I., in "A Word for the Army, and Two Words to the Kingdom" (1647). Edward Nicholas[1] wrote "An Apology for the honourable Nation of Jews, and all the Sons of Israel," in which he said that the then troubles of the country were directly due to England's former treatment of God's chosen people. John Sadler, the Hebraist, politician and master of Magdalene College, Cambridge, boldly championed the cause of the Jews in his "Rights of the Kingdom" (1649). In 1652 Major William Butler, afterwards one of the Major-Generals, in his criticism of John Owen's scheme for a religious settlement, concluded by asking whether it was not "the duty of magistrates to permit the Jews, whose conversion we look for, to live freely and peacefully amongst us." In the same year Captain Norwood, in his "Proposals for Propagation of the Gospel," asked for the readmission of the Jews, and in a sympathetic account of a visit by a sailor to a synagogue at Leghorn, the writer asks, "Shall they (the Jews) be tolerated by the Pope, and by the Duke of Florence, by the Turks, by the

(margin note) Christian Advocates of the Jewish cause.

---

[1] This Edward Nicholas has not yet been identified. He was once thought to have been the same as Sir Edward Nicholas, Secretary to Charles I. Another view is that he was a disguised Marrano, and it has even been stated that "Edward Nicholas" was but a pseudonym for Menasseh ben Israel. See Israel Solomons in the *Jewish Chronicle*, February 9, 1906.

Barbarians and others, and shall England still have laws in force against them ? When shall they be recalled ?" On the same side were ranged John Dury (1596–1680), the Protestant divine, the advocate of Protestant reunion, and writer ; the Baptist divine, Henry Jessey (1601–63), who later distinguished himself by collecting a considerable amount of money for the benefit of impoverished Jews settled in Jerusalem ; and Thomas Fuller (1608–61), the author of "The Holy and the Profane State," "A Pisgah Sight" of Palestine, &c.

The economic argument for the Return.

So far the religious and sentimental aspects. At the same time arguments of a different description, but pointing towards the same goal, were influencing another section of the population. The commercial aptitude of the Jews was singled out for attention, and it was argued that from that point of view as well as on account of the introduction of capital, the incorporation of a Jewish element in the population was especially desirable. Another element in the same campaign was the prevailing fashion to consider the policy of the Stuarts unsatisfactory in every detail, and the question was often asked whether this treatment (*i.e.* the non-admission of the Jews) should be made an exception to the general rule. Was it not the business of the Commonwealth to break with all the traditions of the past ?

The first definite step.

In the midst of all these discussions and academic arguments, the first definite steps were taken for the readmission of the Jews to England. With the success of the Independents in December 1648, the hopes of the advocates of religious freedom appeared to be on the point of realisation, and the Jewish Question immediately became one of practical politics. Close upon the *coup-d'état* popularly known as Pride's Purge came a meeting of the Council of Mechanics at Whitehall, whereat " a toleration of all religions whatsoever, not excepting Turkes, nor Papists, nor Jewes," was voted. The Council of Army Officers in reply voted a resolution, in which the widest scheme of religious liberty was favoured. It was even said (the text of the resolution unfortunately cannot be found) that Jews were specifically mentioned in the reply. The following month (January 1649) a formal petition for the readmission of the Jews was presented to Lord Fairfax and the General Council of War by Johanna Cartwright and her son Ebenezer, two Puritans settled at Amsterdam. After a brief recital of the sufferings endured by the Jews in England before their Expulsion in 1290, and a statement of the belief that the time of the conclusion of Israel's wanderings and sufferings was drawing nigh—in the consequent settlement the hope was expressed that England and Holland would take a leading part—the petition proceeded to pray for the repeal of the statute banishing the Jews from England and for their readmission into the kingdom, with freedom of trade and residence. The petition was favourably received, "with a promise to take it into speedy consideration when the present more publick affairs are despatched." Unfortunately for the petitioners and the Jews these "publick affairs," which included the execution of Charles and the settlement of the State, occupied the whole of the energies of the Government for a long period, and the petition of the Cartwrights bore no practical fruit. So favourably disposed, however, were those in power to the prayer of the petitioners that the repeal of the supposed anti-Jewish legislation was accepted as an indisputable fact by the exiled Royalists, and the Presbyterian opposition at home was also so convinced of the admission of the Jews by Cromwell's government, that in one of the political publications of the time, "The last damnable Designe of Cromwell and Ireton and their

The Petition of the Cartwrights.

Its favourable reception.

Public impression as to Cromwell's philo-Jewish intentions.

Junto or Caball," it is recorded that "their real designè is to plunder and disarme the City of London and all the country round about. . . . and to sell it (the plunder) in bulk to the Jews, whom they have lately admitted to set up their banks and magazines of Trade amongst us contrary to an Act of Parliament for their banishment."

AUTHORITIES :—Lucien Wolf, " Menasseh ben Israel's Mission to Oliver Cromwell" (1901), "The Re-Settlement of the Jews in England" (1888) ; H. S. Q. Henriques, "The Return of the Jews to England" (1905); S. R. Gardiner, "History of the Commonwealth and Protectorate," vols. ii. and iv. (1903); C. H. Firth, "Some Historical Notes, 1648-1680," (*Transactions, Jewish Historical Society*, vol. iv., 1903) ; "Original Letters and Papers of State addressed to Oliver Cromwell," published by John Nickolls, Junior (1743) ; F. W. Maitland, "Apostasy at Common Law" (*Law Quarterly Review*, vol. ii., 1886) ; E. S. of Middlesex (Sir E. K. Spencer), "An Epistle to the learned Manasse ben Israel" (1650); " Dictionary of National Biography"; "Encyclopedia of the Laws of England," articles, "Heresy" and " Uniformity" ; " Statutes of the Realm."

CHAPTER XVIII

THE CRYPTO-JEWS

(1643–1655)

CONTEMPORANEOUSLY with this phase through which English thought was passing, and with this education in philo-Semitism that the English people were undergoing, the small number of Jewish settlers already in the country was gradually increasing. The year 1643 saw a special influx, due to the financial exigences of the Parliamentary Government. They came from Amsterdam, and doubtless immediately joined the little Sephardi[1] colony already settled in the Metropolis. Moreover, it happens that at the same time the Portuguese ambassador in London, Antonio de Souza, was himself a Marrano or Crypto-Jew, and it was in the chapel of his embassy that the small colony of Spanish and Portuguese merchants used to assemble weekly, apparently to hear mass, in reality, however, it seems, to join in divine service in accordance with Jewish rites.

A secret Jewish immigration.

Of this colony of Crypto-Jews the first in importance was undoubtedly Antonio Fernandez Carvajal, known in the community as Abraham Israel Carvajal. Carvajal was born towards the close of the sixteenth century in Portugal, probably at Fundão, a great centre of Marranoism and of considerable commercial consequence. At any rate, it is certain he spent his earliest years there. The oppression of the Inquisition wrought sad havoc with the prosperity of that centre, and it was doubtless in consequence of fear of that instrument of religion that Carvajal, in

Antonio Fernandez Carvajal.

[1] Jews of Spanish or Portuguese origin.

common with many other fellow-Marranos, left
Fundão. The exile settled first in the Canary Islands,
where he acquired some property. For commercial
purposes Carvajal removed to London between 1630
and 1635. He married a daughter of Antonio de
Souza, the afore-mentioned Portuguese ambassador,
and speedily attained a prosperous and leading position among the English merchants. Numerous relatives came over from Spain and Portugal to assist in
the conduct of the great business that was being built
up. Carvajal possessed ships trading with such distant
countries as the East and West Indies, South America,
and Syria, and had representatives in all the important
commercial centres of Europe. Among his fellow-
merchants, although an alien and a successful competitor, Carvajal was undoubtedly popular. He pretended to be a Papist, but was suspected of being a
Jew. Yet, when in 1645 Carvajal was denounced by
an informer for transgressing the Act of Uniformity
by abstaining from attendance at church, all his
competitors in trade, as well as many other prominent merchants, petitioned Parliament to protect
him. This was promptly done. The informer was
summoned before the House of Lords, and the proceedings quashed.

Meanwhile Carvajal continued to prosper. In 1649
he was one of the five merchants entrusted by the
Council of State with the army contract for corn ;
and the following year, on the outbreak of war with
Portugal, his goods and ships were specially exempted
from seizure by a warrant from the same body.
In July 1655 he and his two sons, who had probably
been born in England, were endenizened, and thereby
became the first English Jews of whom there is any
record.[1] This adoption of English nationality, how-

[1] Unless David di Nigarellis of Lucca, naturalised in 1412, was also a
Jew. See page 119.

ever, somewhat endangered Carvajal's fortune, for the outbreak of war with Spain shortly afterwards found a large accumulation of Carvajal's property at the Canaries in considerable risk of seizure by the enemy. The difficulty was overcome with the assistance of English men-of-war, and the property removed to a position of greater security. The great favour that Cromwell's Government displayed towards Carvajal Carvajal's was in acknowledgment of his and his agents' invalu-services to the English able services in obtaining early and reliable intelligence Government. of decisions and events on the Continent likely to be of use to the English Government. Carvajal's character seems to have partaken more of the Spaniard than of the Jew. For instance, being involved at a later date in disputes with the English Customs' authorities, Carvajal collected his friends, broke open the Government warehouses, seized the surveyor, confined him on board one of his vessels, and recovered his merchandise. This action was being inquired into by a commission, under Richard Cromwell's chairmanship, at the time of Carvajal's death in 1659.

The second most important member of the little Simon de community was Simon (Jacob) de Caceres, merchant, Caceres. statesman, and "Chauvinist Jew." He was born in Amsterdam, but had travelled in many parts, and had business connections with Hamburg, the West Indies, and South America. An enthusiastic Jew, he made it his business to go among the Spanish and Portuguese merchants and obtain confidential admissions of Judaism from them. Both Queen Christina of Sweden and the King of Denmark on occasions used their influence on his behalf. De Caceres was of especial assistance to Cromwell in the settlement of the newly-acquired colony of Jamaica, and at a later date submitted to the Protector a scheme for the conquest of Chili, De Caceres offering to command the expedition in person and to raise a force of Jews for the purpose.

Henrique Jorge Mendes (? Henrique Mendes da Costa) was also a great merchant and connected with a famous banking-house, trading in Lisbon and Antwerp. The family to which he belonged was one of the most prominent among the Sephardim. Mendes returned to Antwerp in 1655.

Antonio Rodriques Peremena de Rebello or Robles was, like Carvajal, a native of Fundão, whence he also had been driven by the Inquisition, after having seen his father burnt at the stake, and his mother crippled on the rack. At first he settled in the Canaries, but was once more compelled, by fear of the Inquisition, to emigrate, and removed to London, where he arrived about 1640. A business competitor of his in London was Augustin Coronel Chacon, formerly an agent of Carvajal's in Lisbon. Chacon was born in Portugal, but removed to Bordeaux and Rouen, and afterwards to England. There he acted as a Royalist agent, and as such his services were rewarded after the Restoration with knighthood, subsequent, however, to baptism. Coronel acted as consular agent in London for Portugal, and was the first to suggest the marriage between Charles II. and Catherine of Braganza. From a position of opulence Coronel fell into sore financial straits, and ended his life on the Continent, a pensioner of his rich Jewish relatives.[1] Domingo Vaes (Abraham Israel) de Brito, Abraham Coen Gonzales, Isaac Lopes Chillon, Domingo (Israel Roiz) Francia, Antonio (Abraham) de Porto, Simon de Souza, Duarte Henriques Alvares, who had been royal treasurer in the Canary Islands, Diego Rodrigues Aries, Domingo de la Cerda, and David da Costa, were all merchants and Crypto-Jews settled in

London. These and others, together with their wives and children, formed in 1655 a community of about

---

[1] He seems to have reverted to Judaism when misfortunes overtook him.

two hundred souls. With hardly, if any, exception, they belonged to the Sephardi branch of Jewry. They were all prosperous merchants, many of those mentioned being very wealthy. Their commercial activities extended to all parts of the known world, and some of them possessed estates in the Canaries, the Brazils, and other parts. They dealt in almost every variety of merchandise, and imported a considerable amount of bullion from Spain and Portugal. All the members of the colony dwelt in proximity to one another in the eastern part of the city, a neighbourhood that had long been the foreign quarter of London, in which heretics, papists, apostates from Christianity, and even converts to Judaism, were to be found. Francia lived in Leadenhall Street; Aries in Fenchurch Street; De Porto in St. Mary Axe. A little farther east, in Duke's Place, Coronel Chacon, Duarte Alvares, and Antonio Robles had settled. *Their occupations.*

The members of this little community, subsequent and perhaps in addition to the attendances in the chapel of the Portuguese embassy, were accustomed to meet together on the usual occasions for divine service according to the Jewish rites, in the house of Moses Israel Athias, in Cree Church Lane, Leadenhall Street. Athias, who was a relative of Carvajal, and had come to England in his train, was in fact the rabbi of the little secret congregation, and his house in Cree Church Lane was the synagogue in which the Crypto-Jews worshipped. Officially Athias was a clerk in the warehouse of Carvajal, and, although the real purpose of his house with its carefully guarded entrances may have been sometimes suspected, the congregation was never interfered with, and met regularly without disturbance. The synagogue in Cree Church Lane was, however, not the only one to be found in the Metropolis, while its Jewish inhabitants were still living there in *The earliest synagogue.*

disguise. There was at least one other house of worship in St. Helens, of which David Mier was "priest," but to neither can more than the barest references be found. Of the history of these two places of worship and of any other similar ones that might have existed at the time, nothing is now known.

Cromwell and the Jews.

The exceptional favour shown to these Jews by Cromwell, the connivance at the breach of law effected. by their unauthorised services and abstention from church, were not due merely to philo-Jewish sympathy. Cromwell was, for the age in which he lived, extremely liberal minded and superior to the petty prejudices that influenced his less enlightened associates and fellow-reformers. To him the libels and superstitions of the Jew-haters had little force, and personally he had no objection to the free movement of Jews in the country. Cromwell had, however, two very positive reasons for favouring an unrestricted Jewish settlement. The keystone of his policy was the welfare of the English nation.

Reasons for Cromwell's favour.

His object was to make of England a great nation, prosperous and free. To achieve this object he knew that commercial expansion and success were necessary, and to attain these he hoped to have the co-operation of great Jewish merchants by encouraging them to settle on English soil. Cromwell was by no means unacquainted with the resources and wide activities of the rich Sephardi Jews of the Continent. The Spanish and Portuguese trade was in their hands; the Levant trade also to a considerable extent. Jews had helped to found the Hamburg Bank, and were closely connected with the Dutch East and West Indian Companies. As bullion merchants also, Jews were prominent, and, in addition, many of them owned fleets of merchantmen.

The second reason for Cromwell's favour was the

great assistance these Crypto-Jews of London and their agents on the Continent were to the government of the Commonwealth. And, when employing them on secret service, he was well aware of their true faith. In fact he stated definitely in a letter that "the State, in choosing men to serve it, takes no notice of their opinions; if they be willing faithfully to serve it—that satisfies." If he had believed them to have been papists, it is certain that Cromwell would have had nothing to do with them. His dislike of the Catholic Church was one of the few prejudices Cromwell possessed.

It has already been noticed that the rich London Jews acted as contractors to the Government, supplying it with both money and stores. De Caceres, we have also seen, was called upon by the Government for advice in the settlement of American affairs. In another and more secret capacity Carvajal was of equal if not greater service to Cromwell's government. In his army of continental agents and correspondents, Carvajal possessed the machinery to hand for obtaining early and reliable information concerning designs and movements on the part of foreign powers and also of the exiled Stuart. This invaluable machinery the Jewish merchant placed at the disposal of the government under whose protection he dwelt, with the result that Cromwell was often enabled to forestall hostile designs and to confound the plans of the enemies of the Commonwealth. It was through the intelligence furnished by Carvajal that at least one of the numerous conspiracies against the life of the Protector was laid bare. From one of Carvajal's continental agents came the first news of the secret treaty between Charles and Spain, and it is most probable that it was information from a kindred source which enabled the forces of the Commonwealth to seize

Jewish services to the English Government.

Cromwell's Jewish Intelligencers.

M

the Royalist shipping at Ostend and thereby prevent a renewal of the Civil War.

Advantages to England of Cromwell's toleration.

Cromwell's action in favouring a Jewish settlement was well justified by the immediate results. The commercial benefit to the nation by the acquisition of those Marrano merchants could admit of no doubt. They made their new home the centre of a world-wide commerce. The first Jewish settlers brought with them capital in ready money of one and a half million pounds, and this at a time when one of the special troubles of the country was a scarcity of coin. Their annual turnover in trade equalled a twelfth of the total commerce of the country.

AUTHORITIES:—Lucien Wolf, "Menasseh ben Israel's Mission," "The Re-Settlement of the Jews," "The First English Jew" (*Transactions, Jewish Historical Society*, vol. ii., 1896), "Crypto-Jews under the Commonwealth" (*Transactions, Jewish Historical Society*, vol. i., 1895), "Cromwell's Jewish Intelligencers" (*The Jewish Literary Annual*, 1904).

CHAPTER XIX

MENASSEH BEN ISRAEL
(1648–1654)

OF the many threads that, leading from various direc- The English Colonies. tions, ultimately combined to co-operate in the Re-Settlement of the Jews in England, there are still one or two that deserve mention. The Stuart policy of placing the alternatives of emigration, or conformity to the Established Church, before the dissentient Puritan elements in the population had resulted in peopling the American colonies with the most liberal-minded of the English. It thus came about that the inhabitants of the American colonies were the most advanced and tolerant among all nations then exist-ing, and although the colonists were not altogether self-governing, yet the opinions and feelings of the people did not fail to influence their rulers. Of all the American colonies, that of Rhode Island was most liberally governed. It had been founded by Roger Toleration in the Colonies. Williams, the apostle of religious liberty, whose writ-ings on behalf of toleration of the Jews have already been mentioned ; and in its constitution, adopted in 1641, one of the laws ran : "We agree, as formerly hath been the liberties of the town, so still, to hold for the liberty of conscience." It was under Williams' presidency later, between 1655 and 1657, that the foundations of the remarkably prosperous Jewish settlement of Newport were laid. Williams, who dur-ing his visits to England never omitted to take part in the campaign for toleration, was, as has already been mentioned, ably seconded by another preacher, Hugh

Peters, who had filled the pulpit vacated by Williams at Salem.

Another impulse that came from America was the compulsory emigration of numerous Jewish settlers in South America. The reconquest of the Brazils by the Portuguese in 1654 necessitated a resumption of the perennial wanderings of the exiles. Many of the fugitives, who were numbered by the thousand, fled to the English and Dutch colonies in North America and the West Indies. Some of them founded the Jewish settlement in New York, then known as New Amsterdam. A large body turned to the country from which the place of their sojourn had been torn, and made their way under the lead of their rabbi, Isaac Aboab, to Holland. Those who settled in the English colonies carried their trade with them. No longer on Dutch soil, however, commerce with their relatives and friends in Holland was rendered most difficult, if not impossible, by the commercial policy of England as exemplified in the Navigation Act which protected English shipping and English ports at the expense of those of the Continent. To continue their business relations with their friends living in Holland, it was necessary that the latter should either themselves settle in England or appoint agents there. In either case it was the Jews alone who were affected, and thus the

conquests of Portugal in South America led to an increase of the Jewish population of London.

One other American element in the Re-Settlement was of a more academic character. The problem of

the fate of the Lost Ten Tribes of Israel is one that had already, by the date at which we have arrived, for centuries aroused considerable attention in certain circles. Throughout the civilised world attempts were frequently being made to solve the mystery. In England, references to the Lost Tribes and the supposed place of their concealment are to be found in writers as early as Matthew Paris (1241) and Sir John Mandeville (1322–1357). In the time of the later Tudors and the Stuarts interest in the problem was renewed. Giles Fletcher, Elizabeth's minister to the Emperor of Muscovy, claimed to have discovered them among the Tartars. George Sandys found them in 1610 in the neighbourhood of the Caspian. Meanwhile an entirely new theory as to their fate had arisen with the *In America.* investigations of the Spaniards in America. Numerous writers of that nation contended that the descendants of the Tribes of Israel were to be found among the inhabitants of the New World, and in the controversies that ensued between the Spanish supporters and opponents of that view, a large number of books were written. The controversy after a time reached *An English* England. Its sponsor in this country was Thomas *controversy regarding their* Thorowgood, one of the Assembly of Divines. Eager *fate.* to introduce the missionary work of the Rev. John Eliot among the North American Indians to the sympathetic notice of the English, in order that the latter might accord it financial support, Thorowgood, in 1648, wrote his "Jewes in America." The renewal of the Civil War delayed its publication, and in the meanwhile the proof-sheets were read by John Durie, who had already spoken out on behalf of toleration, and who subsequently took a prominent part in the Jewish Re-Settlement movement. John Durie had, when in Amsterdam, heard other stories of the Israelitish ancestry of the natives of America, and had moreover met Menasseh ben Israel there.

Menasseh ben Israel was born in 1604. He is *Menasseh ben* generally believed to have been born in Lisbon of *Israel.* Marrano parents, but a new theory has been produced that puts forward La Rochelle as the place of his birth.[1] It is certain that his parents suffered severely in either the former or both of the great

[1] See Cardoso de Bethencourt, *Jewish Chronicle*, May 20, 1904.

outbursts of activity displayed by the Inquisition in 1603 and 1605, and in consequence of the sufferings then endured, they, together with a large number of fellow Marranos, left Portugal at that time.   Wherever

Menasseh's early years and education.

Menasseh was born, he and his parents settled in Amsterdam very shortly after their departure from Lisbon.   In Amsterdam, Menasseh's education was entrusted to Rabbi Isaac Uziel of the new congregation, the *Neveh Shalom*.   Uziel was not only skilled in Talmud and mathematics; he had also some reputation as a physician, and was well known as a Hebrew poet.   Under his master's care Menasseh progressed so satisfactorily that at the age of fifteen he was qualified to preach, and three years later he was appointed to succeed his teacher, who had meanwhile died, in the synagogue.   About the same time Menasseh married Rachael Soeira, a great granddaughter of the illustrious Don Isaac Abravanel,[1] and a member of a family reputed to be descended from King David.   By her he had three children, Gracia (Hannah), Joseph, named after Menasseh's father, and Samuel.

His occupations in Amsterdam.

So successful as a preacher did the new rabbi become that he proved a rival to his renowned colleague, Isaac Aboab, between whose oratory and Menasseh's it was difficult to give the preference.   To teaching also, Menasseh devoted himself with zeal. Nevertheless the remuneration he received from his congregation proved insufficient, and it became necessary for him to supplement his ordinary income.   For this purpose Menasseh determined to establish a

His printing-press.

Hebrew printing-press in Amsterdam, the first in the

---

[1] The statesman and Biblical commentator (1437–1508), who, after vain efforts to induce the revocation of the edict of expulsion of the Jews from Spain, himself headed the exodus.   Abravanel was treasurer to Alfonso V. of Portugal.   On the death of that monarch he entered the service of Queen Isabella of Castile, and after the expulsion from Spain that of the King of Naples.   After his subsequent settlement in Venice Abravanel negotiated a commercial treaty between that Republic and Portugal.

Netherlands, and on the 12th of January 1627 he issued his first production, a Hebrew prayer-book according to the Sephardi rite. Other publications that quickly followed were a Hebrew grammar, by his teacher Uziel, and an index to the *Midrash Rabboth*, compiled by himself. This last was Menasseh's introduction to authorship. Meanwhile Menasseh, who was acquainted with ten languages, was engaged on the chief literary work of his life. In his *El Conciliador*, the first part of which was published in 1632, all apparently inconsistent passages in the Old Testament are enumerated, and the recognised Jewish interpretations explained in detail. The book was almost the first written in a modern language by a Jew, of interest to Christian readers, and it did not fail to attract considerable attention in non-Jewish circles. The work was well received by Jewish authorities. The Rabbinical College at Frankfurt-on-the-Main commended the book as the work of "the great and holy man, who is far renowned for his learning." The philosopher and Cabbalist Abraham Cohen de Herrera, the preacher and author Daniel de Caceres a near relative of his namesake Simon, the celebrated physician Zacuto Lusitano, Joseph Bueno another physician of considerable reputation, and Immanuel Nehemias, all received the work with approbation. The last two extolled it in verses. By Dionysius Vossius, the *Conciliador*, which was written in Spanish, was translated into Latin, and by Marco Luzzatto into Italian. Yet the work fell far short of the attainable ideal. Numerous literatures were ransacked for opinions on the subject with which Menasseh was dealing, but of the author's own matured thoughts but little is given. The work was little more than a compilation, and as a compiler—for the *Conciliador* was no exception from the rule followed in Menasseh's theological writings—should he be described rather than as the "Theologian and Philosopher," as he liked to style himself.

Menasseh's writings may be classed under three headings—"Theological Philosophy," "Theological Expositions," and "Historical Writings." In the first class comes *De Termino Vitæ* (1639)—written in Latin, and translated afterwards by Thomas Pocock into English—written at the request of Beverovicius, so that the Jewish side of a question then exercising thinking minds should be heard; *De la Resurreccion de los muertos* (1636), *De la fragilidad humana, y inclinacion del hombre al peccado* (1642), both written in Spanish and translated into Latin; *Nishmas Hayim* (1651) in Hebrew, a work full of Cabbalistic tendencies; and an essay "On Creation" (1635) in Latin. The last-named gave rise, through an eulogistic poem written in praise of it by Barlaeus, to a learned controversy that extended over a long period.

Among Menasseh's "Theological Expositions" are to be placed his *Conciliador* already noticed, the second part of which appeared in 1641, the third in 1650, and the fourth and last the following year. In 1655, however, Menasseh wrote a supplement in Spanish, *Piedra Gloriosa o de la Estatua de Nebuchadnesar*, dedicated to Isaac Vossius, and illustrated with four etchings by the author's friend Rembrandt; and *Thesouro dos Dinim* (1645–47), also in Spanish. Many of Menasseh's theological works were never published. Some were not even finished. Among these are mentioned the "Divine Origin and Authority of the Mosaic Law," "A Summary of Jewish Theology," "Rabbinical Philosophy," "Science of the Talmudists in all its Branches," "Necessity of Tradition," "Image Worship," &c. Among works contemplated were "The Seventy Weeks of Daniel," a *Bibliotheca Rabbinica*, and a Hebrew-Arabic lexicon.

Chief among Menasseh's historical writings comes the "Heroic History," wherein the author proposed to edit and to some extent re-write Josephus, continuing the history of the Jews until the author's own day. The book, if written, was however never published. His other writings in the same class, the *Vindiciæ Judæorum*, the "Hope of Israel," and the "Address to the English Nation," will receive further notice later. One other book from Menasseh's pen that demands mention is his translation of Phokylides into Spanish verse.

The reputation gained for Menasseh by these works rapidly spread throughout Europe, and his correspondents included most of the learned Jews of the day. In addition many Christian scholars, attracted to him by his writings and his renown, joined the circle of his acquaintances and friends. Among these were Gerhard, Isaac and Dionysius Vossius, Hugo Grotius, Caspar Barlaeus, Cunaeus, Bochart, Huet, Blondel, and Anna Marie de Schurman. Among Menasseh's personal friends was also included the great artist Rembrandt van Rhyn. On one occasion Menasseh took a party consisting of Huet the sceptic and theologian, David Blondel the French Protestant theologian and writer, Samuel Bochart the French Protestant minister, theologian, and author, and Isaac Vossius, to the *Neveh Shalom* synagogue, of which he was rabbi. Menasseh's distinguished Jewish friends were also numerous. Their number included the physician Immanuel Bocarro Frances y Rosales (Jacob Rosales Hebraeus), Immanuel Nehemias, the Buenos, Abravanels, Pintos, Raphael Levi, Daniel Abudiente, David Senior Henriquez, the renowned Zacuto Lusitano, Daniel de Caceres, the Marrano scientist and orientalist Diego Barrassa, and others. Joseph Solomon Delmedigo of Candia, the famous philosopher and physician, who, in the course of his wanderings, found himself at Amsterdam, was enabled by Menasseh to publish there a selection of his works.

Although Menasseh had thus obtained a distinguished place in the literary circles of Amsterdam, his private life was by no means devoid of worry and anxiety. The pittance allowed him by the congregation to which he was attached was quite insufficient to supply his needs, and the success of the printing business he had established was imperative. In this sphere of activity, however, competitors had arisen, and the business was no longer so remunerative as when first established. Moreover, Menasseh's relations with his colleagues in the service of the community were by no means friendly, and those with Saul Levi Morteira (*c.* 1596–1660), the Haham of the *Bet Ya'akob* congregation, were especially strained. Morteira counted among his pupils Baruch Spinoza and Moses Zacuto. At a later date he was a member of the Beth Din that pronounced the decree of excommunication against the former. Driven by financial necessities Menasseh determined to enter the commercial world. He

entered into partnership with his brother-in-law, Ephraim Soeiro, who in their joint interests went to Brazil in 1638. The expectations of Menasseh were not realised by this trading mission, and he thereupon determined himself to emigrate and settle in South America. In his determination he was strengthened by a communal reorganisation in Amsterdam whereby Menasseh lost his appointment with the *Neveh Shalom* congregation. In preparation for the change, the second part of the *Conciliador*, published during the crisis, was dedicated to the Jews of Pernambuco and to the General Council of the Dutch East India Company. The Prince of Orange gave him letters of introduction to the President of

the American Chamber of Commerce, and, despite
the remonstrances of his Christian friends, Menasseh
remained steadfast in his determination to emigrate.
He bade farewell to his congregation, and was on the
point of sailing, when Abraham and Isaac Pereira,
wealthy Sephardim recently arrived from Spain,
offered him the appointment of head of a theological
academy they had just established in Amsterdam.
The offer was accepted, and Menasseh remained to
devote himself to authorship and learning (1640).
The printing business was continued for a few years
until 1646, when it was handed over to his elder son
Joseph. The latter was only in control until 1648, in
which year he died, at the early age of twenty, while
on a visit to Lublin.

But is induced to remain in Amsterdam.

Freed from pecuniary embarrassments, Menasseh
commenced to devote his talents to a new object,
that of diplomacy. The precarious political condition
of the bulk of European Jewry and the vicissitudes
through which numbers of Jews were continually
passing had impressed themselves deeply upon his
imagination. Sympathy with his people in their
trouble and their pain made him consider means of
alleviation. A place of refuge for the oppressed
of Israel, a land of liberty for them, appeared the
great desideratum, and in pursuance of this object
an introduction to Queen Christina of Sweden was
sought. This was easily obtained through Menasseh's
friend Isaac Vossius. On the occasion of the queen's
coronation in 1650, Menasseh dedicated to her a
Spanish and Hebrew poem, which was sent to her
and also to her chancellor, Adler-Sabrius. The next
step was to crave permission to dedicate the *Conciliador*, just completed, to the young queen. At the
same time Menasseh offered his services in helping
the queen, who was a student of Hebrew, to extend
her Hebrew library. The offer was gladly accepted,

Menasseh enters diplomacy.

and through Menasseh's instrumentality considerable additions made to the collection.

Menasseh's political objects in this connection were cut short by the abdication of the queen, but the correspondence between them continued after that event. He waited upon her during her stay at Antwerp, and shortly afterwards wrote his *Oracion panegyrica à la Magd. de Christina, Reyna de Suecia.* He also applied to her for pecuniary assistance in the publication of his large Spanish Bible ; the result of the application is not known.

AUTHORITIES :—Lucien Wolf, "American Elements in the Re-Settlement" (*Transactions, Jewish Historical Society*, vol. iii., 1899); H. Adler, "A Homage to Menasseh ben Israel" (*Transactions, Jewish Historical Society*, vol. i., 1895) ; M. Kayserling, "The Life and Labours of Manasseh ben Israel" (" Miscellany of Hebrew Literature," vol. ii., 1877) ; Albert M. Hyamson, " The Lost Tribes and the Influence of the Search for them on the Return of the Jews to England" (*Jewish Quarterly Review*, vol. xv., 1903); M. Gaster, "Manasseh ben Israel's Literary Activity" (*Jewish Chronicle*, Dec. 1, 1905) ; " Jewish Encyclopedia," article, " Manasseh ben Israel."

CHAPTER XX

THE WHITEHALL CONFERENCE
(1650–1655)

MENASSEH had already since some years had his Menasseh's views on English politics. attention directed towards England and the events that were happening there. In the great struggle between the crown and the people his sympathies, in common with those of most of his fellow-Jews of Holland, seem to have been on the side of the Stuarts, and it was to these feelings that he gave expression in an oration on the occasion of the visit of Queen Henrietta Maria to the Amsterdam Synagogue in 1642. Five years later his opinion had hardly altered, for in writing to an English friend he stigmatised the Civil War as a Divine punishment for the expulsion of the Jews from England in the thirteenth century. The seed of his future endeavours for the Re-Settlement had evidently been already sown. Menasseh's dreams and hopes were thus gradually being turned in the direction of England, there to find assistance in his twofold plan for the hastening of the millennium and the immediate relief of Jewish suffering, when he received the letter concerning the Lost Ten Tribes from Dury. Dury was one of the numerous Christian scholars with whom Menasseh was on terms of friendship. During his visits to Holland he had frequently met the Amsterdam rabbi, and among other topics of conversation had been the remarkable " Relation " of Antonio Montezinos. The story of Montezinos, other- The " Relation " of Antonio Montezinos. wise Aaron Levi, which had attracted Menasseh, was to the effect, that while travelling in the interior of

South America he had come across a native tribe claiming descent from Reuben, undoubtedly a remnant of the Ten Tribes that had centuries before apparently completely disappeared. This story of Montezinos had been supported by affidavit, and had obtained the immediate acceptance of Menasseh. Dury's request for information regarding it met with a ready response. Menasseh sent a copy of Montezinos' declaration by return, and on the appearance of Thorowgood's book in 1650 the "Relation" of Antonio Montezinos appeared as an appendix.

Menasseh and the Millenarians.

About the same time a correspondence had been conducted between Menasseh and the enthusiastic Millenarian, Nathaniel Holmes, wherein the views of the latter concerning the impending advent of the Messianic Age were put forward with emphasis. Hitherto Menasseh had troubled little about Montezinos' narrative, but the arguments of Holmes placed it in a new light. He remembered it had been foretold, that before Israel could be restored to the Holy Land their scattering throughout the world must be complete. From the "Relation" of Montezinos and other accounts it appeared that the Israelites had already reached America. In the whole of the then known world Britain remained the only country in which the Children of Israel were not to be found. Once the Dispersion were completed by the admission of the Jews into England, the millennium could no longer be delayed. All other interests were forgotten in the new discovery, and Menasseh henceforth devoted himself to working for the re-settlement of the Jews in England. The receipt of Dury's letter at first inclined Menasseh to write a treatise on the dispersion of the Ten Tribes generally. His plan, however, was speedily changed, and he determined to devote the volume to proving the authenticity of the claim of Israelitish ancestry by the natives of America, and,

after glances at a few other Jewish matters, to con-
clude with a proof that the time of the Messiah was
at hand. The book when completed was entitled
"The Hope of Israel." The Hebrew and Spanish "The Hope
editions did not exceed the intentions Menasseh had of Israel."
expressed. The Latin edition, however, which quickly
followed the others, contained a dedication "To the
High Court, the Parliament of England, and to the
Councell of State." The achievements of that body
were mentioned in eulogistic terms. Reference was
made to favours conferred upon "our Nation" in
the past, and a continuation of them in the future
requested. The dedication was made "upon no other
ground than this, that I may gain your favour and
good-will to our Nation, now scattered almost all over
the earth." The publication created a sensation in
England. The Puritans were flattered by the references to the Government; the Millenarians acclaimed
the learned rabbi as a convert to their views. The
treatise was quickly translated into English, in which
language two editions were rapidly exhausted. The
impression the book made was, however, but transi-
tory. Sir Edward Spencer's somewhat anti-Jewish
booklet, to which reference has already been made,
followed "The Hope of Israel." Sadler, who was
afterwards of great assistance in the Re-Settlement,
expressed doubts concerning Montezinos' Relation in
his "Rights of the Kingdom"; Fuller, in his "Pisgah
Sight" of Palestine, also criticised Menasseh's proposals.

Cromwell had little sympathy with these Messianic Cromwell's
and Lost Tribes beliefs. To him the Jewish Question view of the
Jewish
appealed solely or almost entirely from the practical Question.
side. Merely to hasten the millennium Cromwell was
not likely to stir a foot; but to increase the prosperity
of the country, to extend its influence and its wealth,
and correspondingly to place the English nation in

the forefront of the European powers, was of more consequence. In another chapter Cromwell's knowledge of the Crypto-Jews of London and their services both to the Commonwealth and to commerce have been adverted upon. An increase in the number of men such as Carvajal and De Caceres, Cromwell had very good reason to welcome. For the moment this object of Cromwell's seemed on the point of attainment without any special effort. During the year 1651 negotiations were in progress with the Government of Holland for a treaty of coalition between the two countries, and if this had been effected Jewish merchants would have acquired in England rights similar to those they possessed in Holland. The negotiations, however, fell through, and instead of a treaty of coalition, the protectionist Navigation Act, specially directed against Holland, entered the Statute Book. Under the new conditions it became advisable for Jewish merchants to settle in England, and as their removal would prove mutually beneficial, some means of legalising a Jewish settlement had to be found.

The St. John Mission and Menasseh.

The St. John Mission, consisting of Oliver St. John, Chief Justice of the Common Pleas, and Walter Strickland, who had previously acted as the representative of the Long Parliament in Holland, with John Thurloe, afterwards Secretary of State, as secretary, finding its original mission likely to be a failure, was instructed to study the Jewish Question, and in all probability entered into negotiations with the leading Jews of Amsterdam. Thurloe certainly had frequent interviews with Menasseh ben Israel, and the members of the Mission were entertained by the synagogue. The return of the Mission to England was immediately followed by a letter from Menasseh to the Council of State, which was referred to a committee of which Cromwell himself was a member. A few months later two passes, together with an invi-

Menasseh invited to England.

tation to come to England, were sent to the Amsterdam rabbi. In the meanwhile, however, the long threatened war broke out between England and Holland, and Menasseh's departure was prevented. Moreover more urgent affairs drove the Jewish Question into the background, and although the discussion of the subject continued fitfully in pamphlets and broadsheets, for the moment it was no longer a topic of practical politics. Nevertheless, in 1653 a Puritan extremist, Samuel Herring, in the midst of a lengthy petition to Parliament asking for various reforms in the government of the kingdom, prayed "That the Jewes should be called into this Commonwealth, and have places allotted them to inhabit in, and exercise there lyberty, for there tyme is neere at hand." Similar action was also taken by Robert Rich, and on the motion of Henry Martin that the supposed Act of Expulsion be repealed, a spirited but futile parliamentary debate took place.

The conclusion of peace the following year saw the resumption of the negotiations between Cromwell and Menasseh. The latter, however, still failed to make use of his pass and in person plead the cause of his co-religionists before the English Government. He was dissuaded by his friends from crossing to England, "considering the chequered and interwoven vicissitudes and turns of things here below." The true explanation was the precarious position Menasseh held in Amsterdam, in consequence of his quarrels with colleagues. It was feared that the undertaking of a mission to England, a nation at that time detested by the Dutch fresh from hostilities, might prove fatal to Menasseh's position in Amsterdam. Menasseh therefore stayed at home, and in his place Manuel Martinez (David Abarvanel) Dormido, his brother-in-law, crossed the North Sea.

Dormido had been a Marrano of great wealth and

War with Holland delays the Jewish Question.

Conclusion of peace.

N

David Abar-
vanel Dormido.
a Government official in Andalusia. Like so many of his kindred, however, he had come under the notice of the Inquisition, and to escape the attention of the Holy Office had fled. After eight years in Bordeaux, Dormido settled in Holland, where he openly joined the Jewish community. In Amsterdam Dormido became a wealthy merchant and a leading member of the Jewish community. The conquest of Pernambuco by the Portuguese early in 1654, however, deprived him of the greater portion of his means, and finding it necessary to recommence his career, Dormido determined to do so in England, where he knew many other Marranos to be settled. Thus Dormido came to England in two capacities—privately to mend his fortune, officially as the representative of his brother-in-law Menasseh, and through him as the ambassador of Jewry. Immediately on his arrival in London, Dormido set about preparing two petitions to Cromwell. The former dealt with his own personal affairs. It recorded his sufferings in the past, his desire to become a subject of the Commonwealth, and his prayer for the Protector's intercession with the king of Portugal, so that Dormido's property might be restored. The second petition asked for the re-admission of the Jews to England on terms of equality with the Christian inhabitants. The admission was asked for on the grounds of the advantage to trade and industry of a Jewish immigration, and the consequent increase in the public revenue. Finally, Dormido asked that, in the event of the prayer being granted, the control and management of the new community should be entrusted to him.

Dormido's
petitions
referred to
the Council
of State.
These petitions were most graciously accepted by Cromwell, and immediately referred to the Council of State, with the endorsement : " His Highness is pleased in an especiall manner to recommend these two annexed papers to the speedy consideration of the

Councell, that the Peticion may receive all due satis-
facion, and withall convenient speed." The Council
as a body was, however, not so earnest in the satisfaction of Dormido's petitions as was the Protector.
The petitions were referred to a committee, which,
reporting a month later, the Council, in the absence
of Cromwell, resolved that it " saw no excuse to make
any order." That Cromwell did not agree with this Cromwell and
resolution is obvious from his action. Despite the Dormido.
determination of the Council to have nothing to do
with the matter, Cromwell immediately granted one
of the prayers of Dormido, and sent an autograph
letter to the king of Portugal asking him as a personal favour to restore Dormido's property. This
was only a personal matter, and, from the political
point of view, of no consequence. The larger question still remained unsettled, and, despite the set-back
given to it by the resolution of the Council, Cromwell
was still earnestly in favour of the re-admission of the
Jews. To gain this end it was necessary for the cause
of Jewry to be pleaded by a better known and more
important personage than Dormido. If Menasseh's
scheme were to be successfully accomplished, it was
necessary for him to support it in person. Samuel
ben Israel, who had accompanied his uncle Dormido
to England, was therefore sent back to Amsterdam
with an invitation from the Protector to Menasseh to
come to England. In October 1655 Menasseh ben
Israel arrived in London with the manuscript of his Arrival of
" Humble Addresses " in his pocket. In the interval Menasseh.
between the rejection of Dormido's petition and the
arrival of Menasseh, a scheme was adopted for the
settlement of the Jewish victims of the Portuguese reconquest of Pernambuco and Recife in the English
colony of Surinam. There they were given considerable advantages, in addition to the guarantee of
freedom of conscience and full civil rights, and for

a long period the Jewish community of Surinam was one of the most prosperous in the Diaspora.

Menasseh was accompanied by his son and three rabbis, one of them, Jacob Sasportas, afterwards Haham or ecclesiastical head of the London community. He did not take up his quarters in the eastern part of the city, where the Marranos dwelt, but was lodged in the Strand, the most fashionable quarter of the town, a neighbourhood frequented by foreign ambassadors and other persons of political consequence. His first business was to print the *The "Humble Addresses."* " Humble Addresses," the formal petition to the Government for the re-admission of the Jews. In this document the petitioner no longer put forward the Messianic prophecies and Lost Tribe legends as primary arguments in support of his request. He based his claims on the argument of political expediency. Incidentally he defended the Jews against the charges of ritual murder, usury, and the conversion of Christians. He asked for absolute freedom of movement and settlement for Jews in England, together with the unrestricted exercise of their religion. The prime motive of his previous efforts had been the hastening of the millennium. The renewal of the persecution of the Jews in Poland now rendered him anxious to find a refuge for the fugitives from Eastern Europe, as well as for the victims of the Inquisition escaped from the Spanish and Portuguese dominions.

English opinion. Unfortunately for the cause Menasseh had at heart, the enthusiasm that had been shown in many quarters a decade or less earlier on the Jewish question had considerably cooled. Of the leading English advocates for the re-admission, Williams was in America, Sadler in office and therefore silenced, and Peters with little influence. The conversionists and Millenarians cared nothing about the restrictions imposed on the Jews so long as they were admitted. The political and economic advocates of the re-admission were afraid to publish the reasons of their policy, lest, on the one hand, they should arouse the criticisms of the religious advocates of the same cause, and, on the other, stir up the hostility of the merchants, who would not be likely to welcome the admission of competitors in business. The difficulties were increased Attitude of the Royalists. by the intrigues of Royalists and foreigners. The former did their utmost to prevent the consummation of Menasseh's scheme, first, because it was favoured by Cromwell and therefore ought to be prevented; secondly, because the Royalists were anxious to attach the rich Dutch Jews to their own cause. The foreign hostility came especially from Holland, where it was seen that the new policy, that of attracting the Dutch Jewish merchants to England, was in reality but a continuation of that of the Navigation Act, avowedly directed against that State.

The hostility of these parties took the form of Harmful rumours. the dissemination of rumours. In one quarter it was believed the Jews had made an offer for the purchase of St. Paul's Cathedral and the Bodleian, and, in order to involve Cromwell in the ill effects that ensued, it was alleged that the sale only fell through in consequence of a difference about the price. Attempts were also made to hold Cromwell up to ridicule by the statements concerning a Jewish mission sent to Huntingdon to investigate the Protector's ancestry with a view to proving him to be the Messiah, and by the assertion that Menasseh at his first interview with Cromwell prodded him in the side in order to ascertain whether he were in reality flesh and blood or a spiritual manifestation. It was said that Cromwell proposed handing the customs over to the Jews to farm. Various libels concerning the Jewish character were repeated, and the possibility of the acceptance of Christianity by them declared to be non-existent. In the desire to discourage any sympathy with the Jewish cause on the part of the conversionists, the paradoxical device of engaging the services of a converted Jew, Paul Isaiah, formerly a trooper in Rupert's Horse, was adopted, and it was in the interest of the opposition party that his "The Messias of the Christians and the Jews" was published. The condition of affairs was rendered even worse by the publication of the "Humble Addresses." The religious party among the English advocates of admission resented the emphasis laid on the economic side of the question, while the avowed opponents doubted the reliability of the arguments put forward by Menasseh. The stream of pamphlets on the Jews recommenced, but the direction was changed. The bulk were now devoted to attacks upon the Jews. Only two or three writers dared to use their pens in favour of admission. Both Judaism and the Jews were attacked, and the former advocates of Jewish rights remained silent or advocated restrictions on the proposed Jewish settlement. John Durie was studying Jewish disabilities at Cassel with a view to their introduction into England. Henry Jessey was in favour of restrictions.

The commotion and attacks did not deter Menasseh from his purpose. As soon as his "Addresses" was printed, he took copies to Whitehall for presentation to the Council of State. Unfortunately a day was chosen on which Cromwell was absent, and the books were merely accepted by the clerk on behalf of the Council, and the next business proceeded with. A fortnight later Cromwell placed before the Council another petition, with a similar purport, that he had received from Menasseh. The document asked for the following concessions: (1) Security of life and property; (2) Liberty of public worship; (3) The right to acquire a cemetery; (4) Permission to trade as freely as native merchants; (5) The appointment by Cromwell of an officer to examine the passports of Jewish immigrants and to compel them to swear allegiance to the Government; (6) The jurisdiction of the "Chief of the Synagogue" in disputes between Jews, with right of appeal to the civil courts; and (7) The repeal of any anti-Jewish legislation that might be in force. In Cromwell's presence the Council was more amenable to his influence, and it was on his motion that it was resolved "that the Jews deserving it may be admitted into this nation to trade and traffic and dwell amongst us as Providence shall give occasion." This resolution, together with the petition and the "Humble Addresses," was referred to a committee with instructions to report *The Petitions* without delay. The Council and its committee were *referred to a* in a difficult position. Personally the members were *Committee,* not exactly hostile to the re-admission of the Jews, but they were certainly by no means enthusiastically in favour of it. On the one hand, they had to satisfy Cromwell, who seemed determined on the adoption of his friendly policy; on the other, they had to consider the temper of the nation which seemed, from the expressions of opinion, to be hostile to a Jewish immigration. The committee lost no time in arriving at a decision. It resolved to devolve the responsibility of settling the difficult problem on others, and recommended the convocation of a con- *and a* ference of representative Englishmen to consider the *Conference.* whole question.

The recommendation was adopted by the Council. The list of personages to be summoned to the Conference was drawn up by three members of the Council in conjunction with the Lord President, notoriously devoted to Cromwell. The list was approved by Cromwell, and the Conference convened for the 4th of December 1655. The meetings were

held in the Council Chamber at Whitehall. Judging
from the importance of the people who took part in
it, the Conference was one of the leading events in
the history of the Commonwealth. In addition to
Cromwell himself the statesmen present comprised
Henry Lawrence, the Lord President of the Council;
Sir Gilbert Pickering, one of Charles I.'s judges; Sir
Charles Wolseley, one of Cromwell's peers; John
Lisle, the regicide; Francis Rous, Speaker of the Little
Parliament—all members of the Council; Walter
Strickland, one of the ambassadors to the Nether-
lands four years earlier; Major-General John Lambert,
the leading spirit in the Council of Officers; and
William Sydenham, Cromwellian soldier and states-
man. The law was represented by Chief Justice
Sir John Glynne and Chief Baron William Steele,
Lord Chief Justice St. John, Strickland's colleague
in the embassy, was also invited but did not attend.
The mercantile community was represented by
Alderman Dethick the Lord Mayor, Sheriff Thomp-
son, Alderman Robert Titchborn, Alderman Riccards,
Sir Christopher Pack, ex-Lord Mayor, the leading
mercantile authority in the country, Mr. Cressett
the Master of the Charterhouse, William Kiffen the
wealthy merchant-parson, and the regicide Owen
Rowe then deputy-governor of the Bermuda Company.

The class that had the largest share of representation
at the Conference was that of the theologians. Sixteen of these, the spiritual leaders of Puritan England,
attended the first meeting. They were Dr. Cud-
worth, Regius Professor of Hebrew at Cambridge;
Dr. Owen, most famous of Independent divines and
most fearless of advocates of religious liberty; John
Caryll, the Bible commentor; Dr. Goodwin, President of Magdalen College, Oxford; Henry Wilkinson,
Canon of Christ Church; Dr. Whitchcote, Provost
of King's. The preachers were William Bridge,

Daniel Dyke, Henry Jessey, Thomas Manton, Dr. Newcomen, Philip Nye, Anthony Tuckney, William Benn, Walter Craddock, and Samuel Fairclough. John Carter also received an invitation, but was on his deathbed when it reached him. The Conference was obviously packed. The great majority of the members had already committed themselves to the cause of religious toleration, while several of the laymen were notoriously subservient to Cromwell.

Two questions were placed before the Conference : The Questions. " Whether it be lawful to receive the Jews. If it be lawful, then upon what terms is it meet to receive them ? " The first was a question of law, and, as such, left to the two judges to decide. They had no difficulty in doing so, and gave it as their joint opinion at the first meeting that "there was no law which forbad the Jews' return into England." No legal bar The first point gained, the Conference was adjourned to the Re-Settlement. until the following Friday, the 7th. The second question was discussed on the 7th, the 12th, and the 18th of December, but matters by no means ran so smoothly as Cromwell had hoped. The clergy were not so strongly in favour of the Jewish claims as had been expected. The libels of the pamphleteers had done their work, and on religious grounds strong objections were raised to an unrestricted Jewish settlement. Fears were expressed lest Jesus might be blasphemed at public religious services ; lest the synagogue might become the centre for all the Judaising sects in the country. The risk of English converts to Judaism joining the Jews in sacrificing their children to Moloch was even suggested. The moderate majority was in favour of the admission of the Jews under severe restrictions, thus adopting the opinions expressed by Dr. Barlow, Librarian of the Bodleian, in a memorandum presented to the Conference by Dr. Goodwin. Only a small remnant, consisting of Lawrence, Lambert, and Caryll, contended for unrestricted admission.

The Party for unrestricted admission of the Jews. To strengthen this party Cromwell made a few additions to the members of the Conference on the eve of its third meeting. Hugh Peters, the first of the advocates of unrestricted admission, Peter Sterry, Cromwell's favourite chaplain, and Bulkeley, the Provost of Eton, joined the other members. Cromwell's purpose was hardly served, at least by one of these additional members, for Peters, who had, since his first advocacy of the cause, learnt of the Crypto-Jews of London and their outward conformity to Catholicism, denounced the Jews as a self-seeking generation " who made but little conscience of their own principles." At the final meeting, the commercial aspect of the subject was under consideration, and on this occasion a departure was made from the previous procedure by the ad-mission of the public to the deliberations. The result was that the chamber was thronged by a somewhat unruly crowd of violent opponents of the Jews armed with Prynne's newly published, virulently anti-Jewish tract " A Short Demurrer," which did not fail to interrupt the proceedings and after a time to join in the discussion. The course of the discussion was throughout not in sympathy with the Jewish claims, and it culminated in a vehement anti-

The opposition of the merchants. Jewish demonstration. The merchants, without ex-ception, spoke against the admission of the Jews. They declared that the proposed immigrants would be morally harmful to the State, and that their admis-sion would enrich foreigners at the expense of natives. One of the greatest disappointments Cromwell must have sustained on this unhappy occasion was the adhesion of one of his most devoted admirers, Sir Christopher Pack, the most eminent citizen of his day, to the roll of militant exclusionists. These advocates of exclusion were in reality out of order. It had been decided that there was no bar to the admission of the Jews, and the Conference had only to decide the terms on which that admission was to be permitted. Moreover, the majority of the members—the divines—were averse to the exclusion of the Jews, since the object of the former was their conversion to Christianity. The circumstances were A suggested evidently ripe for a compromise, and, after some compromise. private exchange of views, Henry Jessey, the friend of Menasseh, and considered one of the strongest supporters of the Jewish claims, rose to propose one. His suggestion was to the effect that the Jews should only be admitted to decayed ports and cities, and that they should pay double customs duties on imports and exports.

Cromwell, whose sympathy with the Jews had always been based on economic rather than religious or sentimental grounds, was aghast at the proposal. Suggestions of religious restrictions had but slightly concerned him, but the new proposals were in a far different light. His object was to increase the commercial prosperity of the country by the attraction of Jewish brains, Jewish energy, and Jewish capital to the commercial centres. To banish all these elements of success to decayed ports and cities, and even there to penalise them by double customs duties, meant the total defeat of his plans. It would even mean the removal from London of those Crypto-Jews to whom his government and English commerce were already so deeply indebted. The danger was imminent, for Jessey's proposal appealed to the majority of the Conference. It was necessary for a master-mind to act at once, and Cromwell did not hesitate to do so. Rising from Cromwell the chair of state, he addressed the assembly. After addresses the a review of the various opinions that had been ex- Conference.

pressed, he designated the total as a babel of dis-
cordances. He had asked the divines for advice,
but had only had his doubts increased. He had no
engagements to the Jews, he protested, but "since
there was a promise of their conversion, means
must be used to that end, which was the preaching
of the Gospel, and that could not be done unless
they were permitted to dwell where the Gospel was
preached." Addressing the merchants, he said,
"You say they (the Jews) are the meanest and most
despised of all people. So be it. But in that case
what becomes of your fears? Can you really be
afraid that this contemptible and despised people
should be able to prevail in trade and credit over
the merchants of England, the noblest and most
esteemed merchants of the whole world?" It was
clear that no hope was to be expected from the
Conference. He left his place, and the Conference
was at an end.[1]

AUTHORITIES :—Lucien Wolf, "Menasseh ben Israel's Mission";
Albert M. Hyamson, "The Lost Tribes," &c. ; S. Levy, "Bishop
Barlow on the Case of the Jews" (*Transactions, Jewish Historical
Society*, vol. iii., 1899), "John Dury and the English Jewry"
(*Transactions, Jewish Historical Society*, vol. iv., 1903); Lionel
Abrahams, "Menasseh ben Israel's Mission to Oliver Cromwell"
(*Jewish Quarterly Review*, vol. xiv., 1902); Henry Jessey, "A
Narrative of the Late Proceedings at Whitehall concerning the
Jews" (1656).

---

[1] This speech has been constructed by Mr. Lucien Wolf from fragments
to be found in various contemporary writings.

CHAPTER XXI

THE RE-SETTLEMENT
(1655–1658)

ALTHOUGH the Conference was dissolved, the matter was not yet concluded. The Committee had to report on the subject to the Council which had appointed it. It did so to the following effect. The view of the judges that there was no legal bar to the Re-Settlement was accepted. The following opinions expressed at the Conference were put forward : (1) The grounds on which Menasseh had asked in his recent book for the re-admission of the Jews were " very sinfull for this or any Christian state to receave them upon." (2) The admission would create the danger of apostasy on the part of the Christian inhabitants in the country. (3) The existence of synagogues for public worship according to Jewish practices would be evil in itself and very scandalous to the Christian churches. (4) The Jewish customs concerning marriage and divorce were unlawful, and would set evil examples. (5) Strongly supported charges had been made against the Jews of not considering oaths made to Christians binding or harm done to them evil. (6) The admission of Jews would prejudicially affect the native merchants. Finally, the Committee recommended that the Jews should be admitted provided they had no autonomous jurisdiction ; they should be restrained from blaspheming Christ ; they should not profane the Christian Sabbath ; they should have no Christian servants ; they should be disqualified from holding public office ; they should print

nothing against Christianity; they should not discourage attempts to convert them to Christianity,
while, however, they themselves should make no
attempt at making proselytes.

The Report
rejected.
The report was not, however, accepted by the
Council. Cromwell had apparently had sufficient
discussion and publicity so far as the Jewish Question
was concerned, and was conscious that the only
manner of gaining his way was by unofficial action
and connivance at a Jewish settlement, rather than
by legislative methods. Although there could be no
legal bar to a settlement of Jews in England, in
the then excited state of public opinion it would have
been extremely inadvisable for any number to have
entered the country or even for those already there
to have thrown off their disguise. Consequently from
the outward point of view the opening of the year
1656 saw no difference in the Jewish Question in
London from that of twelve months previous. The
Jewish colony remained undisturbed, but continued
under the guise of Catholicism. The judges' decision
and the obvious partiality of Cromwell towards the
Further efforts
of the
exclusionists.
proposed immigration had, however, not passed un-
noticed by the anti-Jewish extremists, and it appeared
to them by no means wise to relax their efforts towards
exclusion. The campaign of the pamphleteers was
continued. Within a few days of the dissolution of
the Conference a new and enlarged edition of Prynne's
"Demurrer," which had proved so useful in exciting
people's minds, was issued. The argument that the
Expulsion by Edward I. held good until reversed by
Parliament was emphasised and amplified. A month
later the second part of the "Demurrer" was issued.
In this Prynne devoted his pen and his patience to
detailing the disabilities under which the Jews were
tolerated in the country before they were finally
expelled, and the extraordinary crimes of which,

according to his opinion, Jews as a race were continually guilty. Others followed Prynne's lead in his
anti-Jewish campaign. Cromwell's action was to give Cromwell gives
a verbal assurance, through Sadler, to the London an assurance of toleration.
Jews, of his personal protection, and permission to
celebrate divine worship in the Jewish manner, provided it was done privately. Since the repeal of the
Recusancy Acts in 1650, omission to attend service at
the parish church was no longer penalised. By the
Instrument of Government of 1653 no one could
be compelled to profess Christianity. The only forms
of religion the practice of which was illegal were the
papistical, prelatical, and licentious.

This unofficial secret tolerance of Judaism was,
necessarily, but a temporary expedient. It could not
remain secret for long, nor had it any of the elements
of a permanent settlement of the question. The
concession to the Jews speedily got noised abroad,
and in due course reached the ears of those who
had at the Conference shown themselves so bitterly
opposed to any concessions whatsoever. The opportunity for an active display of anti-Semitism soon
arrived. On the outbreak of war with Spain early Outbreak of
in 1656 a proclamation was issued by the Privy war with Spain. The property
Council declaring the property of all Spaniards lawful of Robles
prize. The proclamation had hardly been published seized.
when, at the instigation of an informer, the property
and papers of Antonio Rodriguez Robles, a wealthy
Marrano merchant, were seized. At the time the
affair did not bear a Jewish aspect. Robles appealed
to Cromwell against the seizures, on the ground that
he was a Portuguese and not a Spaniard, and an inquiry was ordered by the Council. It was, however,
soon seen that this attack on Robles might well
extend to an invasion of the interests of the other
Marranos, many of whom were of Spanish birth or
had acquired, when in the Spanish service, that

nationality. The leading Marranos, consequently, hastily drew up a petition to Cromwell in which they asked that the "favours and protection" extended to them, including the right of meeting privately for divine worship, might be confirmed. The document was signed by Menasseh ben Israel, David Abarbanel (Dormido), Carvajal, Abraham Coen Gonzales, De Caceres, Abraham Israel de Brito and Isaac Lopes Chillon. The document was not signed by Robles, whose sympathies lay rather with the section of the community which was attached to the Royalist party. Cromwell referred the petition to the Council.

The next event was the denunciation of further Marranos as Spanish subjects. A crisis was arising in the fortunes of the little community. The anti-Jewish zeal had re-awakened, and, as John Sadler pointed out to Menasseh, the libels of the pamphleteers were unfavourably affecting the interests of the community. Menasseh was urged to reply to the attacks of Prynne and others, and, in compliance, the *Vindiciæ* The *Vindiciæ* *Judæorum* was published. Menasseh had no longer to *Judæorum.* plead for the unrestricted admission of the Jews, nor to prove that by that act the millennium would be hastened. His task was to safeguard the few concessions already made to the Jews settled in England, and moreover to defend the fair name and fame of the whole of the Jewish people. Right worthily did he fulfil his mission, and his *Vindiciæ* has taken its place among the most effective defences of Judaism and Jewry ever penned. The publication of the *Vindiciæ* was followed by a further move on the part of the persecuted Marranos. Robles, following up his previous appeal, addressed a fresh petition to the Protector. After reciting the sufferings of himself, his family, and other Jews at the hands of the Inquisition, he continued that he had sought refuge in England from those tyrannical proceedings, and in order to enjoy the proverbial hospitality of England towards afflicted strangers, he asked for Cromwell's sympathy with himself and his fellow Jews. This further petition was supported by affidavits signed by all the leading Marranos of London. The Marranos had thrown off their disguise and openly confessed Judaism.

The Marranos throw off their disguise.

This bold declaration attained its object. The confidence of the Crypto-Jews was not misplaced. The Robles case was inquired into by the Admiralty Commissioners, to whom it had been referred by the Council. By them the other Marranos were examined. The Commissioners were unable to arrive at a positive opinion with regard to the question referred to them. They admitted that the balance of evidence was in favour of the view that Robles was "a Jew borne at Fundão in Portugall," but they left the responsibility of a decision to the Council, and this body, on the 16th of May 1656, ordered all the warrants to be discharged, and reinstated Robles in the possession of his property. The position of the Jews as a body was strengthened in accordance with the desire expressed in the last petition to the Protector. Rights of "cohabitation and trade in these dominions" were formally accorded to the Jews in writing (the document granting them has been lost). The city authorities were directed by Cromwell to place no impediments in the way of the Jews, and the Jews on their part agreed not to encourage an indiscriminate immigration, not to obtrude their worship and ceremonies in public, not to engage in controversies, and to make no converts. The maintenance of a synagogue was permitted, and the right to acquire a cemetery granted. In February 1657 the lease for a Jewish cemetery in Mile End was granted to Carvajal and De Caceres. Shortly afterwards, Solomon Dormido, a son of David

The right of unrestricted residence granted.

O

Abarbanel Dormido, was admitted a duly licensed broker of the City of London, the Christological oath, in other instances considered essential, being waived in his case.

Results of Menasseh's mission.

All the requests of the London Marranos had been granted, but the goal to which Menasseh ben Israel had directed his efforts at the outset of his campaign was unattained. He had come to England to obtain for the Jews rights equal to those of the Christian inhabitants, to gain an asylum for the persecuted of Jewry. In no sense were those objects attained by the compromise that had been accepted. Opposed to what he must have considered a betrayal of the interests of Jewry, Menasseh refused all adhesion to the settlement. The relations between him and the members of the London community became strained. His position in Holland had also been undermined, for there the Jews, all attached to the Royalist cause, had severed all relations with him on his mission to Cromwell. The Dutch Jews placed their trust in Charles, with whom they opened negotiations. Deserted by his friends, his resources exhausted, Menasseh did not even in these circumstances lose courage, but continued to urge on Cromwell the issue of a proclamation in the terms he had outlined at the opening of the negotiations. Menasseh's monetary troubles were relieved by Cromwell, first by a gift of £25, and later by a pension of £100 a year. This pension was almost immediately commuted. Menasseh continued doggedly on his course until September 1657, when his only surviving son, Samuel, died. Then Menasseh's spirit broke. With the financial help of Cromwell, prematurely aged, he took his son's body to Holland, and there he himself died, two months later, in the house of his brother-in-law, Ephraim Soeira, at Middleburg.

Death of Menasseh.

The battle had, however, been won by the Jews,

and no further attempt to disturb them was made Practical
so long as their protector Cromwell lived. Secure concessions of Cromwell.
in his favour the Jews of London went on their way
untroubled. As merchants they mixed freely with
their fellow-merchants and brokers of other creeds.
As Jews they held divine service, and performed the
various Jewish ceremonies, no longer privately, but
still not in a manner likely to wound the susceptibilities
of their non-Jewish neighbours. There was no longer
need for them to pretend to be other than what they
really were. On the other hand, they were careful
not to obtrude their Judaism on their neighbours, nor
to break the compact by which they had secured
toleration. Unfortunately, Cromwell survived this
settlement but a few months, and on his death the
government of the country, again unsettled, lapsed
rapidly towards chaos. In the general distraction
the position of the Jews again became insecure. The
anti-Jewish party was not slow to take advantage of
what it considered its opportunity. A few weeks
after the Protector's death a petition was presented
to Richard Cromwell by Richard Baker, on behalf
of a hostile party of merchants, asking for the expulsion of the Jews and the confiscation of their
property. The petition was, however, without effect.

AUTHORITIES :—Lucien Wolf, " Menasseh ben Israel's Mission,"
" Crypto-Jews under the Commonwealth " ; M. Kayserling, " The
Life and Labours of Menasseh ben Israel " ; Israel Davis, " The
Re-Settlement of the Jews by Oliver Cromwell " (*Jewish Chronicle*,
November 26 and December 3, 1880).

CHAPTER XXII

THE JEWRY OF THE RESTORATION
(1659–1685)

Restoration of the Monarchy. THE London Jewish community, on the re-entry of Charles II. into his dominions, numbered not less than thirty-five families. Many of the names that had become prominent in the Anglo-Jewish annals of the Re-Settlement period were no longer to be found. From the list of London Jews drawn up in the year 1660, Menasseh ben Israel, Antonio Carvajal, Domingo Vaz de Brito, Isaac Lopes Chillon, Henrique Jorge Mendes, Simon de Caceres, and others are absent, but in their stead are to be found new names, many of which afterwards became prominent in the community. Such are the Pereiras, the D'Oliveiras, Samuel de Veiga, Dr. Mendes Bueno, Rodriques, Franco Gomes, the Gabeys, Rodriques Nunes, Henriques Alvares, and the Lousadas. In addition four converts to Judaism have been traced, of whom Samuel Swinock and Bellamy, the cooper, were formerly connected with Carvajal.

The religious organisation of the community. The small community still had two synagogues, one for Sephardim in Creechurch Lane, and the second apparently for Ashkenazim in St. Helens. Of the former and its organisation the material exists for a fairly detailed description ; of the latter, all that is known is that—as has already been mentioned—its rabbi was named Mier. The Sephardi synagogue had probably been in existence for some time, although its services had been conducted with great secrecy. By the arrival of the Restoration year all attempts at concealment had certainly been abandoned. In The London synagogue of the Sephardim. common with most European synagogues of the period, that of the London Sephardim was to some extent fortified. The protection in this instance took the form of three double-locking doors. The synagogue proper was on the first floor, and occupied two rooms, the smaller for the use of the women, the larger for that of the men. Following the continental custom, as displayed in synagogues existing at that day, the two rooms were separated by a partition into which was fitted a long narrow heavily latticed window. The interior was arranged similarly to those of contemporary Sephardi places of worship.

Concerning the organisation of the community we Moses Athias. know that the rabbi was Moses Athias, a relative of Carvajal, who had been brought over by that merchant. Benjamin Levy filled the combined offices of Hazan,[1] Shochet,[2] Bodek,[3] and Secretary to the congregation. There were also a clerk and a communal physician, Dr. Joseph Mendes Bueno. The community possessed its poor, who even in the infancy of the congregation were attracted from all parts to London, and in the first balance-sheet of the Sephardi community provision is made for their relief. Finally, there was a cemetery at Mile End. The community had dwelt since the settlement of its pioneers in the ward of Portsoken.

The period marked by the death of the Protector Effects of Cromwell's death. and the Restoration of the Royal House was one fraught with much anxiety for the incipient community. Protected by the strong hand of Cromwell its members were safe to go about their business un-

---

[1] The Cantor, or public reader of the prayers in synagogue.

[2] The official who, in accordance with the Jewish ritual, kills cattle, &c., intended for consumption by Jews.

[3] The official who examines meat killed in the Jewish fashion, in order to ascertain whether it is free from disease and consequently fit for consumption by Jews.

Jews and the
Royalists.
concerned by political changes, but when that protection was removed the general uneasiness which
month by month grew more pronounced until it
culminated in the Restoration, affected the London
Jews as well as the population by which they were
surrounded. To the country generally the landing
of Charles II. brought for a time quiet and security.
To the Jews, however, the passing of the Cromwell
dynasty, the success of its injured rival, and the
expected reversal of the whole of the policy of the
previous decade and a half, seemed but the presage
of impending trouble. Moreover, the leading members
of the London community had been closely involved
in several of the projects of the Commonwealth, and
had in many ways rendered assistance to its forces.
Such action was not likely to ingratiate the friends
and colleagues of Carvajal and De Caceres in the eyes
of the new government. On the other hand, it must
not be understood that all the Jews who had any
dealings with England at the time were supporters
of the Cromwellian government. The Royalists also
had their sympathisers among the Jews of Holland
and of France. The Da Costa family, and Augustine
Coronel Chacon (d. 1665) in particular rendered
assistance in restoring the exiled house of Stuart, and
the services of the last named were acknowledged
A Jew
knighted.
on the Restoration by the bestowal on him after his
apostasy of the honour of knighthood.

The arch Jew-baiter of the time was Thomas
Violet's anti-
Jewish efforts.
Violet (1634–1662), a writer on trade, goldsmith and
alderman of the City of London, " a restless meddling
man," who had, under both Charles I. and the Commonwealth, suffered punishment for several offences,
political and otherwise. As early as December 1659,
Violet had opened his campaign by an application to
Mr. Justice Tyril, in the course of which he set forth
the case against the Jews that had been drawn up by

Prynne. The Jewish settlement under Cromwell, Violet contended, was illegal, and his application was that the law should be set in motion against those Jews who were then in the country. The judge was not disinclined to accept Violet's views, but in the then disturbed state of the country he advised the postponement of the application. Violet was however impatient. Unable to have the Jews removed on the grounds of nonconformity, he endeavoured to involve them in a criminal charge. He had already had considerable experience in working up cases against merchants for violation of certain ordinances, and he now devoted his talents to the elaboration of a charge of coining against the London Jews. Unfortunately for Violet, his confederate, whose part it was to have passed a packet of spurious coins on Rabbi Moses Athias, confessed his share in the conspiracy, and the result, as far as Violet was concerned, was failure. His next move (in 1660) was to renew his application to Mr. Justice Tyril, but the only reply he received was the advice to lay the matter before the Privy Council. Violet was not slow to do so, and in his application he emphasised the alleged criminal propensities of the Jews. He did not ask for their expulsion ; he suggested, on the other hand, that the property of the Jews should be confiscated, and they themselves thrown into prison, there to await ransom by their continental co-religionists. *An application to the Privy Council for the harassing of the Jews.*

Meanwhile more influential enemies than Violet appeared upon the scene in the persons of the City authorities. The Corporation had always been jealous of all favours bestowed upon the Jews, but, recognising their inability to move Cromwell from his purpose, had discreetly kept silent. The return of Charles II., however, gave them, they thought, their opportunity, and Violet's remonstrance and other anti-Jewish petitions to the Privy Council were supported by a petition to the same effect from the Lord Mayor and Aldermen. Various charges, economic, moral, and religious, were brought against the Jews. The king was asked to advise Parliament to expel "all professed Jews out of your Majesty's dominions and to bar the door after them with such provisions and penalties as in your Majesty's wisdom shall be found most agreeable to the safety of religion, the honour of your Majesty, and the good and welfare of your subjects." The petition referred explicitly to the privileges conferred upon the Jews by Cromwell.

The Jews appeal to the king.

The petition of the City aroused the Jews to action. The community met in the house of Senora Carvajal, the widow of Antonio, in Leadenhall Street, and drew up a counter petition to his Majesty, praying for permission to continue to reside in his dominions. No attempt was made to disguise the existence of a religious community in London. All the petitions were considered by the Privy Council, and after considerable discussion it was resolved to refer them to the House of Commons for the advice of that body. This decision led to the issue of a further venomous pamphlet by Violet in order to assist the cause to which he had devoted himself. On the 17th of December a Royal Message was presented to the House, but instead of asking for advice whether the Jews should be banished or not, it desired that the question of the protection of the Jews should be taken into consideration. There is no record of any action by Parliament, and the *status quo* as established by Cromwell consequently remained undisturbed. The City received no answer to its petition, but it took no further action in the matter.

Change of Jewish status.

The status of the Jews in England was meanwhile changing. Under Cromwell the Jewish settlers were all of foreign birth, and denizations had been granted in but two or three instances. Charles was far more liberal in this respect, and before the end of 1661 practically all the leading members of the community had in this manner become English citizens. A new generation was also growing up, born in the country, and these were of course Englishmen in every respect, but subject, on account of their religion, to certain disabilities.

The marriage of the king with Catherine of Braganza was of benefit to the community in more than one respect. In the train of the queen, whose marriage was suggested by Augustine Coronel, came the brothers Duarte and Francisco da Sylva, Portuguese Jewish bankers of Amsterdam, to whom was entrusted the management of the dowry that Catherine brought with her. The community had thus powerful friends at court. The marriage also led to a considerable increase in the number of Marrano settlers in London. Some of these came to assist the Da Sylvas in their office. Moreover, the period was one of extreme persecution of the Marranos of Spain and Portugal, and many of the victims escaping from their country came to England. It was about this time that the distinguished families of Mendes and Da Costa settled in this country. They intermarried so frequently that the family became known as Mendes da Costa. Fernando Mendes, a distinguished physician, was the first of the family to settle in England.

Effect of the king's marriage.

After the failure of the attempts of Violet and the City authorities, the nascent community remained on the whole undisturbed for a few years. Early in 1663, it is true, there was some talk of calling in the Jews' letters of denization, and also some trouble concerning the oath of allegiance and supremacy, but both soon passed away, and the publicity and security in which the Jews worshipped are evidenced by Pepys, who visited the synagogue on October the 14th, 1663. Within a few months, however, a new trouble

An attempt to
blackmail the
Jews. threatened. Without any warning a bold attempt
to levy blackmail on the community was made by
the Earl of Berkshire and Mr. Ricaut. These two
gentlemen called one day on the leading Jews of the
metropolis, and told them that the king had placed
the Jews in their care. Unless a large amount were
paid to them without delay, Berkshire and Ricaut
would seize the whole of their property. The threat
did not frighten Manuel Martinez Dormido and
his colleagues. Instead of paying the demands they
brought the conspiracy to light in a petition in which
they prayed the king to continue his protection to
the Jews, and to permit them to remain and trade in
the kingdom. The petition met with the desired
The king pro-
tects the Jews. response, and the king's assurance that he had not
given any order for "the molesting or disquieting the
Petitioners either in their Persons or estates, but that
they may promise themselves the effects of the same
favour as formerly they have had, soe long as they
demeane themselves peaceably and quietly with due
obedience to his Majesty's Lawes, and withoutt
scandall to his Government," finally settled the
pretension of the Earl of Berkshire and Mr. Ricaut.[1]

---

[1] A controversy has arisen around this promise of protection. One
view, the leading exponents of which are the Very Rev. Dr. M. Gaster and
Mr. H. S. Q. Henriques, is that this promise marks the opening of post-
expulsion Anglo-Jewish history, and from the Order in Council of August
1664 should be dated the Re-settlement of the Jews in England. The
petition and its reply together form the Charter of the Jews, by which
alone the right of residence in the country was secured. Previous to the
grant of this " Charter," it is true Jews were settled in the country. These
were, however, merely individuals whose Judaism was more or less concealed ; previous to 1664 no organised community existed or would have
been tolerated. The reference in the king's reply to "the same favour as
formerly they have had" is explained not as relating to any grants or
toleration under the Cromwellian régime, but to verbal promises made to
the Jews of Holland during their pre-Restoration negotiations with the
representatives of Charles Stuart. The view adopted in the text is that of
Mr. Lucien Wolf, who contends that the reference is to the series of marks
of favour and toleration that covered the period commencing with the
Whitehall Conference. Considerable evidence can be induced in favour
of the view that the position of the Jews in England had been legalised
and generally accepted long before 1664. Several of them have been

Ten years later, in 1673, on the occasion of a some-what similar crisis in the history of the community, the king, by means of an Order in Council, again signified his favour.   1664, the year of the first official The Conventicle Act of 1664. extension of the royal protection to the London Jewish community, also saw the adoption of the Conventicle Act, a measure intended to harass the Puritans, against whom the temper of the country had turned.   By its provisions all meetings of more than five persons, except in family gatherings, for any religious purpose not according to the Book of Common Prayer, were declared seditious and un-lawful, and it was enacted that severe punishment should be meted out to offenders above the age of sixteen years. Charles, on his return, had pledged himself to religious toleration, and his own inclina-tions, in addition, were in favour of as liberal treat-ment of Roman Catholic dissenters as could be arranged.   But more powerful forces overcame him, and he was compelled to give his approval to this oppressive measure.   There can be little doubt that no thought was given to its possible effect on the Jews when the Bill was under consideration.   It was directed against Christian nonconformists alone, and it was they who suffered most severely under it.   The Jews, however, met regularly in numbers exceeding five, for religious purposes not according to the teach- Jewish prayer-meetings at first unaffected. ings of the Book of Common Prayer, and conse-quently after the passing of the Conventicle Act those meetings became illegal, and the worshippers participating in them became liable to heavy fines and imprisonment.

mentioned in their proper places in the narrative; the opinion of the Judges given at the Whitehall Conference, the proceedings connected with the Robles case, and the leasing of a cemetery, for instance.   Moreover, the legal settlement of the Jews in England was acknowledged in the petition of the Lord Mayor and Aldermen of 1660, and in the testimony of Violet.

Strange to say, no action was taken against the Jews for several years. Service was held in the little synagogue in Creechurch Lane, and possibly in St. Helens also, with the usual regularity. Violet had died two years after the Restoration ; Lord Berkshire and Mr. Ricaut had apparently been discouraged from any further display of Jew-baiting by their recent abortive attempt to levy blackmail. Almost ten years passed before any attempt was made to harass the Jews in consequence of their continued offences against the Conventicle Act. In 1673, at length the long delayed blow fell. In that year certain members of the community were indicted at the Guildhall for a contravention of the Act by meeting together for worship in Duke's Place. A True Bill was found by the Grand Jury against the defendants, but representatives of the latter immediately appealed to the King in Council for permission either to exercise their religion freely or to retire with their property from the country. Charles showed himself as favourably disposed towards his Jewish subjects as he had been in 1664, and on the 11th of February the Attorney-General was instructed to stop all proceedings at law against the petitioners, and to provide that they be troubled no further in the future on the same account.

The Jews harassed under the Conventicle Act.

Charles II. intervenes in their favour.

Nevertheless, one further endeavour was made to interfere with the conduct of Jewish worship. In 1685, shortly after the accession of James II., at the instance of Thomas Beaumont, writs were issued by the King's Bench against forty-eight Jews, thirty-seven of whom were arrested as they were following their business. The action was taken under a statute of Elizabeth, directed against the Catholics, which rendered abstention from "a church, chapel, or usual place of common prayer" an offence, the penalty for which was a fine of £20 for each month during

Jews arrested under the Act of Uniformity.

which the offence was continued, together with the production of two sureties for due attendance in the future. To meet this attack the precedent of 1673 was followed by the leaders of the community, who petitioned the king to permit them and their co-religionists to continue as heretofore the due exercise of their religion so long as they remained of good behaviour towards his Majesty's Government. James's reply was similar to that of his predecessor, and once more the Attorney-General was directed to stop all proceedings : "His Majesty's intention being that they should not be troubled on this account, but quietly enjoy the free exercise of their religion, whilst they behave themselves dutifully and obediently to his Government." On no subsequent occasion was any attempt made to interfere with the religious observances of the English Jews.

James II. stops the proceedings against the Jews.

AUTHORITIES :—Lucien Wolf, "The Jewry of the Restoration" (1902), "The First Stage of Jewish Emancipation" (*Jewish Chronicle*, Aug. 7, 14, and 19, 1903), "Status of the Jews in England" (*Transactions, Jewish Historical Society*, vol. iv.), "Menasseh ben Israel's Mission"; M. Gaster, "History of the Ancient Synagogue of the Spanish and Portuguese Jews" (1901) ; H. S. Q. Henriques, "The Return of the Jews to England" (1905), "Jews and the English Law" (*Jewish Quarterly Review*, vols. xii. and xiii.) ; "Dictionary of National Biography."

CHAPTER XXIII

THE SEPHARDIM

(1663–1702)

THE increase in the numbers of the community consequent on the Restoration, and the additional security given by the settlement in public affairs, effected by the return of the country to its allegiance to the House of Stuart, rendered some organisation or re-organisation in the government of the London Jewish community necessary. During the year 1663 it appears that extensive alterations were made in the building in Creechurch Lane. Before the close of the same year the amount of the contributions of members to the congregation was fixed, and in November the revision or compilation of a constitution (Ascamoth) was decided upon. This constitution was published on the 5th of April 1664. No experiments were attempted in this work. The compilers were all thoroughly conservative, and were satisfied to model their institutions and regulations on those of the Sephardi community of Amsterdam, from which city the majority of the leading members of the community had come. The lines laid down in Venice, the oldest of the post-Expulsion Sephardi communities, were also followed to some extent. These Ascamoth, in addition to laying down rules for the management of the affairs of the congregation, following the precedent set by Amsterdam and Venice, strictly forbade, under the penalty of *cherem* or excommunication, the holding elsewhere within the city of London and its suburbs, than in the synagogue, of service except in

The community organised.

the case of mourners and bridegrooms. This law in
later years led to much dissatisfaction and consequent
agitation ; but it was not until the middle of the nineteenth century that a second Sephardi synagogue was
established in London. Another matter with which
the Ascamoth dealt was the publishing of books. This
was not permitted to any members of the congregation without the consent of the Mahamad,[1] and in the
case of the publication of any libellous writing the
punishment was also to be excommunication.. The
intention in formulating this rule was doubtless to
avoid any action on the part of members of the congregation which might lead to trouble with the civil
authorities, and consequent unwelcome attention to
the community. Furthermore, it was stated that the
congregation was primarily intended for Spanish and
Portuguese Jews, but any Jew not belonging to that
community, either living in London or who might
subsequently settle in London, could be admitted by
permission of the Mahamad.

The revenue of the congregation depended upon The communal
both direct and indirect taxation. A tax was levied revenues.
on all goods bought and sold by its members, and the
price of all meat consumed was increased by one
farthing per pound for the benefit of the communal
treasury. At the head of the community were the
wardens and a treasurer, and the first known occupants
of these offices were David Abarbanel Dormido, Moses
Baruch Lousada, and Elias de Lima.

The community once definitely organised, steps
were taken to procure a spiritual head. The spiritual
affairs of the congregation had hitherto been in the
charge of Rabbi Moses Athias, but with the increase
in the standing of the congregation it was thought
that the services of a more important personage were

[1] The governing body of the congregation.

required. Haham [1] Jacob Sasportas of Amsterdam was invited to take spiritual charge of the London Sephardi community, and after a little negotiation he consented on the 19th of April 1664, and in due course arrived in London.

Haham
Sasportas.

Sasportas was in many respects well fitted to open the roll of London Hahamim, that has included so many names which have shed lustre on their community. He was born about 1618 in Oran, North Africa, a descendant of Nachmanides. After an education in the place of his birth, in his twenty-fourth year Sasportas was appointed rabbi in Tlemcen in Morocco, subsequently removing to fill a similar post in the more important centre of Fez. While in this latter city the endeavours of the king to extort money from him involved Sasportas in trouble, but after suffering a short imprisonment he managed to escape to Amsterdam. His country, however, still had need of him, and he was recalled by Prince Benbuker, who sent him as ambassador to the king of Spain to invoke his assistance in suppressing a rebellion in Morocco. From Spain Sasportas returned to Amsterdam, and for a time was associated with Menasseh ben Israel in his literary undertakings and also accompanied him to London in 1655. There he met, among other pioneers of the Re-Settlement, Dormido, the warden of the synagogue when, as Haham, Sasportas later took office in London. At the time of his call to England a similar offer came from Leghorn ; Sasportas did not retain his office for long. The Great Plague in

The Great
Plague of 1665.

1665 dislocated all the arrangements of the metropolis, and among those whom it drove from the centre of infection was the Haham. Sasportas returned to Amsterdam, which, after a brief stay, he left for Hamburg. In this latter city he continued the

---

[1] Haham (Wise Man), an old rabbinic epithet of honour, is the title borne by the spiritual head or chief rabbi of a Sephardi community.

campaign that he had already commenced in London against the Sabbathian movement,[1] whose adherents were to be found in every Jewish centre, east and west. For a short time he lived in Leghorn, but once more settled in Amsterdam, of which community he was appointed chief rabbi in 1681. For seventeen years, the remainder of his life, he filled this office, and although so long a period had passed since his departure from London, the announcement of his death was received in that city with expressions of grief and of mourning. Sasportas' attainments were of a high order, and he was considered one of the ablest and most learned men of his time. He earned great respect in all the countries in which he lived, both by his accomplishments and his acts, and his influence was felt in the London community long after his departure. Throughout his life Sasportas corresponded with and retained the friendship of the various Hahamim who succeeded him and one another at the head of the London community.

The establishment of the congregation on a stable basis was speedily followed by the institution of the earliest of the subsidiary societies that have since that date increased to such an extent, and now form so large a cluster round the parent institution. The first of these societies, supplementary to the synagogue, to come into existence was the *Hebra* of *Bikur Holim*, a society for visiting the sick, formed in 1666. The religious education of the children of the community had also not been neglected, and the duties of the Haham, as laid down in the Ascamoth, included the devotion of several hours daily to the imparting of instruction in the tenets of Judaism.

The principal difficulty with which the community

The first Anglo-Jewish charity.

[1] The religious movement commenced by Sabbathai Zevi, the famous pseudo-Messiah (born at Smyrna, 1626, died at Dulcigno, 1676), who wielded a considerable influence, which extended as far westwards as Hamburg and Amsterdam.

Alien immigration.

had to contend during these years seems to have been the problem of alien immigration. The toleration and protection enjoyed by the Jewish settlers in England, their prosperous condition, combined with the uneasiness and disquietude, varied by persecution, with which the fellow-communities in the East were being troubled, served to attract to the British dominions many other children of the Jewish race. Troubles in the Balkans were not slow in communicating their influence to Amsterdam, Hamburg, and London, and London's share in the wave of immigration of that period was almost more than it could digest. At times it seemed that the influx would involve the older settlers and their newly established institutions in one common ruin, and at these periods recourse was had to legislation, in order to discourage the settlement of new-comers incapable—temporarily, at any rate—of self-support. When the flood had abated these ordinances fell into disuse, to be revived perhaps in a later crisis. The forces that attracted to these shores were, however, more powerful than any restrictive measures that the Mahamad could devise, and from the beginning of the reign of Charles II. until the present reign the stream of Jewish immigrants has continued to flow, although it may have varied in intensity from time to time.

Haham da Silva.

The office vacated by the departure of Haham Sasportas from London was filled after the lapse of a short interval by the appointment in 1670 of Joshua da Silva, a friend of the recent incumbent and a prominent pupil of Haham Aboab of Amsterdam. He remained in office until his death nine years later, and was the first Haham to be buried in London. Before that date, however, the community had outgrown its synagogue accommodation, and a new and larger building was inaugurated in 1676. The exact site of this edifice cannot be stated, but it either took the place of the previous synagogue in Creechurch Lane or was erected in the same neighbourhood in Heneage Lane.

On the death of Joshua da Silva, Jacob Abendana (1630–95) was appointed Haham. The new Haham had already held office in Amsterdam, but was born, and spent the greater portion of his life, in Hamburg. He only remained in office four years, but even in that short period his remarkable literary activity bore fruit in the translation into Spanish of the Mishna. His well-known translation of Jehuda Halevi's *Cuzari* was completed before he came to London. The appointment of Haham Abendana was, moreover, the cause of the settlement of another distinguished Jewish litterateur in England. Accompanying or closely following the new Haham came his brother Isaac (1650 *cir.*–1710 *cir.*), who settled at Oxford and taught Hebrew there. With the exception of Menasseh ben Israel and Leon Templo, who published his "Temple of Solomon" in 1675 (although in English, the book was printed at Amsterdam), he was the first Spanish Jew who is known to have published English works, and his calendars evoked so much interest in learned circles that after his death they were collected and republished under the title of "Discourses of the Ecclesiastical and Civil Polity of the Jews."

In 1689 Solomon Ayllon came to London to take over the spiritual charge of the community. He also came from Amsterdam, but his residence in that city had been of short duration. Ayllon was born at Salonica about 1660, but was taken to Safed in the Holy Land shortly afterwards. In Palestine Ayllon settled and remained until, in consequence of the great distress into which the population was thrown by war, earthquakes, and famine, he was sent as a messenger to Europe to collect funds for the relief

Haham Abendana.

Haham Ayllon.

of the Palestinians. His course led him to Leghorn,
thence to Amsterdam, and subsequently to London.
In Safed Ayllon had been notorious for his Sabbathaian sympathies, and these had been but slightly
modified by his journey across Europe. London,
under the influence of Haham Sasportas, had been
ranged on the other side in the far-reaching controversy that raged around the personality of Sabbathai Zevi. These conditions did not tend to the
success of the new Haham, and it is therefore not
surprising that in 1701, after experiencing many
difficulties, Ayllon was willing to retire to Amsterdam. In Holland, however, his troubles were by
no means at an end, and his Sabbathaian proclivities
soon involved him in controversies with Zebi Ashkenazi, his colleague in the Ashkenazi congregation.

Increase in
the Jewish
population.
Meanwhile the Jewish population of London had
been continually increasing. Many causes contributed to the influx. Poverty, political troubles,
religious persecutions, outbreaks of war, all acted as
accessories to the immigration. The quarrels between the Emperor and the Turks, the occupation
and recapture of Belgrade, caused a temporary flow
towards England from that direction. The renewal
of Inquisition activities in Portugal served to increase
the Sephardi population of London. Consequently
the synagogue, although only built in 1676, was soon
uncomfortably full, and it was determined to erect
a still larger one in the same neighbourhood in Bevis
Marks. This decision was arrived at in 1699, and
the new building still used by the congregation was
consecrated three years later.

Haham Nieto.
The previous year the vacancy in the office of
Haham was filled by the appointment of David Nieto,
"without question the greatest of Hahamim" of
London. In numerous paths the new Haham made
a reputation for himself. The work of his life was

the defence of orthodox Judaism, and in its course ^{Nieto's} he did not hesitate to denounce the errors of its ^{activity.} impugners, whether Christian, Sabbathaian, Caraite, or merely the ignorant members of his own congregation. His learning was deep, his energy unbounded. Science, literature, art, and poetry all had attractions for him, and to each he proved a worthy son. Moreover, he showed a conspicuous firmness of character and independence of spirit. Nieto was born in Venice in 1654, and studied theology and medicine. The Leghorn community conferred upon him the dual offices of preacher and physician, and these he filled until his call to London on the eve of the opening of the new and enlarged synagogue.

AUTHORITIES:—Lucien Wolf, "The Jewry of the Restoration"; M. Gaster, "History of the Ancient Synagogue"; J. Picciotto, "Sketches of Anglo-Jewish History" (1875); "Jewish Encyclopedia."

CHAPTER XXIV

THE EXTERNAL HISTORY OF THE COMMUNITY

(1677–1690)

THE period that intervened between the attacks on the London Jew in 1673 and 1685 was by no means without incident, so far as the external history of Anglo-Jewry was concerned. The attempt to interfere with the observance by Jewish settlers of their religion having been foiled in the earlier year, the anti-Jewish party looked about for another opportunity of annoying the colony. In July 1677 the attention of the aldermen of the city was called to the existence

The problem of the poor. of a "number of destitute aliens pretending to be Jews." A Jewish migration from the east of Europe had been in motion for nearly a generation. The persecutions of the Cossacks in the middle of the century had had their natural sequel, and crowds of Jews and Jewesses had been fleeing westwards in order to avoid the cruelties of Chmielnicki and his followers. Hamburg and Amsterdam, the Jewish centres on the North Sea, were filled with fugitive Jews. Menasseh ben Israel, in his endeavours to effect a settlement in England, had been not unmindful of the fortunes of his troubled co-religionists. The first balance-sheet of the London Sephardi congregation shows a considerable amount devoted to the needs of poor Jews. Once the matter was brought before the Court of Aldermen it acted promptly. It was decided that no "Jews without good estate" should be permitted to reside or lodge in London or the liberties thereof. The result of this restriction was not altogether harmful to the struggling community. It is true that it retarded the growth of the Ashkenazi community to a considerable extent, but, on the other hand, it relieved the Sephardi settlers of what might otherwise have been a very serious burden, and gave great encouragement to the foundation of provincial communities, notably at Portsmouth and Hull.

Another matter that arose three years later promised at one time to be fraught with far more serious consequences to the community. Although the Marranos had braved numberless dangers in order to retain their connection with their ancestral faith, at a later period at which to be a Jew was no longer fraught with untold terrors, conversions to the dominant faith became more frequent. The conversion of Rabbi Moses Scialitti in 1663 undoubtedly rendered easier the undisturbed continuation of the Jews in England, for it was hoped that this convert's example would be widely followed by his fellow Jews "to the greater glory of God." These hopes, however, were not realised.

The conversion that almost led to a crisis in the affairs of the community was that of Eve Cohan, the daughter of a wealthy and highly respected Jewish family in Holland. This lady eloped with one of her father's servants and came to England. In London she determined on being baptized, despite the endeavours of her Jewish friends to dissuade her from such a step and to induce her to return to her parents. All entreaties having failed to have any effect, legal proceedings were instituted in order to effect her temporary arrest. The case, as was natural, created a great sensation. The Bishop of St. Asaph made himself especially prominent in calling upon the Lord Mayor to "vindicate the honour of the

Christian religion and of the English nation," and the magistrate did not fail to respond to the appeal. Not only was the case dismissed, but the Lord Mayor threatened to proceed against the whole sect "for daring to offer such an affront to the religion and nation of the land." He ordered an abstract of the "laws in force against the Jews" to be prepared. The whole matter was, however, forgotten after a short interval.

In the same year a suggestion, which if adopted would have had an incalculable influence on the future of the Anglo-Jewry, was made to the Government. The question of the creation of a ghetto had been raised more than once in the preceding years. Menasseh ben Israel himself had asked that the Jews should enjoy a sort of judicial autonomy within their own community, and his brother-in-law, Dormido, believing the establishment of a ghetto in London inevitable, had applied for the post of consul to his nation. Shortly after the accession of Charles II., Jacob Azrik, a Jew of Prague, had offered to farm the special taxes to be levied on Jews. In 1680 the ghetto was again suggested as a solution of the financial difficulties in which the Government then found itself. The scheme was drawn up by the Bishop of Lincoln and Sir Peter Pett, and supported by Lord Anglesey. The system in force in the Pre-Expulsion period was to some extent to be adopted. The Jews were to be isolated civilly, but were to possess greater privileges than their predecessors. A special justiciary of the Jews was to be appointed —and for this office Sir Peter Pett was suggested— and he was to manage their special taxes and be the intermediary between them and the Government. The scheme was referred to the Privy Council and, fortunately, was never approved.

A subject that led to a considerable amount of

excitement in the Jewish colony, during the reign of James II. and the opening years of that of William and Mary, was the question of the alien duties. The Alien duties. patents of the denization, in addition to other advantages, conferred on their recipients exemption from the special duties paid by foreign subjects on the admission of foreign merchandise into England. This exemption, which reduced the handicap of the endenizened merchants as compared with their English trade rivals, led to considerable dissatisfaction on the part of the latter. The wisdom of these exemptions was discussed during the reign of Charles II., and the king was petitioned by several prominent merchants to abolish the privilege. Charles was, however, unable to acquiesce in the views of the petitioners. This favourable attitude towards endenizened Jews continued throughout the short reign of James II. despite the continued opposition of the London merchants. On the succession of William and Mary the case was again re-opened. A custom-house officer, William Pennington, hit upon the ingenious theory that the exemptions from these duties were only granted for the current reign, and that on the accession of a new sovereign they lapsed, and unless granted afresh, the alien duties were payable in full by importers hitherto endenizened.

It was certain that no patents of denization had William Pennington. yet been granted or renewed by William. Nevertheless, the Jews, practically the only people benefited by the exemptions, continued to enter their merchandise in their own names and to pay only English duties on it. For these offences, Pennington contended, the whole of the goods that had thus been illegally imported were forfeit to the crown. This view was for the moment adopted by the Government, and by its direction Pennington commenced proceedings in the Court of Exchequer for

the recovery of £58,000 from certain Jewish merchants. The Jews, however, were also not without
influence, and this was used so successfuly, both at
court and with the Commissioners of Customs, that
long before the date fixed for the hearing of the trial,
an Order in Council was issued for the Attorney-
General to enter up *Noli Prosequis*, not only against
the information brought by Pennington, but also
against any others that might in the same connection be brought against the Jews. Pennington did
not silently acquiesce in this settlement, but made
several fruitless endeavours to have a short petition
that he had drawn up on the subject taken into
consideration.

Development
of the Customs
controversy.
The agitation did not, however, rest at this point.
Further representations were made to the Commissioners of Customs by the English merchants, in
which it was pointed out that the recent decision
would involve a loss by the Government of fully
£40,000 due on past transactions, as well as for the
future an annual revenue of £10,000. If these
amounts were remitted so far as the Jews were concerned, the needs of the Government would render
the supply of equivalent amounts by the people of
England necessary. The remission of these duties
would also, it was contended, disturb the balance of
trade, and unfair advantages would be obtained by
the Jews over English merchants both at home and
abroad. It was also submitted that the Order in
Council was contrary to the spirit of the Act of
Rights, and confirmed pernicious decisions made by
Charles II. and James II. It was pointed out that
English merchants paid taxes not only in connection
with their business transactions, but also on the
estates that most of them possessed. On the other
hand, the "rich Jews were past finding out," and the
English would be very unwilling to pay the additional

taxes that would doubtless be necessary while the Jews were illegally exempted from payment of their just dues.

Convinced by these arguments the Commissioners placed the matter once more before the Council, and after renewed consideration the previous order was rescinded and another issued in its place. This latter order entirely met the wishes of the petitioning English merchants, and was correspondingly unsatisfactory to their Jewish colleagues and trade rivals, who, however, apparently recognising the finality of their defeat, seem to have bowed to the inevitable and to have taken no further steps in the matter. Vacillating policy of the Council.

In the latter stages of this controversy the City of London took part with the English merchants in their hostility to Jewish interests. When the question still remained one of alien versus native, the City authorities had shown little interest in the matter. The knowledge, however, that in this controversy alien was in reality a synonym for Jew aroused the latent concern of the aldermen, and from previous displays of anti-Jewish prejudice on the part of the City little doubt could have existed as to its attitude in the controversy. The Court of Aldermen discovered that, whether the denizations were void or not, the exemptions from payment of alien duties were certainly a violation of the City's privileges, and in consequence Sir Robert Jeffery and the town clerk were directed to wait upon the Lord Chancellor and desire his intercession with the king in a direction unfavourable to the interests of the Jews. The wishes of the City were not gratified on this occasion, although, as we have seen, the desired end was attained two years later.

After this date, however, a more friendly feeling sprang up between the City authorities and the London Jewish community. An outward sign of it was A *rapprochement* between the City and the Jews.

the presentation of a piece of plate and a sum of fifty guineas to every Lord Mayor on his installation. The presentation was made on every occasion by a deputation of the leading Jews representing "the Elders and Ministers of the Dutch and Portuguese Synagogues as a compliment for their protection," and was continued until 1780, when in lieu an extra allowance was made to the Lord Mayor by the Court of Aldermen.

William III. and the Jews. Although in the matter of the alien duties the final measures adopted by the Government pressed very heavily on the Jewish subjects of the crown, William's attitude towards them on the whole was, if at all, little less favourable than that of his predecessors. It has been said that Dutch Jews were largely instrumental in furnishing the means that rendered his descent on England possible, and the famous Dutch Jewish financier of the day, Francisco Lopez Suasso, Baron d'Avernas-le-Gras, who afterwards settled in England, has been singled out for mention as one who advanced large sums to William. The authority for this statement has, however, never been given, and no reference to it can be found in either the State records or in those of the Suasso family.

Immigration of Ashkenazim. The revolution undoubtedly gave a considerable impetus to Jewish immigration, at first from Holland and later from regions to the east of that state, and from the end of the seventeenth century may be dated the beginning of the growth of the Ashkenazi community which was afterwards to cause the pioneer congregation, the Sephardim, to sink, in comparison of numbers, into insignificance.

In the years immediately following the Revolution the drain on the Exchequer was very considerable, and the Government suffered much anxiety in endeavouring to meet the expenditure. The position of the Jews being still somewhat abnormal, the idea occurred more than once that special taxation laid on Suggested special taxation of the Jews. Anglo-Jewry would be both justifiable and remunerative. In furtherance of this idea, a bill was introduced into Parliament in 1689 for putting a tax of £100,000 on the Jews for the purposes of the war. The opposition to it was so considerable that it was ultimately abandoned, not before the Jews had threatened, however, that they would rather remove to Holland than pay the threatened imposition.

The following year a new means of obtaining funds from the Jews was discovered. A request had been made to them for a loan to the Government, but the response of £12,000 only was found disappointing. The Earl of Shrewsbury, the Secretary of State, thereupon instructed the Lord Mayor to send for the leading members of the community and to point out to them the "obligations they are under to his Majesty for the liberty and privileges they enjoy, and how much it is to their advantage to make suitable returns of affection and gratitude for the kindness they have received and may expect." The money was required for payment to Isaac Pereyra, a member of the community, who was acting as Commissary-General of the Army in Ireland, and his Majesty was sure that on second thoughts the Jews would raise their subscriptions to at least £20,000.

AUTHORITIES :—Lucien Wolf, "First Stage of Jewish Emancipation," "The Status of the Jews"; D'Blossiers Tovey, *Anglia Judaica*, "State Papers"; H. S. Q. Henriques, "Jews and the English Law" (*Jewish Quarterly Review*, vol. xii.).

CHAPTER XXV

THE ASHKENAZIM

(1690–1764)

ALTHOUGH the only Jewish settlers during the Commonwealth whose names have come prominently forward were of Sephardi origin, it must not be understood that the founders of the modern Anglo-Jewish community were derived solely from that branch of the Jewish race. The Ashkenazi [1] settlers differed on many points from their Sephardi brethren. The latter were men of substance and of wealth, influential merchants, bringing considerable capital in the form of material wealth into the country. The Ashkenazim, on the other hand, were for the most part of a class of whom Menasseh ben Israel was thinking when he pleaded for the re-admission of the Jews into this country. The Cossack uprising of 1650 had driven Polish and Lithuanian Jews westward. The efforts of Menasseh were watched from the other shore of the North Sea by Polish-Jewish refugees, and although his failure compelled that generation to seek refuge elsewhere, sufficient of their compatriots finally settled on these shores to lay the foundations of the Ashkenazi community. The invasion of these poverty-stricken refugees was a source of some trouble to the Jewish community already established. Although they worshipped in their own synagogue—an Ashkenazi Chevra was in existence in London as early as 1659—and the more aristocratic Sephardim carefully prevented the admission of poor Ashkenazim

[1] Lit. *German*, but applied to Jews worshipping in accordance with the "German" ritual.

238

into their community, the richer community was compelled to assist in supporting the burden of Ashkenazi poverty. The heaviness of this burden increased continually, so that there was at times a danger that the Sephardim would sink under it; but, as we have seen, at that point the City authorities stepped in. By their legislation the pressure was relieved, and of the four hundred Jews in London in 1690 not more than half were in receipt of charitable relief.

Among the earliest Ashkenazi settlers in England, however, there was one in every respect worthy to be classed with the first of the Sephardim. The objection to the admission of Ashkenazim into the Sephardi community was waived in the instance of Benjamin Levy (*d.* 1704), a wealthy merchant of Hamburg, who Benjamin settled in this country about 1670. Levy was content Levy. to remain a member of this community for about twenty years, but at about the end of that period he joined with other Hamburg Jews who had settled in the country in establishing the first regular synagogue with the German ritual. Most of the founders of this synagogue, which was situated in Broad Court, Mitre Square, had come from or through Hamburg, and had obtained some relations with the community of that city. The wealthier ones retained the connection on their settlement in this country. Many of them remained members of the older congregation, and the lines on which the new London synagogue was established were copied from those that had proved of service in Hamburg. The founders were, however, not satisfied to take only their constitution from Hamburg. From the same city came the first religious head of the Ashkenazi community in England. Haham Zevi was requested to send a person suitable to minister to the spiritual needs of the new congregation. His choice fell upon his uncle, Rabbi Jehuda ben Ephraim Cohen, also a relative of Benjamin Levy, and Cohen was thus the first important rabbi of the Ashkenazi Jews of England. According to the constitution that had been adopted for the new institution, the rabbi had considerable power in civil as well as in religious matters. His interest and support were consequently of considerable material value, and it is said that the rabbi's resignation, which followed a few years after his appointment, was forced by a party in the congregation who found it impossible to serve their own ends under his impartial and incorruptible administration. On leaving London, Rabbi Jehudah was appointed Rabbi of Rotterdam.

Rabbi Uri Phaibush (Aaron Hart).

His successor was Rabbi Uri Phaibush (Aaron Hart) of Breslau (1670–1756), a brother of Moses Hart (d. 1756), cousin and partner of Benjamin Levy. Moses Hart was a leading member of the group that had been opposed to the first incumbent of the office of rabbi and had forced his resignation. From the appointment of Aaron Hart this group seems to have obtained control of the congregational affairs, and henceforth all offices in the congregation were filled by its members. In 1696 Benjamin Levy purchased a piece of land in the neighbourhood of Globe Road to serve as a burial-ground for the new congregation. The circumstances that led to the change in the rabbinate were not conducive to the smooth working of the affairs of the new community. Although one party had prevailed, the other had not been entirely subdued, and the latter was not slow to seize every opportunity to gain advantages, moral and material, in the long war that raged between them. Benjamin Levy, a financial magnate, considered himself above the petty quarrels of his relatives in the congregation, and for the most part kept aloof from synagogue affairs. The two parties were headed by the Parnas[1] Aberle and Marcus Moses, a supporter of Rabbi

---

[1] President of the Congregation.

Most learned Aaron Hart Rabby Aged 81.

Done from an Original Painting of B. Dandridge by James M. Ardell.

RABBI AARON HART

Jehudah, respectively. In addition to the political A communal dispute. reasons for an absence of sympathy between these two men, there were personal ones. Both were wealthy East India merchants and trade rivals. The dissatisfaction of the defeated party found expression in criticisms of the orthodoxy of the usurper. On many points complaints were made, and much annoyance caused to those in possession, who were unable to retaliate. Their opportunity, however, came when Marcus Moses sacrificed his discretion to his courage, and openly questioned the legality of a divorce granted by Rabbi Aaron Hart. Although the Jewish layman is permitted to allow his talent for criticism to run to considerable lengths, the validity of a divorce is taboo. The offence of Marcus Moses was not overlooked, and, although he pleaded that an incorrect interpretation had been placed upon his remarks, sentence of excommunication was passed against him. To Moses the punishment was far more considerable than mere exclusion from the synagogue. His business suffered, inasmuch as none of his coreligionists would conduct any transactions with him. Socially, also, he was shunned by those who had until recently been his friends.

After ineffectual endeavours to obtain rescission A secession. of the obnoxious decree, Moses determined upon counter measures. With the assistance of his friends Sampson Mears and Abraham Nathan, an opposition congregation was assembled in Marcus Moses' house in Magpye Alley. Jochanan Höllischau, who had previously been a member of the London Beth Din, was appointed rabbi, and almost his first official act was solemnly to declare Moses free from the ban of excommunication passed on him. Moses then purchased a burial-ground in Hoxton and a site for a new synagogue in St. Mary Axe. At this juncture the party of Rabbi Uri Phoebus took action. Appeal was

made to Moses Hart, who had held aloof from the
party disputes. The dangers of an independent congregation were magnified and emphasised. It was
contended that the new congregation would prove an
encouragement to pauper immigration, and that the
existence of an un-Anglicised body of Jews outside
the general community would prove harmful to the
common weal. Negotiations were opened with the
Sephardi community, and as a result Abraham
Mendez, its president, joined with Moses Hart, in
March 1704, in petitioning the Board of Aldermen to
prevent the erection of the new edifice. After a short
inquiry the Aldermen agreed to act in accordance
with their petitioners' wishes, and an order was issued
forbidding the erection.

This decision, however, did not cause the dispersion
of the new congregation. It continued to meet in
the house of Moses, and worshipped there for twenty-
two years. Rabbi Jochanan obtained the support of
several eminent rabbis, among others Rabbi Jehudah
Loeb, in his decision regarding the excommunication
of Moses ; and the synagogue became gradually known
as the Hambro, either as the representative in London
of the Hamburg traditions, or after Marcus Moses,
otherwise Marcus Hamburger. The founder himself,
leaving his family and the congregation well provided
for, left for the East. In 1721 he returned with an
immense fortune, and commenced to build a synagogue in the garden attached to his house in Magpye
Alley. Once again the older Ashkenazi community
joined with that of the Sephardim to prevent the
erection. The Corporation issued another fiat in
support of the petitioners, but on this occasion Moses
ignored all the efforts of his opponents, and the
synagogue was completed in 1726.

The Hambro
Synagogue.

Four years earlier another Ashkenazi synagogue
had been erected in the metropolis. The congrega-

tion that met in Broad Court had outgrown the accommodation—a private house—originally provided. A new building became an urgent necessity. Moses Hart was still the leading member of the congregation, and his liberality towards it was little less than that of Marcus Moses towards the rival body. His wealth had increased considerably during the twenty years that had passed, and his social status had been raised by the office under Government, conferred upon him by Godolphin, Lord High Treasurer, in the reign of Queen Anne. The site chosen for the new building was in Duke's Place, Aldgate. The first wardens were Lazarus Simon, Isaac Franks, and Abraham Franks. Myer Polak was the treasurer. Following the example set by the Sephardi community a code of laws was drafted for the government of the congregation. The establishment of this synagogue, serving as an attraction to the Jews of the Continent, still further increased the Jewish population of London. Ten years later, in 1732, a Talmud Torah School, the predecessor of the Jews' Free School, was established.

The Duke's Place or Great Synagogue.

The beginnings of the Jews' Free School.

From the date of the establishment of the Great Synagogue, the Jewish population continued to increase, the persecutions in Bohemia in 1744 helping to swell the influx. In 1745 the first Ashkenazi charity was established — the *Hachnosath Berith*. Three years later the cemetery accommodation proving insufficient, a piece of ground was acquired in Alderney Road, Mile End Road, for a burial-ground. In 1752 the three congregations joined forces to deal with a difficulty that threatened danger to both communities in common. Since the resettlement in the middle of the seventeenth century all endeavours for the purpose of the conversion of Christians to Judaism had been severely discouraged. It was a tradition that the return of the Jews to England had only

Conversion troubles.

been agreed to by the English Government provided that no converts were made, and for almost two centuries after that date the synagogues invariably refused to receive into the community any Gentile, no matter how sincere was his desire to enter it. It appears that in the middle of the eighteenth century some foreign Jews, settled temporarily in London, were making proselytes. On this coming to the ears of the synagogue authorities, joint action was taken by them, and the announcement was publicly made that any Jew guilty of the stated offence would be expelled from his synagogue and deprived of all the benefits and privileges pertaining to the Jewish religion. The London Jewish community had by that date grown to eight thousand, a large proportion of whom consisted of poor Jews who had come from Holland.

Rabbi Hirsch Löbel.

Rabbi Uri Phaibush remained in office until his death in 1756. He was succeeded in the following year by Rabbi Hirsch Löbel, a son of Rabbi Aryeh Löb, at the time Chief Rabbi of Resha, and a nephew of Jacob Emden.[1] Born in 1721, on attaining manhood, Löbel threw himself with zeal into the famous Eybeshutz controversy that centred round the alleged adherence of Rabbi Jonathan Eybeshutz to the Pseudo-Messiah, Sabbathai Zevi. The notable part that Löbel took in this controversy was the direct cause of the call he received on the death of the rabbi of the Great Synagogue in London. His tenure of office in London, however, was by no means devoid of worry. Doubts were cast upon the correctness of the Shechita,[2] and in the course of the controversy, one Jacob Kimchi declared that all the

---

[1] Jacob Israel ben Zebi Ashkenazi Emden (Jacob Herschel), born at Altona 1697, died there 1776; Talmudist and anti-Sabbathaian controversialist.

[2] The ritual pertaining to the slaughter of animals for consumption by Jews.

Shochetim under the control of Rabbi Löbel were unfit to hold their offices. The rabbi desired to defend his subordinates, but his wardens refused him the necessary permission to do so, and it was probably in consequence of this action that Rabbi Hirsch Löbel, otherwise known as Hart Lyon, resigned his office in 1764 and retired to the Continent.

Before that date, however, there had been another secession from the Senior Ashkenazi community. This movement does not appear to have been due to any disagreement. It was merely the natural outcome of the increase of the population and the pressure on the limited space provided in the two existing synagogues. In these circumstances some of the members of the existing congregations joined with others newly arrived, to establish a third Ashkenazi place of worship. This action aroused as much hostility as had the foundation of the Hambro Synagogue on a previous occasion. A meeting of the governing body of the chief synagogue was held on the 19th of August 1761, when it was resolved that : "Whereas certain persons unworthy of our Countenance and Protection have lately form'd themselves into a society calling themselves a Congregation at Bricklayers Hall, we do hereby strictly Charge our priest now and hereafter that he does not directly or indirectly or other in his name or with his Knowledge and Permission, officiate either Publick or private in the services of Marriages, Burials, Circumcission or any other act of priesthood for any person whatever belonging to the said society. And to prevent inocent persons from Unverity joyning that society we Order that this resolution be read publickly two Sabbaths successively in our Synagogue so that non may plead ignorance thereof."

The resolution was also communicated to the authorities of the Bevis Marks Synagogue, who were

The New Synagogue.

desired to take similar action. So far, however, as the new congregation was concerned, these resolutions passed unheeded. The following year the erection of a building to accommodate the seceders was commenced and was completed in due course. For a long period the relations between the New Synagogue and the older congregations were severely strained, but all continued to prosper, and in the course of time the gulfs between them were bridged. At the same time as the establishment of the New Synagogue, the Great Synagogue was enlarged in order to afford sufficient accommodation for its growing congregation.

The beginnings of provincial Jewry. While the rich Sephardi merchants settled almost exclusively in the metropolis, the provincial congregations were founded, almost without exception, by Ashkenazim with limited resources, who settled wherever they saw opportunities for earning a livelihood. Thus by the beginning of the eighteenth century most of the ports, especially those on the south and west coasts, possessed a sprinkling of Jews. The poorer members of these communities were pedlars, and obtained their stocks from their more prosperous co-religionists, who were shopkeepers. In this manner Jewish communities were established during the eighteenth century at Portsmouth, Falmouth, Bristol, Plymouth, Hull, Yarmouth, and Liverpool. These pedlars, as they became more prosperous, themselves set up as shopkeepers in towns in the centres of the districts they had hitherto served. Thus communities also sprung up in Exeter, Bath, Birmingham, Canterbury, Cheltenham, Coventry, King's Lynn, and Norwich. These shopkeepers were for the most part jewellers, and in some instances they developed later into bankers and bullion merchants. The influx of destitute alien Jews into London during the eighteenth century assisted the tendency that had shown itself in all parts of the country. The problem that faced the Ashkenazi community of the metropolis was dealt with by means of dispersion. Pedlars were not only sent inland from the coast towns. London was also in many instances their headquarters, and from that centre they went as far afield as Lancashire and Northumberland.

Dispersion of immigrants.

AUTHORITIES :—Lucien Wolf, "The N'vei Tzedek" (*Jewish Chronicle*, April 5, 1895), "Benjamin Levy" (*Jewish Chronicle*, August 7, 1903), "The Hambro Synagogue" (*Jewish Chronicle*, Nov. 18, 1892), "First Stage of Jewish Emancipation," "The History and Genealogy of the Jewish Families of Yates and Samuel" (1901); H. Adler, "The Chief Rabbis of England" (1887); J. Picciotto, "Sketches of Anglo-Jewish History"; "MSS. Records of the Great Synagogue"; "Jewish Board of Guardians Report" (1859), "Jewish Encyclopedia."

CHAPTER XXVI

THE COLONIES
(1625-1800)

ALTHOUGH at the time of Menasseh ben Israel's embassy, re-admission had not yet been gained for the Jews to the soil of England, and no Jew as such had the formal right of residence within the country, in other parts of the British dominions other conditions prevailed.

Barbadoes, the first English colony to admit Jews.

The island of Barbadoes was the first colony in which undisguised Jews settled. Discovered by the English in 1605, it was settled by them twenty years later, and Jews are generally supposed to have been included among the earliest colonists. Three years later, in 1628, it is certain that there were some Jewish inhabitants. As compared with other states and colonies, there was practically no anti-Jewish discrimination practised in the island, the disabilities under which the Jews lay being few and of little importance. In 1656 the Jewish Colony was benefited by the grant of the enjoyment of the privileges of " Laws and Statutes of Ye Commonwealth of England and of this Island, relating to foreigners and strangers," and five years later letters of denization were granted to several Jewish settlers. The dissolution of the Jewish community in Cayenne led to an immigration into the island, whose Jewish colony was thus reinforced. The prosperity of these settlers progressed to such an extent that jealousies were aroused, and endeavours were made to obtain legal restrictions on their commercial activities. These efforts were, however, unavailing ; and, on the other hand, during the Status of the colonial Jews. governorship of Lord Willoughby, in 1671, the free exercise of their religion without any restrictions was granted to the Jews. At the same time the oaths of allegiance and supremacy, objectionable to Jews on account of their wording, were dispensed with in the case of the endenization of Jews. Two years previously the Jews of Barbadoes had petitioned for their evidence taken on the Pentateuch to be accepted in courts of law. Their inability to take the ordinary oath had in the past rendered impossible the acceptance of their evidence, when either party to the suit was a non-Jew. At the same time objections were stated against the endeavours, to which allusion has already been made, to restrict their trade. The petition was supported by the Governor, but no action was taken on it for five years. In 1674 the local legislature allowed the oath to be taken on the Pentateuch, and evidence to be given in cases relating to "trade and dealings and not otherwise." The following year an unsuccessful attempt was made to extend this permission to cover all legal proceedings. This benevolent treatment suffered a slight reaction in 1679, when the jealousy of the rival merchants induced the Assembly to pass an Act restraining the Jews from keeping or trading with negroes.

The Act of 1674 appears not to have been put into Restrictive laws and their removal. operation until 1681, a year of several other anti-Jewish petitions, and of a presentment of the Grand Jury against "the evil done to the island by vagrant and poor Jews." This movement was without success, but seven years later the undenizened Jews were discriminated against. The restrictive Act of this year remained in force until 1756. From 1756 to 1761 special taxes were levied on the Jews. A period of prosperity then ensued, marked only in 1802 by the removal of all political disabilities, and in 1820 by the conferment by Parliament of political advantages over the remainder of the population. In the last mentioned year the Jews were allowed to choose five representatives to determine the share of the taxation of the island that should be levied on them.

The conquest of Jamaica.

The conquest of Jamaica by Cromwell in 1655 found Jews already among the settlers on that island. Jamaica had been given to the family of Columbus, and by marriage brought into the possession of the Braganzas, who afterwards ascended the throne of Portugal. Columbus was favourably disposed towards the Jews, and, excluding the Inquisition from the island, rendered their settlement easy. Jamaica, thus nominally under the crown of Spain, was still to some extent autonomous and Portuguese, and it was under these conditions that Jews first found themselves in the island. The conquest by the English led to the expulsion of the Spanish settlers. Similar treatment would probably have been meted out to the Portuguese, and with them the Jews (reputed Portuguese), if the hostility between the Spanish and Portuguese had not been so keen as to render impossible the withdrawal of the latter to Cuba. Without a near refuge elsewhere the Portuguese were suffered to remain in the island, and consequently the new English government, immediately on the occupation, found Jews among its subjects.

Jamaica under Cromwell and Charles II.

The presence of Jews in the island was considered by Cromwell an important factor in the furtherance of his colonial policy. In his organisation of the colony he received valuable assistance from Simon de Caceres, the colleague of Carvajal. The Restoration made little difference in the condition of the Jews in Jamaica. Their numbers increased and they continued to flourish. Some of them were engaged in retail trade, but the majority were wholesale merchants, and the greater portion of the trade with the Spanish

Main was in their hands. During the term of office of Governor Molesworth, the settlers received permission to erect a synagogue.

As in Barbadoes, however, the commercial success of the Jews aroused jealousy among their neighbours. In the year 1671 the English merchants petitioned the Council of the Colony for the expulsion of the Jews. The petition was in due course transmitted to England, but Governor Lynch in forwarding it argued strongly against the prayer being granted, and paid a striking tribute to the value of the Jews to the colony. The views of the governor were adopted by the King in Council, and the result of the petition was a recommendation that steps should be taken to encourage the settlement of still more Jews in the island. *Jewish colonists welcomed.*

This desire for further Jewish colonists was satisfied by immigrations from Brazil and Surinam. The former colony had fluctuated between Portuguese and Dutch ownership, and the Jews who had settled there and thrown off their masks under the latter were compelled to leave their homes when the Portuguese returned. Many of them came to the English colonies and of these Jamaica received her share.

Jews seem to have first settled in Surinam in 1644,[1] eighteen years before Lord Willoughby received permission from Charles II. to establish an English colony there. In his government Lord Willoughby recognised no difference between Jew and Christian, and the Portuguese Jews whom he found there were given the same privileges as the English colonists. The dissolution of the colony of Cayenne in 1664 led to a Jewish immigration into Surinam, and there the Jews remained under easy conditions until 1675, when the colony passed into the possession of the Dutch. The new Government continued the policy of its predecessor, but many of the Jews, having once tasted *In Surinam.*

[1] The earliest date suggested is 1632.

English rule, seemed desirous of retaining it, and, as the British had evacuated Surinam, they sought a new home elsewhere under the English flag. So valuable, however, were the Jews considered, that the Dutch refused them permission to depart, and the English Government was compelled specifically to demand them as English subjects. This was probably the first official recognition in foreign relations of Jews as British subjects. The cession of 1675 was, however, not permanent, for the colony alternated between Dutch and English rule over a long period. At one time Surinam was exchanged with the Dutch for New Amsterdam, since known as New York. Nor did all the Jewish settlers reject Dutch rule. Many privileges were granted to the Jewish colonists, especially when the English were in control. As early as 1665 they were allowed a court of justice of first instance for civil cases, and they were exempted from prosecution by their creditors on the high festivals. It was specifically stated in a Government proclamation that immediately on reaching the colony "every person belonging to the Hebrew nation . . . shall possess and enjoy every liberty and privilege possessed by, and granted to, the citizens and inhabitants of the colony, and shall be considered as English-born." It was decreed that they should not be compelled to serve in any public office; their persons and their property were placed under the special protection of the Government; they were permitted to practise their religion without hindrance, and land was assigned to them for the erection of synagogues and schools, and for use as a cemetery. All these advantages were granted, "whereas we have found that the Hebrew nation . . . have . . . proved themselves useful and beneficial to the colony."

Despite the somewhat satisfactory position that the Jews held in the island of Jamaica, attempts at per-

Jews recognised as British subjects in Surinam.

In Jamaica.

secution were not entirely wanting. In 1681 an endeavour to effect their expulsion was made by the Council of the Island, on the ground that the Jews were the "descendants from the crucifiers of the blessed Jesus." The crown ignored both the request and the reason for it, but the special taxes levied on the Jews, on the ground of their wealth, were continued. Another reason given for this exceptional taxation was the exemption of the Jews from many public duties and consequent expenses. It was suggested that these exemptions were beneficial rather than of the nature of disabilities. The Jews were at that time excluded from all public office, denied the elective franchise, disqualified from serving on juries, and debarred from the privilege of purchasing white servants. Permission was, however, given them to erect synagogues.

The twofold burden of special taxation and the restriction of privileges was not borne by the community in silence. Petitions against the taxes were sent up every year and invariably rejected. The fiscal burdens, instead of being diminished, were increased, with the result that, by the opening of the eighteenth century, the bulk of the taxation of the colony was paid by the small Jewish population. On the other hand, the greater portion of the industry and the commerce was in the hands of that section. In 1711 the Jews suffered a further disability by being prohibited, in common with mulattos, Indians, and negroes, from being employed in any of the offices created by the Act of that year. In 1702, however, a new demand was preferred by the Jews of the colony, that of the right to vote at elections for the Assembly. The petition and remonstrance were declared to be "erroneous, false, and scandalous," and a proposal was even made to punish the petitioners by imprisonment. A lighter sentence, however, took

Excessive taxation imposed on the Jews of Jamaica.

its place—a fine on the community of £2000. Before ten years had passed a less intolerant policy began to gain adoption. In 1711 the question of the admission of Jews to the elective franchise was considered, and a bill to that effect was introduced into the Assembly. That body, however, amended it so as to prevent the election of Jews, and, in the dispute between the two houses that ensued, the proposed measure was abandoned.

Abolition of the special taxes in Jamaica, 1736.

By 1736 the strength of the Jewish case in regard to special taxation was acknowledged, and the governor received instructions not to assent to any bill in which such taxation was continued. The Assembly, however, was not in the mood to agree to any such alteration in policy, and a lengthy dispute, in the course of which the Assembly was prorogued three times, ensued before the objectionable clauses were omitted from the bill. During the course of the dispute the Jewish community showed itself in a very favourable light, by voluntarily raising the sum of £1000 towards the expenditure of the year, in order that they might not be the cause of a rupture between the governor and the Assembly. When the taxation was finally abolished, it became the practice to give annual presents to the governor and to certain of his officers.

The middle of the eighteenth century saw the Jewish Question again a burning one in the island. Basing their claim on the Act of the British Parliament of 1740, the Jews of Jamaica demanded enfranchisement. The community, however, was not unanimous in the matter, and all applications for votes on the part of the Jews were without exception refused. Henceforth the outer history of Jamaican Jewry had few incidents. As in other parts of the world the community has made it a rule to support its own poor. At the beginning of the nineteenth century, on the ground of the refusal of certain members to contribute to the funds for the benefit of the poor, the heads of the Spanish and Portuguese synagogue petitioned the Assembly to compel the defaulting members to take their share of the burden. A bill was introduced for this purpose, but it was rejected, and nothing more was heard of the matter.

From the end of the seventeenth century Jews were found scattered throughout the other West Indian possessions of England, but in small numbers. Occasional references to them are to be found in the records. For instance, in 1694 an Act was adopted by Parliament for the purpose of preventing the Jews from engrossing commodities imported into the Leeward Islands. On the petition of the Jews it was repealed seven years later, on the promise that in case of war they would assist in the defence of the islands. *In the other islands.*

The date of the first organised settlement on the North American continent is generally given as 1654, when a number of Dutch Jews landed in the Dutch colony of New Amsterdam, now New York, to be followed a few months later (in 1655) by co-religionists who had left Brazil on its evacuation by the Dutch. Before this immigration scattered Jews were to be found occasionally on the mainland, notably in Maryland, and in 1652 it is stated that a colony of Jewish soldiers and sailors was sent to New Amsterdam by the Dutch West India Company. About the same date Jews first arrived in the English colony of Rhode Island, where the most tolerant government then existing was to be found. In that colony all comers, no matter of what nationality, were accorded the same rights and privileges as Englishmen, and, in fact, were granted naturalisation immediately on touching the soil of the colony. *In North America.*

In 1664 New Amsterdam passed under the dominion of the English and became New York. The status

In New York. of the Jews, which had been tolerable, remained the same under the new Government. The colony was entrusted to the Duke of York, who appointed the governors, and it was at the time his policy, as it was that of Charles II., to grant as wide a religious toleration as possible to Christians of all denominations. Consequently the Duke's laws, promulgated in 1665, ordained that no professing Christian should be molested on account of his religious views. Nine years later this tolerance was extended to "all persons of what Religion so ever," so long as they did not disturb the public peace or molest others in the free exercise of their religion.

Towards the end of the seventeenth century the legal disabilities under which the Jews of New York laboured underwent some increase. In 1683 an Act was passed by the Colonial Assembly for the naturalisation of foreigners, from the benefits of which the Jews, as non-Christians, were excluded. Two years later the petition of the Jewish residents for permission to hold public worship was rejected by the Mayor and Common Council of New York, to whom it had been referred by the Governor Dongan, and, in the same year, the precedent set in the West Indies was followed by the prohibition to engage in retail trade. But this last prohibition was not very strictly enforced, and gradually lapsed into oblivion. The

First North American synagogue. refusal of religious toleration was reversed in 1686, after the accession of James II., and the synagogue that was erected in New York in consequence of this change of policy, was the first on the North American continent. The civil, as distinct from the political, situation of the Jews, both in England and in the colonies, was so comfortable towards the end of the seventeenth century, and the results of the tolerance were so satisfactory, that it was quoted by William Penn as an argument in favour of the acceptance by the nation of the larger scheme of tolerance that James placed before it.

For the next forty years the Jewish communities The question in North America had no external history. In 1715 of naturalisation in New legislation for the naturalisation in New York of alien York. residents was specifically confined to Protestants, although one of the sections of the Act enacted that all aliens who were in residence in the colony before the 1st of November 1683 should become naturalised without any formalities. The Act thus prevented the naturalisation of foreign Jews who had settled in the colony subsequent to 1683, but, on the other hand, declared those who had migrated before that date to be naturalised. Eight years later, in 1723, an Act was passed naturalising certain aliens—six Jews—but nothing appears in the statute providing for the omission by the naturalised Jews of the obnoxious phrase, "upon the true faith of a Christian," from the necessary oath. In 1727 the General Assembly of New York adopted legislation omitting the phrase from the oath of abjuration when taken by any of his Majesty's subjects professing the Jewish religion.

Meanwhile it seemed that some Jews had become accustomed to exercise the elective franchise, and had voted in elections to the legislature. These illegal acts became known in the course of the discussion of a disputed election in 1737. The immediate question before the House was the legality of the evidence of Jews in the case, and on both questions it decided against the Jewish claims. The precedents in Great Britain were quoted, and it was unanimously decided that the disqualification that held good in England also had the force of law in the North American colonies.

The first Jews are believed to have settled in Canada In Canada. at the time of its conquest in 1760. Of the first two known, Commissary Aaron Hart and Lazarus David,

R

The first Jewish congregation in Canada. the former was attached to the English army. The first Jewish congregation was formed in 1768, and a cemetery was purchased seven years later.

AUTHORITIES :—Richard Hill, "Lights and Shadows of Jamaican History" (1859) ; W. J. Gardner, "History of Jamaica" (1873) ; E. Long, "The History of Jamaica" (1774) ; Sir R. H. Schomburgh, "History of Barbadoes" (1848); C. P. Daly, "Settlement of the Jews in North America" (1893); A. M. Dyer, "Points in the First Chapter of New York Jewish History" (*Transactions of the Jewish Historical Society of America*, vol. iii.); Dr. B. Felsenthal and Prof. R. Gottheil, "Chronological Sketch of the History of the Jews in Surinam" (*Transactions of the Jewish Historical Society of America*, vol. iv.); R. Gottheil, "Contributions to the History of the Jews in Surinam" (*Transactions of the Jewish Historical Society of America*, vol. ix.) ; Dr. H. Friedenwald, "Material for the History of the Jews in the British West Indies" (*Transactions of the Jewish Historical Society of America*, vol. v.) ; M. J. Kohler, "Civil Status of the Jews in Colonial New York" (*Transactions of the Jewish Historical Society of America*, vol. vi.), "Jewish Activity in American Colonial Commerce" (*Transactions of the Jewish Historical Society of America*, vol. x.), "Beginnings of New York Jewish History" (*Transactions of the Jewish Historical Society of America*, vol. i.); Dr. Charles Gross, "Documents from the Public Record Office (London)" (*Transactions of the Jewish Historical Society of America*, vol. ii.); Andrew C. Joseph, "The Settlement of Jews in Canada" (*Transactions of the Jewish Historical Society of America*, vol. i.) ; "Jewish Encyclopedia"; M. Kayserling, "The Jews in Jamaica and Daniel Israel Lopez Laguna" (*Jewish Quarterly Review*, vol. xii.).

CHAPTER XXVII

FROM THE REVOLUTION TO THE GEORGIA SETTLEMENT
(1655–1750)

THE loosely defined status of the Jews who settled in this country under the later Stuarts led, as we have already seen, to numerous incidents that threatened trouble to the small community. Under the powerful protection of the State the Jews, whenever attacked, had little difficulty in defending the security of their position. The inhabitants of London, however, lived under a dual government. In addition to the powers wielded by the Government of the country, there were those of the City municipality, and these were so formidable, that when they were directed against the Jewish population its position was most adversely affected and its stability endangered.

Under the several charters that the City possessed it was able to keep Jews perpetually out of the freedom, and without the freedom of the City, men were debarred from retail trading, from the plying of handicrafts, from the transaction of business on exchange, and from other almost indispensable privileges. As merchant strangers the Jews of the Re-Settlement could only deal in wholesale, and do so subject to restrictions. The unique position, however, that the Jews held in English trade in the middle of the seventeenth century, and the considerable benefit they were thereby acknowledged to confer upon the country, rendered a change in their status inevitable. As early as 1657 a Jew, Solomon Dormido, a nephew of Menasseh ben

Solomon
Dormido admitted as a
City broker.

Israel, applied to the Court of Aldermen for admission as a broker, and, despite innumerable disqualifications, Dormido, who was notoriously a Jew, was admitted.[1] His example was followed with like success by others, David Aboab in 1671, Samuel de Caceres in 1674, Moses Barrow in 1679, Isaac Lindo, Joseph Ferdinando (a son of Antonio Carvajal), and Samuel Sasportas (a son of the Haham). A group of Jewish brokers gradually collected, and congregating in a particular portion of the Exchange, as other groups did, their corner soon became known as the "Jewes Walk."

Jewish brokers
limited to
twelve.

The laxity in the manner of the admission of the brokers, however, led to many abuses, so that in 1697 the Corporation applied for, and obtained, Parliamentary powers "for restraining the number and ill-practices of brokers and stock-jobbers." The committee appointed to re-organise the Exchange drew up new rules, in accordance with which membership was limited to a hundred English brokers, twelve aliens, and twelve Jews. These last-named were excused from taking up the freedom before admission to the Exchange, and the necessary oath was modified to meet their religious scruples. The Jews were further ordered to provide themselves with silver medals. The twelve Jewish brokers were Moses Barrow, David de Ffaro, Benjamin Nunes, Samuel de Caceres, Elias Lindo, Abraham de Payba, Jacob Arias, David Avila, Joseph Ferdinando, Abraham Ffrancke, Benjamin Levy, and Elias Paz. This was the first grant of freemen's privileges to dissenters and non-freemen that the Corporation made. It placed the Jews in a better position than that of the alien Protestants, and when, in 1708, the authorities of the Dutch and French Churches protested against the preference and demanded similar privileges for their own members,

[1] See page 210.

the Court of Aldermen refused to make any departure from the rules laid down in 1697.

On one subsequent occasion, in 1720, an endeavour was made again to interfere with the admission of Jews as brokers. In that year a petition was presented to the Lord Mayor and Aldermen objecting to the admission of a Jew on several grounds. Among them were the absence from the Act of 1697 of all reference to Jews, and to the immunity of the Jews, as non-freemen, from the liability to pay scott and lott, or otherwise to contribute to the public charge.

Frequently towards the close of the seventeenth century the Jewish settlers came under the notice of Parliament. For instance, in 1698 the Legislature had under consideration a Bill "for the more effectual suppressing of Blasphemy and Profaneness." This measure proposed to enact that any person educated in or having made profession of the Christian religion who might deny the divinity of any of the persons in the Holy Trinity, or assert that there were more gods than one, or deny the truth of the Christian religion or the divine inspiration of the Holy Scriptures, should be liable to punishment. The House of Lords proposed to amend the Bill by the omission of the words "having been educated in or at any time having made profession of the Christian religion," the effect being to render every Jew in the kingdom liable to the pains and penalties laid down in the Bill. When the measure, however, was returned to the House of Commons, objection was raised to the amendment on the ground that it would "subject the Jews who live amongst us to all the Pains and Penalties contained in the Bill; which must therefore, of necessity, ruin them, and drive them out of the Kingdom; and cannot be thought was the intention of your Lordships, since here they have the means and opportunities to be informed of and rightly instructed in the principles

The Act of 1698, the Lords' amendment.

of the true Christian religion." The Lords apparently had no such intention, and on the representations of the other House willingly abandoned the suggested amendment. Another Act of Parliament of this period

Proselytism, a crime.

enabled a criminal prosecution to be brought against Jews who should obtain proselytes from Christianity.

The measure affecting the Jews, however, that is best known is that entitled " An Act to oblige Jews to maintain and provide for their Protestant children," adopted in the first year of the reign of Anne. The avowed purpose of this measure was to assist the conversion of the Jews to the religion of the country. It

The Act of 1702.

provided that " to the end that sufficient maintenance be provided and allowed for the children of Jewish parents who shall turn Protestant be it enacted . . . that if any Jewish parent in order to the compelling of his or her Protestant child to change his or her religion shall refuse to allow such child a fitting maintenance . . . it shall be lawful for the Lord Chancellor . . . to make such order therein for the maintenance of such Protestant child, as he . . . shall think fit."

Jews permitted to hold land.

Another doubt concerning the status of the Jews in England was cleared up by the decision of the Attorney-General, Sir Robert Raymond, in 1718. He was asked to decide whether a Jew born in England but of foreign parentage could purchase and enjoy an estate in fee. The Attorney-General's opinion was that he was fully capable of purchasing and enjoying the lands, and that the law had put no disability upon him on account of his religion. He went further and said that in respect of the matters under consideration the Jew's position was so satisfactory that it would not be improved by denization. This decision obtained definite confirmation a few years later. An Act of Parliament, passed in the year 1722, required all persons in possession of real estates to take the oaths of allegiance and abjuration. The latter oath concluded with the words "on the true faith of a Christian," and Jews were consequently unable to accept it. To remedy this state of affairs a further Act was adopted in the following session. This made provision for the omission of the objectionable words when the oath was taken by a Jew. In the discussion in Parliament it was suggested that the clause was unnecessary, inasmuch as Jews were debarred from holding land. The opinions of the leading lawyers of the day were obtained on the point, and they were unanimously in favour of the opinion already given by Raymond. As a result the Bill was adopted.

Although at this period Parliament was so careful of Jewish susceptibilities, in that respect it was not altogether representative of the nation. The nation had not yet moved from the position that rendered possible the legislation of the first year of the reign of Anne. No legal persecution of the Jews was then existing in England, but the populace, roused by agitators, found other means of giving full play to their prejudice. In 1732 a paper was published by one Osborne accusing Jews of being accustomed to murder those who married outside the community. *Anti-Jewish libels.* One definite instance was quoted, and it was said that the woman and her child had been murdered by Jews lately arrived from Portugal and living near Broad Street. The publication roused the populace, who attacked all Jews who fitted the description given. Mobs were abroad in several parts of the city. At this juncture proceedings were taken against Osborne in the Court of King's Bench, and, despite the defence that no particular Jews could show that they were pointed at more than any others, the accused was found guilty on the ground that the whole community of Jews had been attacked.

The creation of a chartered company under James

Oglethorpe, for the purpose of emigrating needy and respectable families to the American continent, and forming of them a colony between the Altemaha and Savannah rivers, directed the attention of the An emigration scheme. Sephardi community of London to the possibilities of the colonies as a solution of the difficulties arising out of the continued immigration from Eastern Europe. The continual influx of poor Ashkenazi Jews had long been a source of anxiety to the leaders of the community, and many efforts had been made to deal with it.' The governing body of the Georgia Company numbered twenty-one trustees. The funds at their disposal consisted partly of a parliamentary grant and partly of donations from private individuals. These latter were obtained through honorary agents acting under the commission of the Council, and among the agents were three leading members of The Salvador family. the Sephardi community of London, Alvaro Lopez Suasso, Francis Salvador, and Anthony da Costa. To Suasso, who was one of the wealthiest men of his day, reference has already been made. Salvador was at the time one of the directors of the Dutch East India Company, the first Jew to hold such a position. He was a leading financier, and his charities were famous. The firm of Francis and Joseph Salvador (they were known in the community as Jessurun Alvarez) became after the death of Sampson Gideon the leading English financiers of the day. The Salvadors were not only prominent in general public life ; they also took a leading part in the affairs of the . community. The Salvador family was already interested in American enterprises, and owned large tracts of land in South Carolina. In later years they suffered considerable financial losses, in consequence of the earthquake at Lisbon and the failure of the Dutch East India Company. In 1773 a Francis Salvador of a later generation emigrated to South

Carolina, leaving his wife and four children in London. The American colonies were then on the threshold of revolution, and Salvador entered heartily into their cause. He was an active member of the first and second Provincial Congresses of South Carolina, and took his share in the warlike measures that ensued on the determination to oppose the attempts of the mother-country. Three years later, at the early age of twenty-nine, Salvador was killed in battle with the Indians, whom the English had induced to attack the colonists. Da Costa was the first Jewish director of the Bank of England.

The sums collected by these gentlemen, for the most part from co-religionists, should in the ordinary course have been handed over to the Company. Instead of doing so, however, Suasso and his colleagues appear to have devoted them to the emigration to the new colony, of destitute Jews who had arrived in England. The trustees, strongly disapproving of this action, demanded the return of the commissions issued to the three Sephardim. They contended that not only had Suasso and his colleagues exceeded their powers, and violated the instructions that had accompanied their commissions, but their intentions, if consummated, would have proved harmful to the best interests of the colony and the trust. The commissioners at first refused to comply with the demand and persisted in their course. After considerable correspondence and the lapse of several months, however, the commissions were surrendered.

Meanwhile the first batch of settlers under Ogle- thorpe had hardly reached the Savannah river when an unexpected vessel arrived with forty Jews on board. This company consisted of people of two descriptions. The one, for the most part Sephardim, came out as ordinary colonists at their own expense. The second comprised assisted Ashkenazi emigrants.

Oglethorpe had not been advised of the sailing of
this batch of emigrants, a third of the whole number
of the first colonists, and was somewhat at a loss
how to deal with them. According to the charters,
freedom of religious opinion and observance was
guaranteed to all except Papists. The governor
therefore, after consideration, determined to receive
the new colonists and at the same time informed the
trustees of their arrival. The Board in London did
not receive the news with equanimity. A pamphlet
was prepared in order to assure the public that it was
not the intention " to make a Jews' colony of Georgia,"
and complaint was made that the unauthorised action
of the Trust's commissioners had not only prejudicially affected the colony, but had turned aside many
intended benefactions. To Oglethorpe the trustees
wrote in a similar sense, and he was instructed to
give the new arrivals no encouragement whatever,
and by no means to allow them any settlement among
the grantees. Oglethorpe, however, was more liberal-
minded than his fellow trustees, and ignored their
instructions. Jewish names appear in the earliest
lists of those to whom grants of land were made, and
the governor considered the Jewish element in the
population its most valuable portion. In the month

of the arrival of the forty settlers a congregation was
formed and divine service held. The Jewish settlement proved of great value to the colony, into which
viniculture was introduced by one of its members,
Abraham de Lyon; another acclimatised the silk
industry, while the services of a third, Dr. Nunes, in
attending the sick were highly appreciated, not only
by the governor, but also by the London Board.
When a large proportion of the Jewish colony withdrew, temporarily as subsequently transpired, to
South Carolina a few years later, Georgia felt their
loss severely.

Contemporary with this Jewish influx into the New World and closely connected with it was a similar movement within the Sephardi community. That congregation appointed, in 1734, a committee, possibly consisting of Salvador, Suasso, and Da Costa, to apply for grants for an exclusively Jewish settlement in Georgia. This application was not granted, but three years later land was offered for a similar purpose in Carolina. In 1745 the committee was still in existence, and obtained an extension of its powers, and three years later John Hamilton, an irresponsible philanthropically disposed financier, entered into negotiations with the committee with a view to settling Jews in South Carolina. For this purpose he petitioned the Lords of the Committee of Council for Plantation Affairs for a grant of 200,000 acres in that colony. The application was entertained, but mutually satisfactory conditions could not be agreed upon, and the whole scheme was dropped. In 1750 a number of London Jews settled in South Carolina, not as assisted emigrants or in a body, but merely as individual settlers.

Other schemes for Jewish immigration into America.

In 1749 a new colonisation plan was suggested. Nova Scotia was the locality in favour on this occasion, and poor families were enjoined to proceed thither. To induce them to do so an offer was made of three years' charitable allowances, but none seems to have availed himself of it.

AUTHORITIES :—Lucien Wolf, "The First Stage of Jewish Emancipation," "Jew Brokers" (*Jewish Chronicle*, April 16, 1897) ; D'Blossiers Tovey, *Anglia Judaica;* H. S. Q. Henriques, "Jews and the English Law" (*Jewish Quarterly Review*, vols. xii. and xiii.) ; J. E. Blunt, "A History of the Establishment and Residence of the Jews in England" (1830) ; J. Picciotto, "Sketches of Anglo-Jewish History"; C. P. Daly, "Settlement of the Jews in North America"; Chas. C. Jones, "History of Georgia" (1883); George White, "Historical Collections of Georgia" (1855); P. C. Webb, "The Question whether a Jew" (1753); Charles Egan, "The Status of the Jews" (1848); B. A. Elzas, "The Jews of South

Carolina" (1905) ; C. C. Jones, jun., " The Settlement of the Jews in Georgia " (*Transactions, Jewish Historical Society of America,* vol. i.); Leon Hühner, " The Jews of Georgia in Colonial Times " (*Transactions, Jewish Historical Society of America,* vol. x., 1902) ; " Francis Salvador" (*Transactions, Jewish Historical Society of America,* vol. ii.); " Jewish Encyclopedia," article " Francis Salvador."

CHAPTER XXVIII

THE NATURALISATION CONTROVERSY
(1690-1753)

ALTHOUGH the community as a whole kept very much to itself during the two centuries that succeeded the Re-Settlement, from time to time throughout that period some leading member would render himself well known far beyond the walls of Bevis Marks. Such a position was held at the opening of the new era by Carvajal, Simon de Caceres, Augustine Coronel, and others. Under William and Mary, Suasso became famous in political and financial circles, and in the following reign Sir Solomon Medina ("the Jew Medina") was, to the outside world, the leading Jew of his day. Following William III. to England, Medina became the great army contractor in the wars that succeeded his arrival. For his services he was knighted, being the first professing Jew to receive that honour, but his chief title to notoriety consisted in the charges preferred against him, and more or less proved, of having bribed, on an extensive scale, the great Duke of Marlborough. A contemporary of Medina, Menasseh Lopez, was also one of the most prominent financiers of his day.

In that department of activity, however, the leading member of the community was undoubtedly Sampson Gideon, known in the synagogue as Sampson de Rehuel Abudiente (1699-1762). The son of a West Indian merchant, who was also engaged in business in the City, Gideon, by a remarkable display of sagacity,

Gideon and
the English
Government. judgment, and courage, succeeded in raising himself
from very modest beginnings to the position of
trusted adviser of the Government and a member of
the landed gentry of the country. With Walpole
Gideon was on terms of intimate friendship. He
was his adviser in all financial transactions. Under
the later Government of Pelham, when, in 1743 and
1744, the French fleet held the Channel, Gideon's
aid and advice were even more valuable. The
following year, that of the invasion of Prince Charles
Edward, panic seized all classes in London, and the
condition of the City seemed almost more fraught
with danger to the State than even the invasion of
its territories. At this critical juncture Gideon was
one of the few who lost neither their heads nor their
faith. He freely lent his property and his credit to
the Government, and raised a loan of £1,700,000 for
their assistance. Henceforth the Government invariably consulted Gideon in financial matters, and he,
on his part, devoted himself almost entirely to the
welfare of the State.

In an earlier crisis, that of the South Sea Bubble,
Gideon was also among the few who were not carried
away by the whirlwind of speculative excitement, and
consequently stood clear of the crash that succeeded.
The Jews and
the South Sea
Bubble and the
Forty-five. The Jews, as a whole, stood aside from the wild specu-
lations of the time, and were among the few whose
fortunes passed through the ordeal unimpaired. In
the Forty-five the example set by Gideon was followed
by all classes of his co-religionists. The lower classes
enlisted in numbers in the City Militia, and willingly
bore arms in defence of the *Status quo*. The more
prosperous members of the community formed
associations with the same object, while those whose
situations made them more useful in following their
own callings, promoted in every way whatever was
considered most serviceable to the Government. The

run on the Bank of England was stopped by the confidence aroused at the sight of the continuous supply of specie poured into its coffers by Jewish merchants.

The danger caused by the public offer of bank- Patriotic notes at sale at a discount was met by an association Finance. of twelve eminent merchants, two of whom were Jews, who undertook to accept them, whenever offered, at their face value. These twelve immediately obtained the support of all the best elements in the population, and the Jews, to a man, joined the association. The Government was in want of funds, and it was determined to raise a loan on the land tax at a rate of interest less than that otherwise available. One-fourth of the loan was immediately taken up by the Jews. Two members of the community had two vessels in the river ready laden for foreign ports. As soon as it was known that the Government was in need of ships to prevent the possibility of a hostile landing, these vessels were placed unconditionally at the disposal of the State. The patriotic action of the Jews of England in this crisis did not pass unrecognised. When calm was once more restored, it was resolved to present an address to the king, and the small deputation that represented the merchants of London on the occasion included one member of the Jewish community.

Five years earlier a long step in the journey to- A Naturalisa-wards full English citizenship was taken by the tion Act. passage through Parliament without opposition of an "Act for naturalising such foreign Protestants, and others therein mentioned, as are settled or shall settle, in any of His Majesty's Colonies in America." Before the seventh year of the reign of James I., it was possible for a Jew to acquire civil status in England in the same manner as any other alien— that is to say, by naturalisation by Act of Parliament. Legislation in 1609, although directed against Catholics, at the same time excluded Jews from the privilege of naturalisation, inasmuch as it made the acceptance of the sacrament an indispensable condition. In 1663 the law was altered slightly by the provision that any foreigner who should engage for three years in hemp, flax, or cotton manufacture, should enjoy the privileges of natural born subjects upon taking the oaths of supremacy and allegiance.

Jews and the Act of 1740.

Two Sections of the Naturalisation Act of 1740 dealt specifically with the case of Jews. In Section II., "such who profess the Jewish religion" were exempted from the necessity of receiving the sacrament as a preliminary to the act of naturalisation. In Section III. the same persons were allowed to omit the phrase "upon the true faith of a Christian" when taking the oath of abjuration. Beyond those immediately affected by it the measure aroused little interest, and for thirteen years its working proved as smooth as its passage had been. Nearly two hundred Jews, the majority of them residents in Jamaica, took advantage of the Act and became English citizens. A similar Bill was introduced into the Irish Parliament in 1745, and passed through the Lower House. It was, however, rejected by the Peers in 1746, and again on its re-introduction in 1747, and ultimately it was dropped. An effort made to establish a Jewish theological seminary also failed. By the terms of the will of a rich member of the

Judaism and the Law.

community, Elias de Paz, £1200 was set aside for the maintenance of a "Yesiba," or assembly for daily reading the Jewish law, and for advancing and propagating Judaism. The bequest was brought under the notice of the courts in 1744, and Lord Hardwicke, the Chancellor, decided that the legacy was invalid, on the ground that it was intended for superstitious purposes. The king, on petition, ordered that £1000 of the amount be paid to the governor of the Foundling Hospital, for the purposes of assist- ing to support a preacher and to instruct the children under his care in the Christian religion. The balance of the money, if it represented more than the law expenses, was probably devoted to a similar purpose. The judgment in this case was followed in 1786 in that of *Isaac* v. *Gompertz*, when a legacy of £40 per annum, for the support and maintenance of the syna- gogue in Magpye Alley, was similarly disallowed.

The absence of all opposition to the Act of 1740 probably emboldened the Whig Government to take a further step in the direction of Jewish emancipa- tion, and, no doubt, in this determination they were strengthened by a feeling of gratitude for the great services rendered by English Jews to the State in the critical period that succeeded the adoption of that measure. In 1753, therefore, the Duke of Newcastle, on behalf of the Government of his brother, Mr. Pel- ham, introduced a Bill into the House of Lords " to permit persons professing the Jewish religion to be naturalised by Parliament." The measure in reality proposed to do much less than its predecessor of 1740. Under the latter, Jews could become English subjects merely by taking the necessary oaths before some local official. The Bill of 1753 proposed to render Jews resident in England qualified for natural- isation by special Act of Parliament. The Government in its action had the support of a number of mer- chants, manufacturers, commanders of vessels, and others, who in their petitions in its favour argued that the passage of the measure would benefit English trade, in which Jews had for many years been deeply interested. It was suggested that the adoption of the measure would encourage rich foreigners to settle in the kingdom, and that the new-comers would set a laudable example of industry, temperance, and frugality. The Lord Mayor and City Corporation, however, held different views. They also petitioned Parliament, and opposed the Bill on the ground that it would tend greatly to the dishonour of the Christian religion, endanger the Constitution of the realm, and be highly prejudicial to the interest and trade of the kingdom in general and of the capital in particular. These views were supported in other petitions by merchants and traders.

The Bill in the Commons.

Before these petitions had been presented, the Bill had passed through the House of Lords without any serious opposition, and had been introduced into the Lower Chamber. There it was met by a storm of hostility. The source of this opposition was for the most part political, and it was intensified by the imminence of a General Election. The Tory party, believing that by playing upon the prejudices of the populace it would render easier the defeat of the Government at the polls, adopted anti-Semitism in all its extravagances. In the Commons a leading part in the opposition to the measure was taken by Sir John Barnard, one of the members for the City, a private enemy of Sampson Gideon. Counsel were heard on both sides of the question, and witnesses examined.

Violent debates.

The debates were violent, the speeches embittered, and the pamphlets, which outnumbered them, more so. It was argued that the proposed naturalisation would deluge the country with brokers, usurers, and beggars ; that the rich Jews would purchase lands and even advowsons, and thus not only acquire an interest in the Legislature, but also influence the constitution of the Church, of which they were inveterate enemies ; that the poorer Jews would oust the natives from their employment, and, by the exercise of extreme frugality, under-sell them ; that the adoption of vagrant Jews into the community would rob the natives of their birthright, disgrace the character of the nation, endanger the Constitution both in Church and State, and be an indelible reproach on the established Church of the country. The Jews would multiply to such an extent, would acquire so much wealth and consequently also power and influence, that their persons would be revered, their customs imitated. In short, Judaism would become the fashionable religion of the land. Moreover, the proposed legislation would be a direct contravention of that prophecy which declared that the Jews should be a scattered people, without country or fixed habitation. The Bill was an unchristian one, and as a distinct abandonment of Christianity would draw upon England all the curses that Providence had attached to the Jews. The House was reminded that after four hundred and thirty years the Jews in Egypt had mustered 600,000 armed men, and that, according to the Book of Esther, when they gained the upper hand in the land of their sojourn, they had "put to death in two days 76,000 of those whom they were pleased to call their enemies, without either judge or jury." The possibility of a repetition of this exploit in England was hinted at. From the House the agitation spread to the streets. The question of the advisability of permitting Jews to apply for naturalisation monopolised the public mind. The old story of the crucifixion of children by Jews was revived. The Bishops who had voted for the measure were libelled and insulted in the streets. Despite all opposition, however, the Government persevered with the measure, which in due course passed through the House of Commons and received the royal assent.

The agitation did not cease with the passage of the Bill. On the contrary, it seemed to grow in volume. During the recess the opposition became almost more violent than it had been during the session. Petitions were widely signed for the repeal of the obnoxious

Public dislike of the measure. measure; effigies of Jews were carried about the streets ; and the walls were placarded with the legend, "No Jews, no wooden shoes." It is not certain whether the latter portion of the popular cry expressed hostility to the foreign Protestants, especially Huguenots, whom the Government had endeavoured, without success, to naturalise in 1751, or whether it was merely added to the cry for the purpose of euphony. The storm was too powerful for a Government on the eve of an election to withstand. When Parliament re-assembled no time was lost in re-opening the question. The moment that the reply to the Address had been agreed to in the Upper House, the Duke of Newcastle introduced a measure to repeal the Act of the preceding session. In explaining his motion, the Duke said that the disaffected had made a handle of the Act to raise discontent among many of his Majesty's good subjects, and, as the Act was of itself of little importance, he was of opinion that it ought to be repealed. This new Bill passed through the House Action of the House of Lords. with little discussion. The Act of 1753 had contained a clause disabling all naturalised Jews from purchasing, inheriting, or receiving any advowson or presentation or right to any ecclesiastical benefice or promotion, school, hospital, or donative. It was intended not to repeal this section by the new measure, but the majority feared lest the clause, if unrepealed, might suggest that the Jews, by being expressly excluded from the possession of any ecclesiastical right of presentation, had the power and privilege of purchasing and inheriting any lay property in the kingdom. These views prevailed, and the clause was sacrificed, together with the remainder of the measure.

The Lower House was even more urgent for the repeal of the Act than the Peers. On the first day of the session, before the motion for the Address had been adopted, Sir James Dashwood, one of the leaders of the Opposition, gave notice that he would make a motion of very great importance at the very first opportunity. As soon as that arrived, Dashwood, after referring to the just and general indignation that the Act of the previous session had aroused among the people, moved that the House be called together on the fourth of December to take the Act into consideration. The motion was seconded by Lord Parker, a member of the other party, and agreed to without opposition. Meanwhile the Bill that had been introduced into the Peers had passed through that chamber, and had come down to the Lower House. On the whole its terms suited the Commons. Exception, however, was taken to the preamble, which recited that "Whereas an Act of Parliament was made and passed in the twenty-fifth year of his Majesty's reign, intituled, An Act to permit persons professing the Jewish religion to be naturalized by Parliament, and for other purposes therein mentioned: And whereas occasion has been taken, from the said act, to raise discontents and disquiets in the minds of his Majesty's subjects, be it enacted," &c. The wording of the preamble was considered by the Opposition an unjust reflection on the body of the people in general and on the Parliamentary opponents of the measure in particular. Sir Roger Newdigate proposed as an amended form " Whereas great discontents and disquietudes had from the said Act arisen." A long discussion ensued, in the course of which the amendment was opposed by Mr. Pelham and Mr. Pitt, and defeated, whereupon the measure was adopted *nemine contradicente*, and in due course received the royal assent.

The opponents of Jewish naturalisation were, however, not yet satisfied. The Act of 1740 still remained on the statute book. A return of those Jews who had

obtained naturalisation under the Act was called for
and presented to the House. A motion was then proposed by Lord Harley and seconded by Sir James
Dashwood, to the effect that so much of the Act of
1740 as related to persons professing the Jewish
religion, who should settle in a British colony should
be repealed. The motion was opposed by Mr. Pelham
and Mr. Pitt and rejected.

The agitation and Sampson Gideon.

This unsuccessful attempt at Jewish emancipation
had one peculiar personal result. Among the prime
engineers of the movement was Sampson Gideon.
The indebtedness, not merely in a financial sense, of
the country to him was doubtless one of the principal
reasons, if not the only one, for the Government policy,
and, on the other hand, the rivalry of commercial
competitors was among the causes of the embittered
opposition to the Government's proposals. Gideon's
overpowering ambition was to take his place among
the landed gentry of the country, a position he was
well qualified to occupy by his wealth, his influence,
and his services. Despite decisions of counsel already
noted, there was still considerable doubt whether
Judaism did not debar its professors from holding
land in England. The balance of opinion was at
that time opposed to the Jewish claims, and in this
view Gideon concurred. His influence with Walpole
had been sufficient to induce that statesman to obtain
an Act of Parliament enabling Gideon, although a
Jew, to hold estates, but the disabilities under which
Jews laboured still proved a bar to the full attainment of the ambition of Gideon, who felt that his
status was inferior to that of those among whom
he moved. If the legislation of 1753 had remained
undisturbed Gideon's troubles would have disappeared, and he could, while still a member of the
Jewish community, have gratified his ambition in
full. The unsuccessful conclusion of the campaign

seems, however, to have assured him that his ambition and his faith were irreconcilable. One had to be sacrificed, and the latter was chosen as the victim. Gideon had already married a Christian lady, and their children were brought up in her faith ; and their eldest son was, at the age of fifteen, created a baronet. In 1754 Gideon, who had gradually abandoned the deep interest in communal affairs he had previously held, resigned his membership of the synagogue. Gideon, however, continued a Jew, albeit a secret one. On his death in 1763 it was found that he had *Death of Gideon. His will.* left a legacy of £1000 to his old community, with a request that he should be buried in their cemetery as an ordinary member of the congregation. It was announced that for the previous ten years since his resignation, Gideon had continued anonymously to subscribe to the funds of the community. The request was granted, and in accordance with the terms of the will, on the evening of the Day of Atonement every year, the congregation in Bevis Marks is still reminded of the memory of Sampson de Rehuel Abudiente.

The year of the Naturalisation Controversy was witness to the adoption of another measure that finally established the legality of Jewish marriages, *Jewish marriages.* on which hitherto a considerable amount of doubt had rested. The marriage law of the country as a whole was in a very unsatisfactory condition when Lord Chancellor Hardwicke turned his attention to it. His Marriage Act of 1753 rectified many abuses, and enacted among other provisions that, with the exception of Jewish and Quaker marriages, no marriage should be valid in England which was not celebrated by a priest in orders, after due notice, or unless a license had previously been procured. By this measure a privilege was conferred on the Jewish population that was withheld from the Catholics and the bulk of the Nonconformists.

AUTHORITIES :—J. Picciotto, "Sketches"; P. C. Webb, "The Question," &c.; H. S. Q. Henriques, "Jews and the English Law" (*Jewish Quarterly Review*, vols. xii.-xiv.); T. G. Smollett, "The History of England," vol. iii. (1790); W. E. H. Lecky, "History of England in the Eighteenth Century," vol. i. (1883); A. M. Hyamson, "The Jew Bill of 1753" (*Jewish Chronicle*, April 6, 1906); M. Margoliouth, "The History of the Jews in Great Britain," vol. ii. (1857); The Hon. S. W. Rosendale, "An Act allowing Naturalisation of Jews in the Colonies" (*Transactions of the Jewish Historical Society of America*, vol. i., 1893); "Dictionary of National Biography"; "Jewish Encyclopedia."

CHAPTER XXIX

THE SEPHARDIM

(1699–1784)

The Bevis Marks Synagogue, 1702.

THE first year of Haham Nieto's residence in England was signalised by a movement for the further enlargement of the synagogue. The building, constructed twenty-two years earlier, had already proved insufficient, and a pressing necessity for more accommodation showed itself. On the 12th of January 1699, Antonio Gomez Serra, Menasseh Mendes, Alfonso Rodriguez, Manuel Nunes Miranda, Andrea Lopez, and Pantaleao Rodriguez signed a contract with Joseph Avis for the new building. The price agreed upon was £2750, but on the completion of the structure, Avis, who was a Quaker, returned the profit, as he was unwilling to obtain any pecuniary benefit from so sacred a labour. The new building was consecrated in 1702. Many of the benches were brought from the old synagogue and some of the candlesticks from Holland. A beam was presented to the congregation by Queen Anne.

The troubles of Haham Nieto.

The early years of Haham Nieto's ministrations were not untroubled. Exception was taken to a sermon preached by him in November 1703 on the ground of its alleged tendency towards Spinozism. A protest was made against it to the Mahamad by Jehosuah Zarfatti, and the Haham, as a portion of his reply, wrote his treatise on the Divine Providence. But this publication did not close the controversy, and the subject of dispute was referred to the Beth Din of Amsterdam for decision. The hostile faction in

London, however, had already gained over the authorities in Amsterdam. These latter made conditions which the Mahamad considered inadmissible, and, objecting to what they described as the personal motives and considerations that influenced the Beth Din of Amsterdam, the Mahamad of London decided in the future never to appeal on any question whatever to that body or to have any further communication with its members. This action still further embittered the dispute in London. Zarfatti had already been excommunicated. The next step was to exclude the reputed authors of the " libel " from the synagogue and to threaten them also with excommunication. The pamphlet, of which complaint had been made, had been issued anonymously, but when this last decision of the Mahamad was published, thirteen members of the congregation sent a joint letter protesting against the action of the Mahamad and their description of the pamphlet. They contended that it had been written in the interests of their religion. The Mahamad stood by their decision, and were supported by the great bulk of the congregation, including all the scholars it contained. At the instance of the Haham a truce was arranged over the High Festivals, and the offenders were re-admitted to the synagogue. The mutual approach on this occasion led to the arrangement of a *modus vivendi.* The dispute was referred to the Beth Din of the Spanish community of Hamburg, but no decision could be obtained from that source, as the office of Haham was vacant. The spiritual head of the neighbouring Sephardi community of Altona, however, was Haham Zevi Ashkenazi, and to him the Mahamad turned, and by him a reconciliation was effected.

Haham Nieto died at the beginning of 1728. The twenty-eight years that he had spent in England were full of activities, ministerial, communal, and literary.

These last covered a wide range. In Italian, Spanish, David Nieto's works.
Hebrew, and Portuguese, Nieto's pen was equally
fluent. Philosophical and theological treatises,
Hebrew poems, scientific works, sermons and historical inquiries were all included in the bibliography
of his works. In addition, he was engaged on a
Talmudical concordance which was never completed.
Nieto's scholarship was profound, his interests wide,
his intellect keen in the advancement of freedom and
liberty. He was not afraid to expose the weak points
in the Greek Calendar nor to turn the light upon the
horrors of the Inquisition. Neither mystical hallucina-
tion, self-deception, nor the enslaving of the mind
would he tolerate. Wherever his teachings reached
they succeeded in checking Karaism, in destroying
Sabbathaism, and in strengthening the faith in Jewish
tradition.

Magnetically, Nieto attracted around himself a circle Anglo-Jewish scholars.
of Jewish scholars. Dr. Jacob de Castro Sarmento, a
native of Portugal, studied Greek philosophy at Evora
and medicine at Coimbra. Driven from his native
land by the Inquisition, he came to England in 1720.
He was admitted a Licentiate of the College of
Physicians in 1725, and a Fellow of the Royal Society
five years later. In 1739 the degree of M.D. was Dr. Sarmento.
conferred upon Sarmento by the University of Aberdeen. His first publication was a funeral oration
in Portuguese on his friend the Haham. He also
wrote several volumes on medical subjects and moral
meditations for the Day of Atonement. In another
publication Sarmento dealt with the story of Mordecai, Esther, and Haman.

Daniel Israel Lopez Laguna, also a fugitive from Daniel Laguna.
the Inquisition in Portugal, came to London *via*
Jamaica. He brought with him a versified translation
of the Psalms. In London he found a patron in
Mordecai Nunes Almeyda, a man of literary tastes and

Laguna's
Psalms.

a member of a cultured and intellectual family. The book was published in 1720, accompanied, as was the custom in literary circles at the time, by recommendations in prose and verse by fellow-scholars. The list of recommendations of this description contained in the volume shows the extent of the scholarship of the Anglo-Jewish community in the second decade of the eighteenth century. Laguna's volume had no less than twenty-two such introductions, three of them written by ladies, Sara de Fonseca Pina y Pimentel, Manuela Nunes de Almeida, and Bienvenida Cohen Belmonte. The other contributors included Haham Nieto, Rabbi Joseph Abendanon, Dr. Isaac de Sequeira Samuda, and Sampson Gideon. In the polemical discussions that were then raging throughout Jewry, London became the centre of publication, and from that city went forth the repeated blows that assisted in demolishing the last vestiges of Sabbathaism.

Prosperity of
the community.

In these years the community flourished not only intellectually, but in other respects also. Its membership, its prosperity, and that of the members all increased. But as the years succeeded one another the separation between Sephardim and Ashkenazim became more acute. As a symptom of the attitude of the Portuguese to the Germans even during the lifetime of Haham Nieto, it is recorded that on one occasion the Yehidim of the congregation were convened in order to instruct the Mahamad to inflict punishment on a member who had committed the repeated offence of attending the services of the other community.

Isaac Nieto
appointed
Haham.

The office of Haham was left vacant for five years after the death of David Nieto, until in 1733 his son Isaac Nieto (1702–74) was appointed to succeed him. Less accomplished than his father, he was yet worthy to fill the high office he held, but his tenure did not last for long. In 1741 Isaac Nieto resigned the office and went abroad, and a successor was found in Haham Mosshe Gomes de Mesquita (1688–1751), who was already in his fifty-eighth year. Mesquita lived a further seven years and then died. Two of the orations at his funeral were delivered by the Ashkenazi Rabbi Hart and Mesquita's predecessor in office, Isaac Nieto.

Haham Mesquita.

The number of charitable institutions established by the Spanish and Portuguese Jews of London received from time to time frequent additions. Besides the two already mentioned, an orphan asylum, "The Gates of Light and the Father of the Fatherless," was founded in 1703. In 1724 a society was established for providing fatherless girls with dowries and for other charitable objects. Six years later Isaac da Costa Villareal devoted a sum of money to the foundation of an educational institution. The poorer girls of the congregation had always kindly thought and consideration from their more opulent fellow-Jewesses. Six years after the foundation of the Villareal school yet another society for providing dowries was established. In 1747 the Beth Holim was instituted. This charity combined the offices of a hospital, lying-in hospital, and home for aged poor. Two years later a charitable society with multifarious objects, the *Mahasim Tobim*, came into existence. A rather long term of years passed away before the establishment of the next Sephardi charity, one for the distribution of bread. This work was initiated in 1778. The community, however, did not confine its good deeds to its own members. Jewish settlers in other parts of the country were assisted by it to form congregations, and a cemetery was acquired for the Dublin congregation in 1748 by the munificence of the Spanish and Portuguese community in London.

Charitable institutions.

The Mahamad and the community.   Throughout the eighteenth century the Mahamad continued to hold a very strict control over all the doings of the members. Their financial transactions were subject to very close supervision, betting was prohibited, all interference in Parliamentary and municipal elections was forbidden. The congregation during these years occasionally produced a member whose fame or notoriety spread beyond its narrow limits and attracted attention in spheres other than those of Jewry. Emanuel Mendez da Costa (1717–1791) was known as a scientist, philosopher, and author, in all the cultured circles in London. He was a Fellow and Secretary of the Royal Society and of the Society of Antiquaries, and a member of several other scientific associations, English and foreign. A relative of his, Benjamin Mendez da Costa (1704–1764), was famous for his charity, which knew neither race nor faith. A person of a far different description was the eccentric and miser, Ephraim Lopez Pereira, Baron d'Aguilar (1739–1802), who married a member of the Mendez da Costa family.

On the death of Haham Mesquita, Isaac Nieto again became the spiritual head of the congregation, but with the title öf Ab-beth-din, instead of the more important one of Haham. He retained the office for only five years, and then again retired. This resignation was due to dissensions, which were increased by it. Nieto seems to have objected to the appointment of one of his pupils, Moses Cohen d'Azavedo (d. 1784), a son-in-law of the late Haham Mesquita, as Dayan.[1] Nieto from his retirement protested against the actions of the new Beth Din,[2] and declared that it was sanctioning the consumption of "terefah"[3] meat. An endeavour was made to

Dissensions.

---

[1] Ecclesiastical judge.   [2] Ecclesiastical court.
[3] Forbidden by Jewish law.

meet the wishes of the ex-Haham, but it failed, and for a time there was danger of a secession from the parent community.

The policy of the congregation, to take no part in State affairs, suffered a change towards the middle of the eighteenth century. The Jewish question was then becoming a matter of practical politics in England, and in 1746 a Committee of Diligence, consisting of Benjamin Mendez da Costa as President, Daniel J. Rodriguez, Jacob Fernandez Nunes, Jacob de Moses Franco, and Jacob Moses Pacheco, was formed, to watch the interests of the Jews of Great Britain and Ireland. The committee was only of a temporary nature and was soon dissolved, but it proved the forerunner of a permanent body, in which both branches of English Jewry were ultimately represented, for the Board of Deputies commenced its career fourteen years later. Before the admission of the representatives of the German congregations, however, the duty fell to the " Deputies of the Portuguese Nation " to present an address to George III. on the occasion of his accession. *A forerunner of the Board of Deputies.*

The sequel to the appointment of D'Azavedo as Dayan, feared by Isaac Nieto, occurred in 1761. In that year Moses Cohen d'Azavedo was appointed to the office of Haham, vacant since the death of his father-in-law ten years earlier. Without delay Nieto protested against the appointment, and as his influence and the respect in which he was held were considerable, it was determined to delay the completion of the appointment until the opinion of the Beth Din of Amsterdam had been obtained on the candidate's qualifications. The decision controverted all the objections raised by Nieto, and D'Azavedo was accordingly given the office that his critic had formerly held, and retained it until his death in 1784. Nieto survived this defeat twelve years, and died in *D'Azavedo appointed Haham.*

1773. His last years were devoted to a translation into Spanish of the Sephardi ritual. The first volume of this work was published in 1740; the last shortly before his death. In so scholarly a manner did Nieto perform this task that no later translation into any language has surpassed it in accuracy or elegance of style.

Sephardim and Ashkenazim.

Before Nieto's death the breach between the Portuguese and German communities, so far as intermarriage was concerned, which had ever been growing wider, seemed to have become impassable. Until the middle of the eighteenth century the attitude of the heads of the Sephardi community towards such marriages, although by no means encouraging, was not determinedly hostile. By 1745, however, a change had come over their policy in that respect. In that year the treasurer of the congregation, Jacob Israel Bernal, suddenly resigned his office without apparent cause, and shortly afterwards applied for permission to contract a marriage with a member of the German community. The matter was referred to the elders, who, after due deliberation, gave permission for the marriage, but, in order to discourage imitators, laid down conditions that were almost humiliating. In consequence of his marriage Mr. Bernal no longer took a leading part in the affairs of the congregation, and his descendants ultimately left the community.[1] By 1772 the regulations of the congregation regarding marriage had become even more stringent. In that year Asser del Banco was peremptorily refused permission to marry a Tudesca,[2] the Mahamad not troubling to furnish any explanation of their decision.

Relations with foreign communities.

The congregation, being one of the most important in Europe, was the recipient of frequent applications

[1] They included Mr. Ralph Bernal, M.P., and Mr. Bernal Osborne, M.P.
[2] An Ashkenazi Jewess.

for assistance. Loans, a portion of which was never Aid to foreign repaid, were made to the community of Venice, and Jews. financial assistance rendered to the Jews of the Holy Land, Persia, Bohemia, and other countries. The influence of the community was used to relieve their co-religionists in Jamaica from the burden of oppressive taxation, and when disputes arose among the Jewish settlers in Barbadoes they were referred to London for settlement. Applications also came from the United States and the colonies for the supply of readers and ministers, and the Bevis Marks synagogue always did its best to fill the appointments. Another good work performed by the congregation Ransom of was the ransom of Jewish captives in foreign lands, captives. and a special office, that of Warden of Captives, was created to deal with all appertaining to that subject. In 1772 a difference arose between the synagogue authorities and the City as represented by the Lord Mayor. The latter issued instructions to the heads of the Sephardi community to render assistance to one of their members, an incorrigible, who was without visible means of support. The opinions of some of the leading lawyers of the day were obtained, and they were to the effect that the Jews could not be compelled to provide for their own poor. Five years later the synagogue successfully surmounted another trouble. An attempt was made to impose church rates upon it, but the imposition was resisted and the attempt failed.

But the high-water mark in the communal affairs The ebb of had been reached, and the prosperity of the com- prosperity. munity was gradually ebbing. Dissensions broke out and were with difficulty composed. Secession after secession took place, and the community suffered a continual drain of some of its best blood. Sampson Gideon, the Pereira Lopezs, the Francos, the Ximenes were drawn away by ambition. The

Bernals left for probably the same reason. David Ricardo was converted to Christianity. His brothers at the time remained in the fold. Nevertheless most of their descendants are now outside. The Furtados withdrew because the ritual was not sufficiently orthodox. They also lie buried within the shadow of the Church. Among those who remained a continually increasing disinclination to hold honorary office in the community was displayed. So widespread became this tendency that before the end of the eighteenth century a number of public-spirited members undertook to accept any office that might be conferred upon them owing to refusal by other members. The Ascamoth were revised in 1784, but the revision only served to render the new regulations more narrow and tyrannical. In these circumstances it is not surprising that relations between Ashkenazim and Sephardim became strained.

The founders of the London community of Spanish and Portuguese Jews were almost without exception either Marranos coming direct from the Peninsula or the descendants of Marranos who had fled to Holland, Hamburg, Italy, or America. In course of time the number of Marranos dwindled, the descendants of the original *nuevos Christianos* merging with the surrounding population. The supply of recruits from this source grew more feeble and still more feeble, but even before it had entirely ceased their place was taken by descendants of those who had fled in the first instance from before the Inquisition, and had settled on the shores of the Mediterranean, and by others only connected with the Sephardim through the similarity of their *Minhagim*.[1] This new source of immigration caused differences insensibly to grow up in the congregation. The older settlers began to discriminate against

[1] Rituals and customs.

the new-comers. The Berberiskos and Italianos were grouped with the Tudeskos and Polaccos. They were equally considered Foresteiros, and as such at first denied and afterwards only grudgingly admitted to the full privileges of the community. The siege of Gibraltar in 1781 furnished an appreciable addition to this element in the Anglo-Jewish population. Jews, coming for the most part from Morocco, had settled in that fortress on its annexation by the English in 1704, and had gradually formed a considerable community there. During the privations of the lengthy siege, several shiploads of Jews managed to escape and to reach England, where they settled.

Gibraltar Jews settle in England.

AUTHORITIES :—M. Gaster, " History of the Ancient Synagogue," " Presidential Address delivered before the Jewish Historical Society" (*Jewish Chronicle*, 23rd Nov. 1906); J. Picciotto, "Sketches of Anglo-Jewish History"; "Dictionary of National Biography"; "Jewish Encyclopedia."

CHAPTER XXX

THE ASHKENAZIM
(1765-1797)

Appointment of R. Tewele Schiff. ON the resignation by Rabbi Hart Lyon (Zevi Hirsch) of the rabbinate of the Great Synagogue, Rabbi David Tewele Schiff of Frankfort-on-Main was appointed his successor. He came to London in 1765, and shortly after his arrival assisted at the re-opening of the synagogue which had been rebuilt and enlarged in order to afford accommodation for a congregation that was continually growing. The membership of the congregation, however, although it increased in numbers did not proportionately become wealthier. On the other hand, the great bulk of the new members came from the poorest classes in the community, and the congregation in its corporate capacity had for a long term of its existence an arduous struggle to preserve itself. In these circumstances a legacy of £3500, left to the synagogue in 1769 by Lazarus Simon, one of its oldest members, must have been especially welcome. The whole of that amount was not to be devoted to general purposes, but as at that period the synagogue was not merely a house of prayer but also a centre of communal life in all its branches, no matter to what specific communal objects the legacy was devoted, the funds of the congregation were none the less relieved. Of the legacy of Lazarus Simon, the interest on £1000 was to be applied to clothing and providing doles for six destitute men and the same number of destitute women, while the interest on a similar amount was to be

handed half-yearly to the overseers of the poor, fourteen days before the holy-days. At a later date it was
decided to confine the benefits of the first trust to
needy members of the congregation and their widows.
This decision was doubtless due to the pressure of
alien immigration and the alarming increase in the
numbers of the Jewish poor solely dependent for
relief on the synagogues and a few rich members.
This pressure on the synagogue finances was so heavy
that in 1772 the very serious step of mortgaging the *The synagogue*
synagogue buildings was decided upon. The amount *mortgaged.*
raised was small, only £1700, of which £1300 was
due to the builder. The synagogue had been already
greatly indebted to Mrs. Judith Levy (1706–1803),
daughter of Moses Hart, the founder of the congregation, and possibly a sense of this indebtedness
prevented the governing body of the synagogue from
informing her of their trouble. Judith Levy, who was *Judith Levy.*
married to a son of Benjamin Levy, survived her
husband fifty-three years. Her two children long
predeceased her, the son in childhood, the daughter
on the morning of her wedding-day. Judith Levy
removed to the far west of the metropolis, and divided
the remainder of her long life between communal
benefactions and intercourse with the fashionable
world. In society she was known as "The Queen
of Richmond Green," her country house being in
that locality. When Judith Levy heard that money
had been borrowed she expressed some annoyance.
At a subsequent date she gave another considerable
amount to the congregation, and chiefly through her
instrumentality the community was enabled to erect
a new and larger building in Duke's Place in 1790.

The causes of the continued and increasing migra- *The causes of*
tion of foreign Jews to England were several. To *immigration.*
those who were, for the moment, comparatively free
from persecution although burdened by oppressive

The attraction
to England.
disabilities, England appeared as the land of freedom, wherein, to the Jew, there were no restrictions of domicile nor other interference with his private affairs. To the ambitious among younger Jewry, therefore, England appeared almost as El Dorado. The history of the Jews of the Continent in their relations with the other peoples was, however, by no means without incident, and every one of the disturbances that from time to time convulsed Europe during the eighteenth century reacted with twofold force on the Jewish communities within its area. The war that culminated in the partition of Poland in 1772 added considerably to the burdens of the London Jewish community. The inroad of poverty-stricken immigrants became so considerable that in 1771 the Wardens of the Great Synagogue took steps to discourage further immigration by refusing relief to foreign Jews "who had left their country without good cause." This decision effected no improvement in the state of the community. In fact, it continued to get worse until a culmination was reached the same year, when a group of Jewish malefactors was found

Immigration
troubles.
Restriction
advocated.
guilty of serious offences, and an agitation was set on foot against alien Jewish settlers. The Home Office remonstrated with the synagogue, and the authorities of the latter replied that the migration was due to the disturbed condition of Poland and to the fault of the Government in not restricting immigration. The synagogue appealed to the Government to adopt the policy of restriction, and, in consequence of the Jews' representations, instructions were issued to prevent for the future the settlement in the country of Jews, unless they possessed passports and had paid their full passage money—many foreign immigrants at that time were able to obtain considerable deductions from the ordinary passengers' charges. At the same time the Lord Mayor offered to pay the expenses to

the coast of any foreign-born Jews wishing to return
to the country of their birth.

There was then no organised system of poor relief Ashkenazi
in existence in the Ashkenazi community. The only charities.
charities beyond those of the synagogues were the
Berith (Circumcision Society), an association for clothing orphan children, and the *Talmud Torah*, afterwards
the Jews' Free School. The great distress prevalent
in the country towards the end of the eighteenth
century fell especially on the Jews of London, with
their largely disproportionate number of poor. The
Sephardim met the increased burden by establishing
the society "That giveth Bread to the Hungry." The
Ashkenazim were not long in following the example
set by their brethren of Bevis Marks, and in 1779 the
Meshebat Nephesh, a society for the distribution of The *Meshebat*
bread, meat, and coal among the poor, the first *Nephesh.*
Ashkenazi charity of importance was established.
Its first president and one of its founders was Levi
Barent Cohen, the founder of a family from his time Levi Barent
prominent in communal affairs, and the father-in-law Cohen.
of Sir Moses Montefiore and Nathan Mayer Rothschild.
Cohen was a leading member of the Ashkenazi community, and devoted himself with unsparing zeal to
the benefit of his less favourably situated co-religionists.
A few years later a Jewish soup kitchen was also
instituted in London.

In 1788 Jews were brought into prominence in the A *Shechita*
Courts of Law by an action for libel undertaken in libel action.
consequence of a decision of the Sephardi Beth Din
on a question of *Shechita*.[1] A Jew named Levy
reported to that authority that one of its licensed
butchers, Rodriguez, was in the habit of selling meat
unauthorised for consumption by Jews. The case was
investigated, and the Beth Din being satisfied of the
truth of the charge, Rodriguez was deprived of his

[1] The ritual slaughtering of cattle for purposes of food.

licence. This decision was, in the ordinary course, published from the synagogue pulpit, and members of the community were forbidden to purchase meat of the delinquent. Rodriguez thereupon brought an action for libel against Levy and claimed heavy damages. The case was heard in the Court of Common Pleas and decided in favour of Levy, the action of the Beth Din being justified on a second occasion also when a motion was made for a new trial.

This question of *Shechita* engaged the earnest consideration of the synagogue authorities on several occasions. The first proposal for joint action by the London congregations for the supply of meat for consumption by Jews was made in 1792, when a meeting was held of representatives of the three Ashkenazi synagogues. At that meeting, at the suggestion of Mr. L. de Symons, a scheme was drafted for the formation of a Joint Board, to deal with all matters arising out of the subject, on which all the London congregations were to have been represented, and also for the construction of a central hall for the sale of meat. The plan, with details, was submitted to the Sephardi authorities, who, it was contended, would benefit considerably by giving their adhesion. The Sephardim raised great objections to the establishment of a central hall, but expressed their willingness to join the other congregations on the proposed board. The Ashkenazim, however, were unwilling to sacrifice any part of their scheme, and contended that the several portions were inseparable. The three Ashkenazi synagogues, it was stated in the course of the correspondence that ensued, had determined to establish the hall, and the Sephardim could join them whenever they desired. Bevis Marks, on its part, replied that it had already undertaken to re-organise its own *Shechita*, and saw no reason for altering the decision regarding the hall at which it had already arrived. A subscription was set on foot among the Ashkenazim for the purpose of establishing a hall, but it met with little success. A further attempt was made the following year, but funds sufficient for the adoption of the scheme were never obtained. With the disappearance of the proposal there also passed away that for the establishment of a Joint Board, and it was not until more than a decade later that the Board of Shechita was established.

Two years later, however, in 1794, an agreement was arrived at between the Ashkenazi congregations for the relief of the unattached poor. As has already been pointed out, the pressure on the congregations of the burden of the foreign poor was heavy, but the synagogue authorities strove bravely to support it. An arrangement existed for the division of the burden between the three Ashkenazi synagogues and was generally observed. Occasionally, however, misunderstandings and disputes arose, and this was especially the case when some poor alien had to be buried. On more than one occasion the Mahamad had to be called in to arbitrate between the dissentient synagogues. It was in consequence of one of these disputes and its subsequent settlement by the Mahamad that in 1794 the Hambro Synagogue undertook to pay £50 for six months to the Duke's Place Synagogue on condition that the latter relieved it of its burden of the foreign poor during that period. The Mahamad was to decide whether this amount was to be increased for future periods. In the same year the four city synagogues combined for the purpose of arranging for the supply of the necessary Passover cakes.

Co-operation of the Ashkenazim for the relief of the poor.

After twenty-seven years' service Rabbi Tewele Schiff died in 1792, and his funeral was conducted with marked honours. The office of Rabbi of the Great Synagogue was not filled for several years,

Co-operation of the New with the Great Synagogue. although candidates were invited in 1794. The delay in the appointment was due to financial causes. Meanwhile the Great Synagogue availed itself of the services of Rabbi Moses Myers of the New Synagogue, which were freely placed at its disposal. The feud that had raged so fiercely on the occasion of the establishment of this seceding congregation in 1761 had by this time been completely healed, and the courtesy displayed by the New Synagogue on this occasion was but a symptom of the state of affairs that now ruled.

A self-denying ordinance. The year 1794 was signalised in the history of the Duke's Place Synagogue by a remarkable undertaking on the part of a number of its members not to withdraw from the congregation under a penalty of forfeiting a hundred pounds. It was possibly feared that the numerous important secessions which were at the time severely affecting the Sephardi community might induce similar withdrawals among the Ashkenazim, and to counteract any such tendency this undertaking was offered. The policy of the Ashkenazim differed widely from that of the Sephardim in regard to the establishment of new synagogues. The first of the Ascamoth still rendered members of the Sephardi community subject to severe penalties for conducting service within a radius of four miles of Bevis Marks. The Ashkenazi authorities, on the other hand, now readily granted permission to small congregations of Jews to meet *A Polish synagogue founded.* for prayers, and a small Polish synagogue was built near Cutler Street, Houndsditch. The growth of the community necessitated the supply of further synagogue accommodation. The cemetery that had been in use by the Great Synagogue was gradually becoming filled, and in 1795, mainly through the instrumentality of the brothers Abraham and Asher Goldsmid, another piece of land was purchased for a similar purpose. Services had been held for many years in the private house of Baron de Symons of The Western Bedford Row, since his arrival from St. Petersburg in Synagogue. 1768. On his death those who had grown accustomed to meet in his house determined to establish a small synagogue. At first rooms were taken in Bedford Row, but the congregation soon removed to Denmark Court, Strand, where a synagogue was established in 1797. The congregation removed some years later to St. James's Place, Haymarket. The founders of the new synagogue received every display of sympathy from the authorities of the city synagogues, and an agreement was made between the new community and its older colleagues for burial and other purposes.

AUTHORITIES :—Lucien Wolf, "The N'vei Tzedek"; Benjamin Levy, "The *Meshebat Nephesh*" (1879); H. Adler, "The Chief Rabbis of England"; J. Picciotto, "Sketches of Anglo-Jewish History"; Matthias Levy, "The Western Synagogue" (1897), "MS. Records of the Great Synagogue," "Jewish Board of Guardians Report (1859)."

CHAPTER XXXI

THE OPENING OF THE NINETEENTH CENTURY

(1792–1824)

AT the opening of the nineteenth century, according to the authority of Mr. Patrick Colquhoun, the magistrate, the Jewish population of London amounted to 20,000, and various provincial centres held five or six thousand Jews in addition. Those in London worshipped in six synagogues. In the provinces twenty were to be found. Another writer of the period, W. de Archenholtz, drew a very sharp distinction between the Sephardim and Ashkenazim of London. " Dress, language, manners, cleanliness, politeness, everything distinguishes them, much to the advantage of the former, who have little to distinguish them from Christians. The difference is discernible even in their public worship and prejudices ; the physiognomy is the only thing they have in common." All the Jews who were forced to leave Holland and Germany, he said, took refuge in England, and proved a most undesirable addition to the population.

Anglo-Jewish celebrities. The period, however, was not unprolific in Anglo-Jewish celebrities, both Ashkenazi and Sephardi. Myer Lyon, professionally known as Leoni, the opera-singer, was in 1790 a chorister in Duke's Place Synagogue, where his voice often attracted distinguished auditors. A pupil of his, John Braham or Abrahams (1774?–1856), also a chorister at the same synagogue, attained an even greater fame on

the operatic stage. Lewis Goldsmith (1763?–1846), Lewis
publicist, diplomatist, &c., had one of the most Goldsmith.
adventurous careers in that era of adventure, the
French Revolution. Journalist in London and Paris,
employed and denounced in turn by both the English and French governments, he was present at the
capture of Frankfort by the Hessians in 1792, was a
spectator of the Polish struggle under Kosciusko, and
witnessed several of the battles in the Napoleonic wars.
By Napoleon, Goldsmith was frequently employed on
many confidential and responsible services, and at an
earlier date he was commissioned by the Polish revolu-
tionists to obtain British intervention on their behalf.

A personage of an entirely different description was Lord George
the erratic Protestant stalwart, Lord George Gordon, Gordon.
who, towards the close of his career, adopted Judaism,
it is suggested, in order to give celebrity to his financial schemes. Although he conformed strictly to the
ordinances of Judaism, Gordon's adhesion met with
no welcome from the community, and in its life he
took no part. A valued member of the Sephardi
community and at the same time a cultured member
of society was David Alves Rebello. He filled several
offices in the synagogue, and outside of it showed
himself a patron of the fine arts and a benefactor of
the poor. He devoted himself with enthusiasm to the
study of natural history, his writings on which he
published, and formed a considerable collection of
coins as well as of objects relating to all branches
of his favourite science.

The same period was one of Jewish literary activity Anglo-Jewish
in many directions. The Pentateuch was translated literature.
into English by S. Alexander in 1785 and by David
Levi in 1787. Various portions of the Sephardi
and Ashkenazi rituals were published, the translators
being A. Alexander and David Levi, and the Hagadah [1]

---

[1] The Passover Service.

was translated by the same writers in 1787 and 1794 respectively. In the field of theology David Levi published, in 1782, an account of the rites and ceremonies of the Jews, in 1790 a volume of discourses, and, in 1796–1800, a dissertation, in three volumes, on the Prophecies. In 1786 he published his *Lingua Sacra*, also in three volumes, and in 1807 there appeared H. Hurwitz's "Elements of the Hebrew Language," which went through many editions and was for a long time the standard Hebrew grammar among English Jews. Among the Hebrew works published were *Asara Maamarot*, a volume of three essays on philosophical and biblical topics by Eliakim ben Abraham, and issued in 1794.

David Levi.

David Levi (1740–1799), by occupation a shoemaker and subsequently a hat-dresser, was never far removed from indigence. Nevertheless, he succeeded in placing himself in the front rank of Anglo-Jewish scholars of his day, and by his translations of the prayer-books of the two Jewish communities rendered all successors in that field under obligations to him. Levi was also involved in several controversies. To Joseph Priestley's "Letters to the Jews, inviting them to an Amicable Discussion of the Evidences of Christianity," Levi replied in his "Letters to Dr. Priestley." The controversy was continued on both sides, and numerous other writers were subsequently involved in it. In 1795 Levi took part in the Anglo-Israel controversy that centred round the writings and prophecies of Richard Brothers. Two years later he turned his attention to Paine, the militant atheist, to whom he addressed, in a series of letters, a defence of the Old Testament.

The Baal-Shem of London.

An earlier celebrity was the cabbalist and mystic, Hayyim Samuel Jacob Falk (1708?–1782), generally known as the Baal-Shem of London, who obtained a great reputation for possessing occult powers, and concerning whom many remarkable anecdotes are related.

The era of the French Revolution was one fraught with influences on the fortunes of all the European states. England, as one of the nearest neighbours of France, was early drawn into the vortex of French politics, and the hostility towards the French people, at the best only slumbering among the English, quickly burst into flame. As the struggle between the two nations became more intense, the bitterness with which they regarded one another grew more acute. Even before war had broken out, foreigners, especially Frenchmen, who were unable to give satisfactory accounts of themselves were regarded with suspicion, and a condition of affairs supervened somewhat similar to that which prevailed when England under Elizabeth was the scene of the machinations of the Jesuits and of Spain. This suspicion of all foreigners, never entirely removed from the English mind, spread from the people to the Government, which consequently introduced a measure into Parliament in 1792 to deal with what was then considered the alien peril. The object of the measure was to make all foreigners arriving in the kingdom furnish accounts of themselves and give up whatever arms they might possess. They were required to obtain passports at their ports of landing, so that by those means their movements in the country might be followed. The measure also gave the Government the power of expulsion. Despite the opposition of the Whigs under Fox the Bill became law, and during its continuance poor foreign Jews were frequently expelled from the country on the ground of being undesirable.

A continuation of the same policy was to be seen in the action of the City authorities in July 1798. At the instance of the Duke of Portland, one of the Secretaries of State, the Wardens of the City synagogues were ordered to furnish a return of all aliens in the community, and any foreign Jews not included in the list were rendered liable to imprisonment and transportation. The authorities of the synagogues made haste to furnish the desired information, which was probably needed in connection with an Aliens Bill, then under the consideration of the House of Commons.

A few years later a more serious danger threatened the welfare of the community. The increase of the poor had been continual. It was due not only to natural causes, but also to the sustained immigration from the Continent. This deplorable condition of the lower classes was to a great extent due to a widespread want of employment among them. From the occupations filled by members of the same class in the general community Jews were excluded, by their want of technical knowledge as well as by religious scruples. The Jew was unable, even if qualified, to work more than four and a half days a week, as against the six of his non-Jewish competitor. With such a handicap it was hardly possible for the Jewish working man to find employment among Christians, and the number of Jewish masters, not all eager to employ co-religionists, was inconsiderable.

The problem of the Jewish poor.

Although the synagogues and a few of the richer members of the community were by no means unmindful of the claims of their poorer brethren, the majority of the rich Jews of the day were heedless of their condition. Idleness is invariably accompanied by a laxity of moral control, and the last years of the eighteenth century, as a natural consequence, saw crime somewhat widespread in the London Jewish community. This deplorable condition of affairs attracted the attention of Abraham Goldsmid (1756 ?–

The Goldsmid family.

1810), the fourth son of Aaron Goldsmid (*d.* 1782) who came to England from Holland in 1765. Aaron Goldsmid and his four sons, George, Asher, Benjamin (1755–1808), and Abraham, became leading financiers in the City. Benjamin and Abraham were also prominent in philanthropic matters, both Jewish and general, Benjamin being the founder of the Naval Asylum.

Once the attention of Abraham Goldsmid was directed to the condition of the Ashkenazi poor, he determined that the example of the Sephardi community, as illustrated by its establishment of an hospital and asylum, should be followed. With this object he quickly succeeded in collecting a sum of £20,000, the eighty-seven first subscribers to the fund consisting of forty-six Jews (two of them Sephardim), and forty-one Christians. When the amount had been collected, however, considerable differences arose among the subscribers as to the purpose to which it should be devoted, and the fund remained untouched for several years. *Abraham Goldsmid.*

Meanwhile the very undesirable state of affairs was attracting attention beyond the narrow circle of the community. In a treatise on the Police of the Metropolis, published by a London magistrate, Patrick Colquhoun, in 1795, of which numerous subsequent editions appeared with great rapidity, in the course of a consideration of metropolitan affairs from the point of view of a police magistrate, some of the tendencies that displayed themselves in the Anglo-Jewish community were animadverted upon, and the urgent necessity for the profitable and industrious employment of a number of lower class Jews emphasised. The strictures contained in this book were not without effect. Among others they attracted the attention of Joshua Van Oven, who entered upon a correspondence with Colquhoun on the subject of *Colquhoun's account of the London Jews.*

Joshua Van Oven.

U

the condition of the lower classes of Anglo-Jewry. Van Oven agreed with others who had studied the question that the cause of all the trouble lay in the ignorance, on the part of the bulk of the Jewish population, of any skilled trades. As a remedy Van Oven considered that it was highly necessary to deal with the state of affairs by taking steps for relieving the helpless, instructing the children, and diffusing among them a knowledge of trades "without any infringement of their religious customs." To carry out this scheme he suggested the allocation by Parliament of a portion of the poor rates paid by Jews. The amount obtained from this source was to be supplemented by funds derived from the synagogue surpluses, and also from a special poor rate levied on Jews. The total of the funds thus collected was to be administered by a Board representative of the synagogues. The scheme was approved by Colquhoun and also by Abraham Goldsmid and other communal leaders, and it was incorporated in a Bill presented to Parliament. By this measure it was proposed to establish an institution to educate the young for useful industry, to restore health to the sick, and to establish an asylum for old age and infirmity.

Scheme for a Jewish " Poor Fund."

The first opposition to the proposed measure came from the authorities at Bevis Marks, who claimed that, so far as they were concerned, it was quite unnecessary, inasmuch as their congregation already sufficiently provided for all the needs of its poorer members. Great objections were also raised by the local authorities concerned to that portion of the scheme which recommended the allocation of a proportion of the poor rates. This part of the measure was quickly abandoned, and the remainder did not long tarry behind it. The Jewish scheme having been abandoned, the missionaries to the Jews, who were then just beginning to organise their forces under the lead of Frey, himself a converted Jew, began to consider how to deal with the problem. The failure of the scheme of Van Oven, however, did not mean the cessation of all effort on the part of the Jews themselves. The fund collected by Abraham Goldsmid was still in existence, and it was at length, in 1806, devoted to the purpose for which it had been intended, by the establishment of an institution in Mile End for the care of five aged men, five women, ten boys, and eight girls. For the children technical as well as elementary education was provided. This institution, by subsequent extensions of its usefulness, ultimately became the Jews' Hospital and Orphan Asylum.

Some years before this satisfactory conclusion had been reached the office of Rabbi of the Duke's Place Synagogue, which had been vacant for many years —in fact, since the death of Rabbi Tewele Schiff in 1792—was filled. The new incumbent, who was appointed in 1802, was of English birth, the only one since the Re-Settlement who could claim that advantage, but in education and training he was entirely foreign. Rabbi Solomon Hirschell (1761–1842) was the son of Rabbi Hirsch Levin (Hart Lyon), at the time of Hirschell's birth the occupant of the office to which his son afterwards succeeded. The father, after his departure from England, filled several offices on the Continent, and when in Berlin collaborated, at the request of Frederick the Great, with Moses Mendelssohn in the translation of the rabbinical code of Jewish ordinances into German. Rabbi Hirschell arrived in England at a time when, despite the temporary lull in active hostilities, the struggle between Napoleon and the English statesmen was unabated and undecided. In all directions throughout the country ran a well developed vein of patriotic ardour, rendered all the more intense by the fear of French invasion. Deep love of country and willingness to sacrifice on her

Jews' Hospital and Orphan Asylum founded.

Appointment of Rabbi Solomon Hirschell.

behalf were displayed by all classes. On the resumption of hostilities, towards the end of 1803,
volunteers for the defence of their country were en-

Patriotism of
the Jews. rolled in great numbers. The Jews of London showed
themselves no less eager to accept service than their
Christian countrymen, and, at the great review by
George III., on the 26th of October 1803, several
hundreds of Jews were present under arms. Jewish
volunteers were excused from attendance at divine
service, and allowed to take the oaths of allegiance
and fidelity on the Book of Leviticus instead of on
the New Testament.

Long periods in the history of the three city
Ashkenazi synagogues passed without any, or with
few, occurrences of interest to a later generation.
Many years elapsed before the wounds received and
given at the births of the two seceding synagogues
were finally healed. The disagreements, however, if
extending over lengthy periods, were still but temporary, and when generations grew up to whom the
original causes of the disputes were merely traditions,
the disputes themselves were gradually forgotten.
The subsequent histories of the synagogues were
marked by alternate agreements and disagreements.
When the necessity of joint action for dealing with
the poor, or matters such as *Shechita*, became urgent,
the heads of the several congregations would meet
and co-operate. But these understandings seldom
lasted long, and disputes arising over some details
that, from the distance of time, appear of little or no
consequence, relations became strained, until the
necessity for joint action again grew urgent.

Thus in 1804 a conference of representatives of
the three synagogues was held for the purpose of

Proposed union
of the
Ashkenazim. devising a means of union among them. The time
for such a combination had, however, not yet come,
and despite the efforts of Rabbi Hirschell, who him-

self presided over one of the conferences, the sole
result was a new and temporary arrangement for
sharing the burden of the Ashkenazi poor. Twenty
years later another effort was made to forestall the
union that was not finally effected until 1870. The
suggestion on this occasion came from Nathan
Mayer Rothschild. The conferences, which extended leisurely over four years, were held at his
residence, and resulted finally in an agreement
between the three City synagogues. By this certain
charges and revenues were shared in common, and
a committee of arbitration was appointed to adjust
any differences that might arise between the three
participating bodies. A short time earlier Rabbi
Hirschell had been accepted as the spiritual head
of the three congregations.

Rabbi Hirschell appointed Chief Rabbi.

AUTHORITIES :—Lucien Wolf, "The N'vei Tzedek"; Joseph
Jacobs and Lucien Wolf, *Bibliotheca Anglo Judaica* (1888);
J. Picciotto, "Sketches of Anglo-Jewish History"; H. Adler, "The
Baal-Shem of London" (*Jewish Chronicle*, Dec. 4, 1903); J. W. von
Archenholtz, "A Picture of England" (1797); P. Colquhoun, "A
Treatise on the Police of the Metropolis" (1797), "The State of
Indigence and the Situation of the Casual Poor in the Metropolis
explained" (1799); Joshua van Hoven, "Letters on the Present
State of the Jewish Poor in the Metropolis" (1802); "Parlia-
mentary History," vols. xxx., xxxiii.; "Dictionary of National
Biography"; "Jewish Encyclopedia."

CHAPTER XXXII

THE REFORM MOVEMENT
(1802–1885)

The troubles of the Sephardim. BY the close of the eighteenth century the continual inflow of foreign Ashkenazim had gradually placed their community, from the point of view of numbers, in a position of excessive superiority over the Sephardim. These had lost their boasted priority, of which they had been so proud, and had gradually sunk to a position of but a fraction of the Jews of England. That fraction, however, still contained almost the whole of the better class of English Jews. The position of the Bevis Marks congregation, moreover, had become unsatisfactory. The finances fell away to such an extent that a subscription had at one time to be opened, by which an amount of £2500 was raised. The number of members as well as the revenue had decreased. The services were not conducted to the satisfaction of the congregants. Such a pass did affairs reach, that in the second year of the nineteenth century an inquiry was made into the ecclesiastical state of the Sephardi community.

The general dissatisfaction was voiced at a meeting of the elders in 1803 by Isaac Mocatta, who condemned the spiritual decay of the community. He complained especially of the neglect into which Reforms suggested. education had fallen. He suggested a thorough change in the methods, and especially the substitution of English for Spanish as the language into which the prayers were to be translated. The Council of Wardens, in their reference to a committee appointed

to consider the state of the community, complained
that "in this Kahal, which had shone brilliantly for
more than a century as one of the principal of
Europe, the study of the Law will be entirely lost,
and the Kahal will become an object of contempt and
ridicule." The committee in its report, presented the
following year, recommended that a Haham should
be appointed, that the charity schools should be
re-organised, and that the *Medrash* (religious college)
should be managed in a manner calculated to induce
the members of the congregation to send their
children to it as well as to a *yeshiba* or school, the
establishment of which was recommended. The
report had one immediate result. The community
had had no spiritual head since the death of Haham
d'Azavedo in 1784. Within a year of the issue of the
report a successor was appointed in the person of
Rabbi Raphael Meldola of Leghorn (1754–1828).

The new Haham came from a family that had for
many centuries furnished scholars and rabbis of
repute to the larger Jewish community. His father
was Moses Meldola, Professor of Oriental Languages
at the University of Paris. The new Haham was
born at Leghorn, where he acted for a time as Dayan,
and· where the first-fruits of his learning had been
published. He came to London at a critical moment
in the affairs of the community, and the task that lay
before.him was beset by many difficulties. The community, however, had been fortunate in its choice,
and, with the assistance of its Haham, it recovered
the stability that had for a time been in jeopardy.
The congregation, however, was not yet out of the
financial wood. In 1809 a meeting of the members
was convened to take into consideration the state of
its finances. It was then decided to re-organise the
taxation of the members, and at the same time the
radius of four miles, within which no rival Sephardi

congregation was allowed to meet, was extended to six. These measures proved successful, and after a few years the revenue and expenditure balanced once again. This fortunate state of affairs was to some extent induced by legacies due to the munificence of Joseph Barrow and Abraham Lopes Pereira.

Isaac D'Israeli. The year 1813 is noteworthy in the annals of the congregation for the election of Isaac D'Israeli as involuntary *parnass*, and the consequent withdrawal of his family from the community. Until 1819 Portuguese was the sole official language of the congregation, but in that year English was raised to an equal position, and both languages remained for many years side by side in importance. Earlier efforts with regard to the congregational education had not solved all the problems that had to be faced, and the subject still continued to trouble the community. In 1821 the old school management was abolished, and the *Shaare Tikvah*, or Gates of Hope, a society for the support of the congregational charity school, was founded. Meldola's term of office was also noteworthy for the introduction to England of probably the most learned Hazan the community has Hzaan de Sola. yet possessed. David de Sola was born in Amsterdam in 1796, and came to London as assistant reader in 1818. Although at the time entirely unacquainted with the English language, he speedily became one of the most accomplished writers of English in Anglo-Jewry, and one of its leading men of literature. During the forty-two years that he spent in the country he introduced English sermons into the community, translated the liturgies of both his own community and that of the Ashkenazim into English, translated, in conjunction with Dr. M. J. Raphall, a portion of the Mishnah, helped to found the *Jewish Chronicle*, edited the ancient melodies of his community, and took a leading part in the literary revival in Anglo-Jewry that marked the middle of the nineteenth century.

The year 1822 furnished a warning of the hurricane that was about to break forth. The community had gradually become divided into two parties—the one on the whole English and liberal in religious matters, the other foreign and orthodox. In that year the first of the Ascamoth was transgressed, apparently without intention, by a section of the latter party, who, after spending together the evening of the Feast of Weeks in the study of the Law, had held divine service at its conclusion within the proscribed distance from Bevis Marks. The English party was then in power, and the offence was visited with severe penalties. The offending members were heavily fined, denied all synagogue honours for a term of two years, and refused admission to their seats, in place of which others behind the reading-desk were assigned to them. The offenders, however, did not accept their punishment with meekness. Law proceedings were at one time threatened, and the affair led to the temporary withdrawal of the delinquents from the congregation. A reconciliation was, however, ultimately effected. Moses Montefiore (1784-1885) had already by that date attained a leading place in the community, and had obtained a reputation for a remarkable display of philanthropy. Montefiore's influence also served to break down the prejudice that had lasted for more than a century against marriages with members of the Ashkenazi community. Montefiore had himself married a Tudesca, a daughter of Levi Barent Cohen, and by 1825 the *rapprochement* between the two communities had progressed so far that a German was actually called to the law in the Sephardi Synagogue.

Haham Meldola died in 1828. After his death another committee was appointed to consider the

spiritual condition of the community. As a result
the children in the school were taught to chant.
More reforms. Various suggestions were made to improve the
decorum at the services, the length of which was to
a slight extent curtailed. At the same time the importance of the study of Hebrew was emphasised.
All proclamations were in future to be made in
English, in which language also sermons were to be
delivered every Saturday afternoon. Before delivery,
however, these sermons were to be submitted to three
elders. The Medrash or Theological College was
overhauled. The first English preacher among the
Sephardim was the Rev. D. A. de Sola, although he
had been preceded in the sister community in 1817
by the Rev. Tobias Goodman of the Western
Synagogue. In 1839 a permanent choir was formed,
and at the same time the infant school was founded.

Meanwhile the new forces that had gradually been
arising in the community were collecting into one
stream, whose strength increased with its progress.
Symptoms of a Jewish awakening, such as the re-
organisation of the community, the introduction of
English sermons, and the establishment of the Society
A Jewish for the Cultivation of the Hebrew Language and
Renaissance. Literature have already been noticed. Soon the
new spirit grew bolder. It was no longer content
to bring its influence to bear only upon the extra-
synagogal communities. It desired also to pass
through the portals of the House of Prayer, but, on
its threshold, all the forces of Conservatism had
drawn up, and the final struggle took place without
rather than within the sacred fane. The small efforts
that had been made to render the services more in
accordance with the tastes of the more advanced
section of the congregation, had met with slight
success. The removal of many of the Anglo-Jewish
families, from the immediate neighbourhood of Bevis

Marks to districts at some distance from the City, created a new want among those who desired to attend the synagogue, but who lived at too great a distance to do so.

In 1836 a memorial was placed before the elders of the congregation, pointing out the continued want of decorum in the services, and the constant, and, in the opinion of the memorialists, unnecessary repetition of certain prayers. The memorialists went further. They suggested the introduction of an organ into the synagogue, and the abolition of the second days of the festivals. Such suggestions aroused the horror of those holding opposite views. The ultra-orthodox section of the congregation banded themselves together in the *Shomere Mishmeret Hakkodesh*, a society for upholding and preserving the Jewish faith as it had been handed down. The new society presented a memorial in thorough opposition to the recommendations of the previous one, of whose objects they said they approved, but to whose methods they were most strongly opposed. The excessive zeal of this new society, however, aroused in the minds of the wardens fears of its possible effects, and it was forced to dissolve. Steps were thereupon taken to improve the synagogue decorum, but the results gave little satisfaction, and by no means succeeded in removing the differences of opinion between the two parties.

In the sister community there were similar causes of dissatisfaction. As early as 1821 several of the leading members of the Great Synagogue pointed out to the authorities measures that they thought should be adopted in order to improve the decorum. The alterations that the petitioners had advocated in the first instance in both communities had been innocuous and even conservative, but, as time passed, extremists gained control of the party of reform.

The beginning of the Reform movement.

The demands increased, so that at length there could be no doubt that they had passed beyond the stage at which any representatives of orthodox Judaism could accept them. Throughout the European world there was at that time a wave of violent reform. In England the era was that of the Reform Bill and

Influence of German reform.

the Anti-Corn Law movement. In German Jewry the reform element had just raised its head. Geiger had burst forth with his assaults on rabbinic Judaism and his attacks on the orthodox liturgies. His on-slaughts were not without effect on both camps in Anglo-Jewry. The Conservatives were made still more opposed to change; the Reformers increased their demands. To increase the misfortunes of the community the place of 'Haham Meldola had not been filled. Hirschell, the Chief Rabbi of the Ash-kenazim, was sinking in extreme old age towards the grave. Montefiore, sympathetically disposed towards the earliest demands of the progressive party, had, by their subsequent advances, been frightened back into the ranks of the Conservatives. The dis-satisfaction of the Reformers continued to increase until, on the 15th of April 1840, twenty-four gentle-men, eighteen of whom were Sephardim, decided to establish the West London Synagogue of British

The Reform Synagogue established.

Jews. On the opening of the new House of Prayer the Sephardi seceders sent a very temperate letter to the parent synagogue, reciting the alterations they had effected in the service and observances and the reasons for them, and stating their desire to partici-pate in the work of the various communal societies with which they had hitherto been connected. The communication received scant consideration. An edict, signed by Chief Rabbi Hirschell and the members of the Sephardi Beth Din, was issued denouncing the secessionists. They were deprived of all their rights and privileges in their communities,

and a solemn excommunication was, after an interval, passed upon them.

In the meanwhile Chief Rabbi Hirschell died. It was thought that the breach might have been healed on the election of a successor. The vacant position was filled, after a short interval, by the election of Nathan Marcus Adler (1803–1890), Chief Rabbi of Hanover, and a collateral descendant of a predecessor in the English Rabbinate, Rabbi Tewele Schiff. The hopes raised by Adler's election, however, were doomed to disappointment. The excommunication was not withheld, and the breach between the seceders and the parent community became definite. Repeated efforts were made to have the excommunication withdrawn, and, so far as the civil offence, the holding of worship within six miles of Bevis Marks, was concerned, it was removed in 1849. The new congregation, however, as distinct from its members, was refused recognition as Jewish, and the struggles over the attempt to obtain representation on the Committee of Deputies re-acted unfavourably on the contest that was then being waged for the admission of the Jews to Parliament. In 1864 the congregation at Bevis Marks rescinded the resolution forbidding the acceptance of offerings and legacies from members of the Reform Synagogue. Ten years later members of the West London Synagogue were permitted to represent synagogues other than their own on the Committee of Deputies. In 1885 the last trace of dissension passed away, when, on the occasion of the reform of the constitution of the Committee of Deputies, representation was no longer denied the Reform congregation.

The movement for reform, although resulting in the withdrawal of many of the greatest of the Sephardi families, was not without effect on the

N. M. Adler elected Chief Rabbi.

parent congregation. The condition of the Sephardi congregation was investigated, and, as a consequence, many minor reforms were adopted. Among the other steps taken was the opening of a branch synagogue in West London. If this step had been taken twenty years earlier the secession of 1840 would, in all probability, have been avoided, or, at any rate, considerably postponed.

AUTHORITIES :—M. Gaster, " History of the Spanish and Portuguese Congregation " ; Lucien Wolf, " The Queen's Jewry," (*The Jewish Year-Book,* 1897) ; J. Picciotto, " Sketches of Anglo-Jewish History " ; " Dictionary of National Biography " ; " Jewish Encyclopedia."

CHAPTER XXXIII

THE DISABILITIES OF THE JEWS
(1830–1855)

IN the year 1830, that of the accession of William IV., The distribution of the community. the Jewish population of England was computed at 30,000 individuals, of whom two-thirds were resident in London and the remaining 10,000 in the provinces. In the metropolis there was a fairly large number of rich families, a very small middle class, and a very great preponderance of poor. So large was this preponderance that it is computed that of the 2500 members of the Sephardi community in 1829, 1200 were in receipt of relief from the synagogue, and a further number were on the verge of pauperism. The rich class consisted, for the most part, of financiers and stockbrokers, such as N. M. Rothschild, Moses Montefiore, Isaac Lyon Goldsmid, and one or two others; of prominent merchants engaged in the West India and China trades; of diamond merchants; and of a few general merchants. Jewish professional men were few. Jews were still excluded from the Bar, and, although they had been found in the other branch of the legal profession for many years, the number of Jewish solicitors was small. The same might be said of another profession in which Jews have always taken a leading place—medicine. A solitary Jewish architect is known to have existed in England at that period.

The regulations of the City of London, which pre- The City of London. vented any but freemen from engaging in retail trade within its boundaries, and refused admission to the freedom to all of Jewish birth, whether converted to Christianity or not, were the chief reasons for the small dimensions to which the Jewish middle class extended. The City regulations, however, had no force beyond its boundaries. East of Bishopsgate and west of Temple Bar Jews were as free as other sections of the population to engage in retail trade, and, in order that they might do so, a slight dispersion was effected. One result of this was apparent in the establishment of the synagogue in Denmark Court.

Jewish
disabilities.

The number of disabilities under which the Jews of England laboured was considerable, but they varied in their pressure. Several were theoretical rather than practical, and the sole inconvenience to which they gave rise was the doubt in which the position of the Jews was placed. For instance, varying opinions were held as to the right of Jews to hold land, and no definite interpretation of the law on the point was accepted. There were, however, a number of definite legal enactments that differentiated against the Jewish inhabitants as compared with their Christian neighbours. Of these disabilities some were invariably enforced, others were sometimes enforced and at others ignored, while still others had apparently been allowed to become dead letters but were always liable to revival. Summing up, English law as it affected Jews in 1830 excluded them from Parliament, from high rank in the army and navy, from membership of the University of Oxford, and from degrees, scholarships, fellowships, and positions of emolument in the University of Cambridge. There were, in addition, positions from which they might be excluded if those in authority so wished. Jews might be debarred from voting at parliamentary elections if the returning officers cared to exercise their powers to the full. Their admission to the Bar depended entirely upon the attitude of the Inns of Court. It was only at the will of individual corporations that Jews could be admitted to offices connected with them.

The University of Oxford, by requiring candidates for matriculation to subscribe to the Thirty-Nine Articles, excluded all but members of the Church of England. Cambridge allowed Jews to become undergraduates and to go through the University examinations, but that was the limit of toleration. No Jew could take a degree or obtain a scholarship, exhibition, or fellow-ship. The University of London had not yet been founded, and it was not until 1836 that Dublin, for the first time, conferred a degree on a Jew—Nathan Lazarus Benmohel. University College, London, the first unsectarian establishment founded for the purpose of higher education, was established in 1826, mainly by the efforts and through the munificence of Isaac Lyon Goldsmid, but its creation was too recent to influence the current generation of Jewry. *At the Universities.*

The era of political emancipation that marked the close of the third decade of the nineteenth century raised high the hope of the Anglo-Jewish leaders that, when all other classes were being admitted into the full privilege of English citizenship, the discrimination against the Jews was about to pass away. The Test and Corporation Acts were repealed in 1828, and the following year the Catholics were accorded political freedom. The agitation that resulted in these successes had not been without the active sympathy of the Jews. If the former measures had been merely repealed, the gate that barred the way of the Jews to many privileges would have been unlocked, but the action of the House of Lords in inserting in the new declaration required on the acceptance of public office, the phrase, " on the true faith of a Christian," prevented any such consummation. Although the Catholics and other Christian dissenters were admitted into the body politic, the Jews were still kept without its limits. *Catholic emancipation.*

X

Minor disabili-
ties removed.

With regard to the disabilities, whose removal needed not the sanction of the legislature, more success was secured. In 1831 the restrictions imposed by the City of London on Jewish trade were removed—it was only three years earlier that the Corporation would unbend so much as to admit converts from Judaism to the freedom. Another barrier was removed in 1833 when Lincoln's Inn, without in any way exceeding its legal powers, called Mr. (afterwards Sir) Francis Goldsmid (1807–1878), son of Isaac Lyon Goldsmid, and a great-nephew of Benjamin and Abraham Goldsmid, to the Bar after he had taken the usual oath, modified so as to be binding on his conscience, on a copy of the Old Testament. Two years later another difficulty was removed by an Act to simplify election to Parliament. Until that year an elector might be required to take the Oath of Abjuration, in a form unacceptable to a Jew, before being permitted to exercise the franchise. The Act of 1835 relieved all voters of the necessity of taking any oath. In 1836 a Jew was elected a governor of Christ's Hospital.

Jews admitted
to the office of
Sheriff.

In another sphere the battle for municipal eman-cipation was brought without much delay to a successful issue, mainly by the exertions of one man, David Salomons (1797–1873). In 1835 he had been elected Sheriff of London and Middlesex. Objections were raised to his serving, on the ground that it would be necessary for him to take the declaration required from the holders of corporate offices. The question was speedily settled on the initiative of Lord John Russell, who introduced and passed through Parlia-ment a measure declaring that for admission to the office of sheriff the declaration was unnecessary. Salomons accordingly served his year of office, and was succeeded two years later by another Jew, Moses Montefiore.

David
Salomons.

The next step in the campaign was the election

of Salomons in 1836 as an alderman of the City of London. After his election he, in due course, presented himself for the purpose of taking the municipal oaths of office, but asked to be excused from making the statutory declaration in the prescribed form. The Court of Aldermen had full power to grant the desired dispensation, and if they had done so would only have been following the example set by the Corporations of Portsmouth, Birmingham, and Southampton, which had already admitted Jews. The Court of Aldermen, however, took a different course, and refused to admit Salomons. He was repeatedly elected by different wards of the City, but the Court of Aldermen refused to vary its decision, and Salomons thereupon decided to appeal to the courts of law. The legal authorities were asked to compel the Court of Aldermen to admit Salomons after he had taken the municipal oaths without the declaration. The Court of Queen's Bench decided in his favour, but this decision was reversed on appeal. Salomons then petitioned Parliament to enable him to perform the duties for which he had been elected, but from which he was debarred by the Court of Aldermen. His petition had considerable effect, and in 1841 a Bill was introduced into the House of Commons " For the Relief of Persons of the Jewish Religion elected to Municipal Offices." Prominent among the supporters of the measure were Lord Lyndhurst and Lord Bute. Nevertheless the Bill was thrown out by the Lords, but four years later it was re-introduced by Sir Robert Peel's Government and became law. The Act threw open every municipal office to Jews, who by degrees took advantage of it. Salomons was immediately received into the Court of Aldermen, and served with distinction as Lord Mayor in 1855. Several important provincial corporations also welcomed Jewish bur-

The Court of Aldermen.

Municipal offices opened to Jews.

gesses to their deliberations. Many Jews became magistrates and high sheriffs of their counties, and no less than three, Moses Montefiore, Isaac Lyon Goldsmid, and Anthony de Rothschild, had the

dignity of baronet conferred upon them before the portals of Parliament were opened to sons of the synagogue.

Throughout the whole of this period the agitation for admission to the legislature had been continuous. The first step was taken immediately after the consummation of Catholic Emancipation in 1829. At that great moment in the history of toleration in England, it was thought that the completion of the victory by the admission of English Jews to full English citizenship could not long be delayed. This seems to have been the opinion of even the Tory Prime Minister, the Duke of Wellington, for, addressing a deputation of leading Jews, who, on the incentive of Mr. I. L. Goldsmid, waited upon him in the year of Catholic Emancipation, he showed himself by no means unsympathetic. Catholic Emancipation, however, he said, had created a great turmoil, and he advised the Jews to wait a short time until it had subsided. The advice was taken, and no action decided upon until 1830.

In that year Robert Grant, the Liberal member for Inverness, introduced a Bill for the removal of all disqualifications which prevented Jews from enjoying the same " civil rights, franchises, and privileges " and from holding the same " offices, places, employments, trusts, and confidences " as had, by the measure of the previous year, been thrown open to Catholics. The Government raised no objections to the introduction of the Bill, but opposed the motion for its second reading, and the Bill was defeated by a majority of 115 votes over 97. Parliament had been prayed to adopt the measure in numerous petitions

from Jews and Christians, and an able exposition of
the Jewish case had been drawn up and published by
Mr. Francis Goldsmid. The Liberal leaders on the
whole were in favour of satisfying the Jewish claims.
There was, however, one important exception. Earl
Grey, the Premier who had carried the Reform Act,
remained throughout his life a steadfast opponent
of Jewish emancipation. The supporters included
members of both parties in the State, Lord John
Russell and Macaulay among the Liberals, Huskisson
leading the moderate Tories. Of all the non-Jewish
advocates of emancipation none surpassed in devotion and persistence Lord Holland, the nephew and
disciple of Charles James Fox. On the other side
were ranged, however, Sir Robert Peel, Mr. Gladstone, and Lord Shaftesbury, in addition to a
number of other less distinguished politicians.

The arguments in favour of the Bill were based Arguments
on the principles of religious liberty. The opponents pro and con.
also took their stand on a principle. They contended
that a country that was not governed by an exclusively Christian legislature could not be considered a Christian country. It was also argued
that the Jew was cosmopolitan rather than English
or French or Prussian, and did not look upon the
country of his domicile in any light but that of a
temporary resting-place; that the Jew considered
Palestine as his only permanent home, and, in consequence, should not be entrusted with full citizenship
in any other. The opposition was, for the most part,
based on these lines, and few traces of a persecuting
spirit could be found in it. Arguments on a lower
plane, however, were not altogether excluded from
the controversy. For instance, one member urged
that if the Jews were admitted to Parliament "a
few of the leading men among them would soon
obtain as much influence there as they already

Religious
opposition to
Jewish
emancipation.

possess over Three Per Cent. Consols." Another begged the House "in the name of the Lord Jesus Christ to preserve the religion of Christianity, the religion of the State, from being defiled by the introduction of the Bill."

AUTHORITIES :—Lucien Wolf, "The Queen's Jewry"; B. L. Abrahams, "Sir I. L. Goldsmid and the Admission of the Jews of England to Parliament" (*Transactions of the Jewish Historical Society of England*, vol. iv., 1903); Sir Spencer Walpole, "A History of Twenty-Five Years" (1904), "Parliamentary Debates, 1830–1845," "Jewish Progress in the Victorian Era" (*Jewish Chronicle*, May 7, 14, 21, 1897), "MS. Records of the London Committee of Deputies."

CHAPTER XXXIV

POLITICAL EMANCIPATION OBTAINED
(1830–1866)

THE defeat in the House of Commons of the Bill of 1830 was merely an incident in the struggle. The step taken on this occasion was never repeated by the Lower House, for when a measure with a similar purpose was introduced in 1833, it was adopted by the Lower House and sent to the Lords, to whom, however, it proved unacceptable. This process was repeated in 1834 and 1836, but in the latter year the measure was no longer in charge of a private member, but of the Chancellor of the Exchequer of a Liberal Government. For the next ten years the emancipation movement made little progress. For five of them a Conservative Government was in power, and although it was during that period that municipal emancipation was obtained, all efforts to obtain corresponding legislation concerning the legislature were considered futile. Moreover, the cause lost two of its most valuable parliamentary spokesmen by the deaths of Lord Holland and Sir Robert Grant, and both the general and the Jewish communities, engrossed in other troubles, allowed their interest in the struggle to relax. In 1837 a very definite step was taken, which, if it had proved successful, might have appreciably reduced the thirty years of agitation. It may be said that the Jewish advocates of political emancipation were divided into two parties, one constitutional and the other parliamentary. The first consisted of the overwhelming majority of the communal leaders, who laboured to attain their object regularly and by parliamentary means. The other party was comprised in the person of David Salomons. Too impatient or impetuous to await the slow motion of the parliamentary machine, he wished, by his own effort, to assist it along its path. The example of Daniel O'Connell and the satisfactory consequence that followed it were before him, and Salomons desired to emulate the exploits of the Catholic leader. He obtained the nomination for the representation of Shoreham in the legislature, and fought the constituency, but was defeated. Four years later, in 1841, he stood for Maidstone, but was again unsuccessful.

Although Salomons' views regarding the conduct of the campaign were not adopted by his fellow-reformers in the first instance, they were ultimately accepted as more likely to lead to success. The victories that had been obtained by Salomons in the municipal area had no doubt convinced all parties among the reformers that the only means of obtaining admission to the House of Commons was through a constituency. It was determined to nominate a representative Jew for election in the Liberal interest for a constituency in which that party had some chance of success—Salomons had on both occasions made attacks on Tory strongholds. Accordingly, Baron Lionel de Rothschild (1808–1879), the head of the Anglo-Jewish community and an acknowledged leader in the City, was nominated in conjunction with Lord John Russell, the Liberal Prime Minister, for the City of London at the election of 1847. Of the four members elected Rothschild was third. Salomons stood at the same election for Greenwich, but was again defeated.

When Parliament assembled the new member for

(margin notes:) Salomons' first parliamentary contest.

Baron Lionel de Rothschild elected M.P. for the City of London.

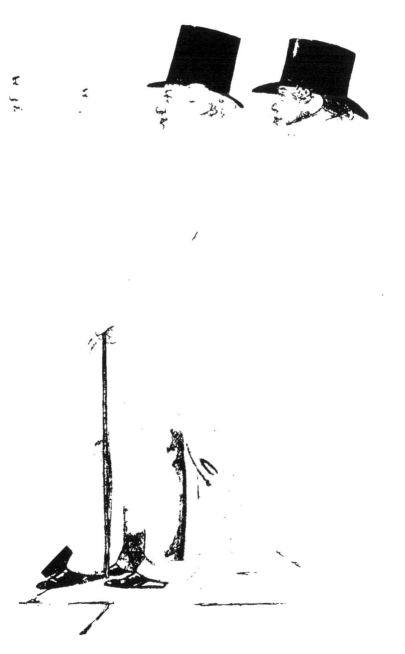

BARON MAYER BARON LIONEL SIR ANTHONY   NATHAN MAYER

N. M. ROTHSCHILD AND HIS THREE SONS

the City presented himself at the table of the House Rothschild unable to take his seat in the House of Commons. of Commons to be sworn, but being unable to take the oath "on the true faith of a Christian," he was refused permission to take his seat. Almost the first business of the new Parliament was the consideration of a Bill, introduced by the Prime Minister, for the removal of the disabilities that excluded Jews from Parliament. The circumstances in which the Bill was on this occasion introduced attracted considerable attention to it outside of Parliament. Petitions for and against it came from all parts of the country. Those in favour of the Bill bore 300,000 signatures, while 56,000 petitioned against it. Among the petitions in favour of the Bill, one from the citizens of London was presented by the Sheriffs at the Bar of the House. The Bill was strongly supported by Lord George Bentinck and Mr. Disraeli, the leaders of the Tory party, as well as by Sir Robert Peel and Mr. Gladstone, who no longer opposed the extension of political rights to the Jews. Bentinck was so much in advance of his party in this matter that, in consequence of his action on the Bill, he was worried into resigning the leadership, in which he was succeeded by Mr. Disraeli, a still more ardent advocate of the measure. The Bill passed through all its stages Another enfranchising Bill rejected by the Lords. in the House of Commons, but was rejected by the House of Lords. The same fate overtook a similar measure introduced the following year. Rothschild thereupon resigned his seat, stood for re-election, and was again returned to the House.

Despite the result of the election, the Government decided for the time being not to urge forward the legislation necessary to enable the member for the City to take his seat. His constituents thereupon held a meeting, and resolved to ask their member to present himself at the House of Commons and offer to take the oath in the form binding on his conscience.

Rothschild again presented himself at the House, and his request to be permitted to be sworn on the Old Testament was granted after debate. He then proceeded to take the oath, but on omitting the phrase to which he took objection he was requested to withdraw. The House proceeded to discuss the situation, and resolved that, though Rothschild could not act as a member of the House until he had taken the oath in the prescribed form, his seat was not vacant. Finally, it adopted a resolution to the effect that, at the earliest opportunity in the following session, the House would take into consideration the form of the Oath of Abjuration, with a view to relieve Jewish subjects.

The resolution was acted upon in 1851, with the result that had attended previous efforts in the same direction. In the meantime, however, a second Jew had been elected to Parliament. David Salomons' first three attempts to obtain parliamentary honours had proved unsuccessful. On the fourth attempt,
however, he had obtained election, and it was as the member for Greenwich that he presented himself at the House of Commons the day after the rejection of the Emancipation Bill by the Peers. Being refused permission to take the oath after omitting the objectionable phrase, he withdrew from the House in obedience to the direction of the Speaker, but he left an inquiry whether, if he took his seat without having taken the full oath, the Government would sue him for the penalties provided by the Act of Parliament so that the question of right might be tried in a court of law. The Government intimated that in such an eventuality it intended to take no such action. Thereupon, amidst great excitement, Salomons entered the
House and took a seat on one of the benches on the ministerial side. Sir Robert Inglis, the veteran foe of emancipation, immediately rose to protest, but gave way to the Speaker, who directed Salomons to with-

draw. Salomons ignored the direction, and considerable uproar ensued, in the course of which the Leader
of the House, on the appeal of the Speaker, moved
that Mr. Alderman Salomons be ordered to withdraw. and is ordered
The adjournment was moved by Mr. Anstey and to withdraw.
He votes in the
defeated, but Salomons managed to take part in the division and
division. In the further discussion one of the speakers speaks.
asked Salomons what he intended to do, and to the
consternation of half the House the new member rose
to explain his position. In a few well-chosen words
he appealed to the indulgence of the House "in the
peculiar position" in which he was placed. While
disclaiming a desire to do anything that might appear
contumacious or presumptuous, he defended the
course of action that he had thought right and proper
to adopt, and concluded with an expression of the
hope that in the then doubtful state of the law the
House would not hastily arrive at any conclusion.
The speech made a good impression and was received
with cheers, but the Premier's original motion was
carried, and Salomons removed by the serjeant-at-
arms.

By voting in three divisions without having previously taken the oath in the prescribed form, the
member for Greenwich had rendered himself liable
to a cumulative penalty of £1500. The Government
had announced that it did not intend to take any
proceedings for their recovery, but that decision
did not prevent action being taken at the instance
of a common informer. The case was tried in the
Court of Exchequer and decided against Salomons.
Baron Alderson, in delivering judgment, expressed
his regret at being compelled "as a mere expounder
of the law" to come to that conclusion. Two of
his colleagues concurred, but the third, Mr. Baron
Martin, expressed his conviction that the defendant
had lawfully taken the oath. A similar conclusion

to that of the Court of Exchequer was reached in a higher court, and Salomons would have carried the case to the House of Lords, if he had not been defeated in the general election that supervened. By these decisions Salomons was not only mulcted in heavy fines, but also became liable to deprivation of the right to be a party to any civil suit, to be a guardian of a child, or an executor, and to the loss of several other rights of citizenship. The Conservative Government, however, immediately introduced and carried through Parliament a measure removing all these penalties, excepting the fine to which members of the House of Commons were liable for taking their seats before taking the oath, and, in order to cover the case of Salomons, the Act was made retrospective.

The Conservative Government was short-lived, and in 1853 Lord Aberdeen introduced the old measure, which met with the usual fate. It was thereupon decided to adopt a new course of action. In the course of the last generation all the disabilities, with the exception of one, under which the Jews laboured, had been removed. The Bill, in the form in which it had been continually introduced, was no longer necessary. Accordingly, it was determined to deal with the parliamentary oaths alone, and Lord Lyndhurst introduced a Bill into the House of Lords for the purpose of striking out from them such portions "as were inoperative, idle, and absurd." He, however, failed to induce the Peers to accept his proposal. In the three successive years the Oaths Bill was defeated by the Lords, although in 1857 the Government accepted an amendment providing that no Jew should hold the office of Regent of the Kingdom, Prime Minister, Lord Chancellor, Lord Lieutenant of Ireland, or Commissioner to the General Assembly of the Church of Scotland. In the session 1857–1858

The question in the Law Courts.

A new proposal.

the Bill was introduced again, and on this occasion not rejected by the Lords. They amended it, however, by omitting the clause that provided that a Jewish member of Parliament, when taking the oath, might omit the words containing the reference to Christianity. The Bill, if adopted in the amended form, would have merely consolidated the oaths to be taken by members, and would have left the Jewish question untouched. The Commons refused to accept the amendment, and appointed a committee to draw up the reasons for their disagreement. On this committee Rothschild was fully qualified by the Rules of the House to serve, and he was made a member of it. A conference ensued between the two Houses, but the Peers insisted on their objections, and would not even accept a compromise suggested by a Conservative Peer, Lord Lucan. This was to the effect that either House should be empowered by resolution to determine the form of oath to be administered in that House by persons professing the Jewish faith. This suggested compromise, however, formed the basis of legislation adopted on the motion of Lord Derby's Government in 1858, and, in consequence of it, Baron Lionel de Rothschild was enabled to take his seat in due form in the House of Commons on the 26th day of July of that year, eleven years after his first election for the City of London.

Rothschild a member of a parliamentary committee.

Political emancipation gained.

The position was rendered more secure in 1866 by the passage in that year of another Act replacing the three oaths, necessary to be taken on admission into Parliament, by one in which no phrase to which a Jew could object appeared. By this measure Jews were admissible to both Houses without any further resolution. Under it Lord Rothschild, a son of Baron Lionel, was raised to the peerage in 1886 and duly took his seat. In 1890, in the course of a

A Jewish peer.

Eligibility of Jews for certain offices.

discussion on a Bill that proposed to open the offices of Lord High Chancellor and Lord Lieutenant of Ireland to all English citizens, irrespective of their religious beliefs, it transpired that, so far as Jews were concerned, the proposed legislation was unnecessary.

AUTHORITIES :—Lucien Wolf, "The Queen's Jewry"; Sir Spencer Walpole, "A History of Twenty-Five Years," vol. ii.; "Jewish Progress in the Victorian Era" (*Jewish Chronicle*, May 28, June 4, 1897); "MS. Records of the London Committee of Deputies," "Parliamentary Debates, 1833–1858"; "Dictionary of National Biography."

CHAPTER XXXV

GROWTH AND REORGANISATION OF THE COMMUNITY

(1840–1906)

IN illustration of the influential position that the Anglo-Jewish community had attained by the middle of the nineteenth century, the story of the Damascus affair may be recounted. In 1840 the whole of Syria, including Damascus, was under the control of Mehemet Ali, the Pasha of Egypt, who had rebelled against his Turkish sovereign. The dispute between the whilom viceroy and his master had been drawn within the vortex of the Eastern Question, and all the Great Powers of Europe found themselves intimately interested in the struggle. The Powers formed two groups. On the one side France lent the whole of her platonic support to the rebellious viceroy. On the other, Great Britain, Russia, Austria, and Prussia stood between Mehemet and the goal towards which he was striving, the sovereignty of the Turkish Empire.

In the midst of this condition of affairs, on the 5th of February 1840, Padre Tomaso, a Franciscan friar *The Damascus affair.* who was well known in the Jewish and Mohammedan quarters of Damascus as well as among the Christians, disappeared. There was every reason to assume that he had been murdered by a Mohammedan with whom he had had a serious dispute some days earlier. The Catholics, however, thought fit to accuse the Jews of the commission of a ritual murder. Supported by the French consul—the Catholics of the East were under the protection of France—representations were made to the authorities, and as a result the leading Jews of Damascus, men of position, wealth, and character, were thrown into prison and cruelly tortured with a view to forcing a confession of the crime. Several died on account of severities they endured. The example set by the officials was followed by the populace. The Jewish quarter of Damascus was attacked and sacked, and indescribable atrocities committed upon its inhabitants. The French consul held what he presumed to designate a trial, decided that the Jews were in the habit of using human blood in their Passover ceremonies, and found all the prisoners guilty. Urgent messages were thereupon sent to Mehemet Ali for permission to execute the prisoners. The news of these events reached London early in April. At the instance of Sir Moses Montefiore a meeting of the leading men of the community, of all parties, orthodox and reform, was convened to consider the situation. The British Government was approached, and Lord Palmerston promised a Jewish deputation to use every effort for the protection of the Jews of the East. The sympathy of the English people with the victims was aroused, and a great undenominational meeting was held in the Mansion House, at which the Blood Accusation was denounced and the sympathy of the English people offered to the Jews. The Jews of England and France, working in unison, sent a mission, consisting of Sir Moses Montefiore, Isaac Crémieux, the French statesman, and Salomon Munk, the orientalist, to Alexandria to plead the cause of the Jews before the viceroy. Despite the difficulties placed in their way by the French Government and its representatives, a brilliant success was achieved. The imprisoned Jews were declared innocent, and the survivors of those originally imprisoned, released. Moreover, Mehemet

The Jews appeal to the British Government.

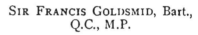

Sir David Salomons, Bart.,
M.P.

Sir Francis Goldsmid, Bart.,
Q.C., M.P.

Sir Moses Montefiore, Bart.

Lionel Louis Cohen, M.P.

Ali himself assured the mission that he placed no credence whatever in the Blood Accusation. On the way home Sir Moses Montefiore visited Constantinople, and obtained from the Sultan the *Hatti Humayun*, by which the disabilities peculiar to the Jews of Turkey were abolished, and they were placed in the eyes of the State on the same level as other non-Mohammedans.

The co-operation of the Jews of the west in the Damascus affair marked a new departure in the history of Jewry. The tendency started on that occasion was strengthened eighteen years later by the Mortara affair,[1] and resulted, in 1860, in the establishment of the *Alliance Israélite Universelle*, an association for the defence of Jewish interests whenever and wherever attacked. When, ten years later, the position of this international Jewish association was jeopardised by the Franco-Prussian War, a similar organisation, the Anglo-Jewish Association, was founded in England. The intercession in the Damascus affair, and the prominent position occupied in regard to it by England under Palmerston, led that statesman to consider the practicability of taking the Jews of the East under English protection, in the same manner as the Catholics were under the guardianship of France. The project was never carried through, although, after Montefiore's return, Lord Palmerston obtained from the Porte a recognition of the right of England to watch over the fulfilment of the conditions of the new *Hatti Humayun*. At the same time a circular was addressed to the British agents in the Levant and Syria, instructing them to protect the Jews, and to notify to the local authorities the interest felt by England in the welfare of the Jews.

The whole of the energies of the Anglo-Jewish

The Anglo-Jewish Association.

Palmerston and the Jewish question.

[1] The kidnapping of a Jewish child and his forcible conversion to Catholicism.

Y

community during the nineteenth century were not absorbed by the movements for ritual reform, political emancipation, and the protection of the Jews of the East. In many other directions also, remarkable activity was shown. The great increase in the numbers of the Jewish population rendered communal re-organisation necessary. The machinery that had served a small community collected around Aldgate and Bevis Marks proved inadequate for the large one scattered throughout the metropolis and the British Empire. In many directions re-arrangements were necessary. The appointment as Chief Rabbi of Dr.

Dr. N. M. Adler's improvements. N. M. Adler in 1845 proved most apposite. He was not only a Jewish scholar and rabbi, he was also a graduate of the Würzberg University and a Doctor of Philosophy of Erlangen. Despite his opposition to the Reform party, he was not one who considered all change harmful and unnecessary. Shortly after taking up his duties, he formulated " A Code of Laws and Regulations for the Ordering of our Synagogue Services." The condition of education, and especially higher education, also attracted his attention. He called upon the synagogues to take measures for providing for the religious education of the children of both sexes, and independent of the pecuniary resources of their parents. Another movement to which he devoted himself was that for the establishment of a training college for the Jewish ministry. This bore fruit in the establishment of Jews' College in 1855.

The problem of poor relief was also dealt with efficiently during these years. The schemes urged and discussed at the beginning of the century had had little result beyond the establishment of the Jews' Hospital and of the Jews' Orphan Asylum in 1831. The Jews' Free School was re-organised in 1817, and, through the munificence of members of the Rothschild family, arrangements made for the apprenticing to useful trades of many of its pupils. The relief of the poor was still in the hands of the synagogues, and consisted rather in the encouragement of pauperism than in the assistance of the recipients to become useful members of society. The somewhat disorganised condition of communal affairs at this period led to a statesmanlike suggestion by H. Faudel Faudel's in 1842. Dr. Adler had not yet settled in the country, suggested reforms. and the improvements that were due to his initiative were still unconceived. Faudel suggested the establishment of a general council which should be "the governing body of the Jews in this country in all secular matters." The intention was that it should administer all the existing Jewish charities, undertake the education, maintenance, and industrial training of all the children of the Jewish poor, and provide a higher class Jewish school for those of the better classes. Many of the points in his programme were subsequently adopted. The establishment of a Jewish representative organisation to consider the problems that affect the community as a whole, is still to come.

The adoption in London of a scientific treatment Charity of the Jewish poor was delayed for several years. In organisation. this respect the provinces were in advance of the metropolis. Liverpool, the most progressive of the provincial Jewish communities, as early as 1845, established a society "for the suppression of mendicancy and the more effectual relief of the deserving itinerant poor." The nucleus of this new institution was derived from the relief machinery of the two local synagogues, but the institution itself was an independent organisation. The lesson taught by Liverpool did not pass unobserved in London. The adoption of the new system was urged by the distinguished mathematician, Benjamin Gompertz, in an open letter to the Secretary of the Hambro Synagogue, but for the time being his representations met with no response. Gompertz was in advance of his time, but by less than two decades. In 1858, on the occasion of the exceptional distress and the consequent strain on the synagogue resources, the moral of the Liverpool experiment was again pointed. Lionel Cohen, a great grandson of Levi Barent Cohen, and Ephraim Alex were the pioneers on this occasion. The failure of Gompertz was retrieved by them, and on the 16th of March 1859 the first meeting was held of the Board of Guardians for the Relief of the Jewish Poor. So signal has been the success of this institution in all departments of philanthropic work, that its methods and organisation are held up as patterns to all similar institutions in the general community.

The Jewish Board of Guardians.

Having succeeded in this direction, Lionel Cohen turned his attention to another movement of concentration that was urgently needed. Repeated efforts had been made in the past to effect some combination between the Ashkenazi synagogues of London, but the mutual rivalries had invariably prevented their success. In 1863 Cohen, who was at the time an overseer of the Great Synagogue, endeavoured to arrange a union between that synagogue and the Hambro, but without success. Three years later, however, the chief rabbi seized an opportunity that occurred for urging a combination of all the metropolitan synagogues under his jurisdiction. The suggestion was adopted by Cohen, and as a result of a series of conferences over which he presided, the United Synagogue was brought into existence by Act of Parliament in 1870. A further step in the same direction was taken in 1887, when the majority of the small synagogues in the East End of London were, at the instance of Sir (then Mr.) Samuel

The United Synagogue.

Montagu, brought together in the Federation of Synagogues.

Meanwhile a gradual *rapprochement* had grown up between the orthodox and the reform parties in the community. The old bitterness had passed away, and in all branches of communal work outside of the synagogue there was hearty co-operation. Efforts were even made to effect a thorough and final reconciliation, but it was found impossible to arrange a compromise in matters of ritual, that would have rendered possible an extension of the chief rabbi's authority so as to include the West London Synagogue. In the orthodox community a progressive spirit had begun to show itself, and efforts were continually made from within to render the ritual, according to which the services were conducted, more in accordance with the times. The authorities showed themselves not unreasonable, and from time to time minor alterations and omissions were sanctioned. The claims of Jewish literature were also recognised, and both branches of the community, Sephardi and Ashkenazi, added many names to the roll of Jewish scholars. In the political world Anglo-Jewry retained and strengthened the position she had gained at the time of the Damascus outrages. In participating in that affair she obtained universal recognition as the leading community of the Diaspora, and when the persecuting tendencies displayed themselves in Roumania and Russia, England, both through her Jewish community and by means of the regular vehicles of expression of public opinion, placed herself in the forefront of those who showed their detestation of anti-Jewish outrages and their practical sympathy with the victims.

With the removal, in 1858, of the last bar to the full emancipation of the Jews, every road in the state was opened to members of the Jewish community,

Jews in English public life.

and there are none that have not been traversed. Every Parliament since the time of Baron Lionel de Rothschild and Sir David Salomons has had its professing Jewish members, many of whom have attained high office. One, Sir George Jessel (1824–1883), was Solicitor-General, and afterwards Master of the Rolls; another, Lord Pirbright (1840–1903), was Parliamentary Secretary to the Board of Trade, and Under Secretary for the Colonies; a third, Sir Julian Goldsmid (1838–1896), was a Deputy Speaker of the House of Commons; and a fourth, Mr. Herbert Samuel (*b.* 1870), Under Secretary in the Home Department. Four professing Jews have been raised to the peerage; several have been sworn of the Privy Council, and a number created baronets. The Council of India, the higher branches of the Civil Service at home and in India, have had their Jewish members; and another member of the community, Sir Matthew Nathan (*b.* 1862), has been entrusted with two colonial governorships.

Jewish Colonial Premiers.

In the colonies Jews have helped to build up new English communities, and have taken their share in their government. One, Sir Julius Vogel (1835–1899), was Prime Minister of New Zealand; a second, the Hon. V. L. Solomon, held a similar position in South Australia, and several others have held high office in other colonies. Among colonial judges more than one Jewish name appears. In science, art, literature, as well as in commerce and finance, individual Jews have taken a prominent part, and brought credit not only upon themselves but also upon their community.

AUTHORITIES :—Lucien Wolf, " The Queen's Jewry "; " Jewish Progress in the Victorian Era" (*Jewish Chronicle,* May 7, June 18, 1897); " MS. Records of the London Committee of Deputies"; " Jewish Encyclopedia."

Inverness

Aberdeen

Dundee

Distribution of

THE JEWS OF THE BRITISH ISLES

in 1907

Greenock

GLASGOW Edinburgh

Londonderry

Belfast

Lurgan

NEWCASTLE ON TYNE   North Shields
                     South Shields
Gateshead   SUNDERLAND
Durham   West Hartlepool
Darlington   Middlesbro'
                     Stockton

Barrow

                     York
Preston Blackburn
         Burnley Bradford
Blackpool   LEEDS   HULL
Southport   Bolton Dewsbury
         Wigan   Huddersfield
LIVERPOOL   Barnsley Grimsby
Birkenhead   MANCHESTER
Rhyl   Widnes Stockport Sheffield
Bangor Chester   Hanley

DUBLIN

Wrexham
                       Derby
                              Nottingham
Limerick   Yarmouth
                Burton on Trent
Waterford Wolverhampton Leicester Norwich
Cork   Dudley BIRMINGHAM
                     Coventry   Cambridge
                     Northampton
                              Bedford

                Cheltenham
Merthyr Newport?
Aberdare Brynmawr   Oxford
Llanelly   Stroud
Swansea Abertillery   LONDON
Aberavon Tenby Bristol Reading Rochester Southend
         Pontypridd   Chatham Ramsgate
         Cardiff Bath Aldershot   Canterbury
         Newport   Dover
                Basingstoke
                     Southampton
                Bournemouth Portsmouth Brighton
Exeter

Plymouth

Scale of Miles
0   50   190

London: Macmillan & Co. Ltd.

Stanford's Geogl Estabt London

ANGLO-JEWISH CHRONOLOGY

YEAR

Tallage of £60,000 (one quarter of the movables of
the Jews) levied 1188
Jews of London massacred on the occasion of Richard I.'s
coronation 1189
Massacres at Lynn, Norwich, Stamford, York, Bury St.
Edmunds, Colchester, Thetford, and Ospringe . . 1190
Jews of Lincoln attacked, and protected by Bishop Hugh . 1190
Jews expelled from Bury St. Edmunds 1190
Blood accusation at Winchester 1192
Richard investigates the massacres : official inquiry into
the wealth of the Jews 1194
The Ordinances of the Jewry 1194
First mention of the Justices of the Jews 1198
Jacob of London appointed Chief Presbyter . . . 1199
The Charter of the Jews 1201
The king protects the Jews of London 1204
John commences to persecute the Jews 1209
The whole of Anglo-Jewry imprisoned 1210
Jews tortured and despoiled to the extent of 66,000 marks.
Exodus of Jews from England 1210
House of Converts established in Southwark . . . 1213
Jews again imprisoned and taxed 1214
London Jewry sacked by the Barons 1215
Jewish rights invaded by Magna Charta 1215
The Jews encouraged by the Regent Pembroke . . . 1216
Burgesses held responsible for the safety of the Jews . . 1217
Jews ordered to wear badges as a precautionary measure . 1218
Attack on the Jews of Lincoln 1220
The Dominicans open a mission in the heart of Oxford
Jewry 1221
Church Synod recommends the imposition of disabilities on
the Jews 1222
The Bishops of Lincoln and Norwich place Jews under an
interdict 1222
A deacon burnt at Oxford for accepting Judaism . . . 1222
The Crown intervenes on behalf of the Jews . . . 1222
Tallage of 4000 marks levied 1226
Tallage of 6000 marks levied 1230
Charge of circumcising a child brought against the Jews of
Norwich 1230
Jews expelled from Leicester 1231
Blood accusation at Winchester 1232
Two tallages of 18,000 marks levied 1232–34
Synagogue in London confiscated and given to the Brethren
of St. Anthony of Vienna 1232

YEAR

House of Converts opened in London	1233
Jews expelled from Newcastle	1234
Thirteen Jews of Norwich charged with the assault of 1230	1234
Christian officers of the Jewish Exchequer dismissed on account of corrupt practices	1234
Christian women forbidden to enter the service of Jews in East Anglia	1234
Jews expelled from Wycombe	1235
Jews expelled from Southampton	1236
Tallage of 18,000 marks levied on the Jews	1236
Aaron of York appointed Chief Presbyter	1237
Further tallage	1237
Elias of London appointed Chief Presbyter	1238
Jews taxed to the extent of a third of their property . .	1239
The Parliament of the Jews	1241
Jews taxed to the extent of 20,000 marks	1241
Jews of Norwich hanged for the offence of 1230 . . .	1241
Jews expelled from Berkhampstead	1242
Aaron of York fined 32,000 marks	1243
Jews expelled from Newbury	1244
Blood accusation at London	1244
Clerical debtors attack Oxford Jewry	1244
The Barons obtain the right to appoint one of the Justices of the Jews	1244
Jews taxed to the extent of 20,000 marks . . .	1244
Jews taxed to the extent of 60,000 marks . . .	1245
Jews threatened with expulsion to Ireland . . .	1245
Jews taxed to the extent of 10,000 marks . . .	1246
Jews taxed to the extent of 5525 marks . . .	1247
Jews taxed to the extent of 10,000 marks . . .	1249
The property of the Jews seized	1250
Alleged act of sacrilege by Abraham of Berkhampstead .	1250
Jews taxed to the extent of 5000 marks of silver and 40 marks of gold	1251
Jews taxed to the extent of 3500 marks . . .	1252
Jews pay 5000 marks for exemption from further tallage for nine months	1253
Jewish rights of residence restricted	1253
The Jews of England, through their spokesman, the Chief Presbyter Elias, request permission to leave the country	1254
The Jews again ask for leave to depart . . .	1255
The Jews sold to Earl Richard for a term of years .	1255
Chief Presbyter Elias imprisoned as surety for a tallage .	1255
Blood accusation at Lincoln (Little St. Hugh) . . .	1255

YEAR

Attempt by Jews to prevent the apostasy of Eve Cohan
  leads to legal proceedings   1680
The creation of a Ghetto suggested, and the matter referred
  to the Privy Council   1680
Jacob Abendana appointed Haham   1680
Unsuccessful attempt to expel the Jews from Jamaica   .   1681
James II. protects the Jews against vexatious legal pro-
  ceedings.   1685
Jewish rights in New York restricted   1685
The first American synagogue opened in New York   .   .   1687
Solomon Ayllon appointed Haham   1689
Bill introduced into Parliament for the levy of a special tax
  on the Jews   .   ʻ   1689
Alien dues imposed on endenizened Jewish merchants   .   1690
A forced loan levied on the Jews   1690
Ashkenazi community established   .   .   .   .   . 1690 c
Jehuda ben Ephraim Cohen appointed Rabbi of the Ash-
  kenazim.   1690
The number of Jews on the London Exchange limited to
  twelve (twelve per cent. of the native Christians)   .   .   1697
David Nieto appointed Haham   1701
The Jews of Jamaica ask for political emancipation and are
  fined   1702
Bevis Marks Synagogue opened   1702
An Act to oblige Jews to maintain and provide for their
  Protestant children   1702
Ashkenazi secession (Hambro Synagogue)   .   .   .   1704
The Wardens of the two older synagogues petition the Board
  of Aldermen to forbid the establishment of a third
  community.   Prayer granted   1704
Jewish disabilities created in Jamaica   1711
The Attorney-General decides that English-born Jews are
  capable of holding land   1718
Uri Phaibush (Aaron Hart) appointed Rabbi   .   .   .   1722
Great Synagogue opened   1722
Hambro Synagogue opened   1726
Death of Haham Nieto   1728
The Villa-Real School founded   1730
Jews' Free School established   1732
Anti-Jewish riots in London   1732
Isaac Nieto appointed Haham   1733
Jews take part in the colonisation of Georgia   .   .   1733
The special taxation of Jews abolished in Jamaica   .   .   1736
Colonial Jews naturalised   1740
M. G. de Mesquitta appointed Haham   1741

YEAR

Death of Haham Meldola	1828
The Duke of Wellington expresses his sympathy with Jewish political emancipation	1829
The first Jewish Emancipation Bill	1830
Restrictions on Jewish traders in the City of London removed	1831
A Jew called to the bar	1833
Jewish Emancipation Bill passes the House of Commons	1833
David Salomons elected Sheriff of London and Middlesex. Act of Parliament qualifying Jews to hold the office of Sheriff	1835
Hirschell appointed Chief Rabbi of the three City Ashkenazi Synagogues	1835
Movement for reform in the Sephardi community	1836
A Jew elected a Governor of Christ's Hospital	1836
A University degree conferred upon a Jew at Dublin	1836
David Salomons elected an Alderman of the City of London	1836
Jewish Emancipation Bill becomes a Government measure	1836
Moses Montefiore, Sheriff, knighted	1837
Jews' Infant School established	1839
The Reformers secede from the parent communities	1840
England expresses her sympathy with the persecuted Jews of Damascus	1840
The first Jewish baronet (Sir Isaac Lyon Goldsmid) created	1841
West London Synagogue (the Reform Synagogue) established	1842
Death of Chief Rabbi Hirschell	1842
Reformers excommunicated	1842
N. M. Adler elected Chief Rabbi	1845
Act for the relief of persons of the Jewish religion elected to municipal offices	1845
A Jew (Baron Lionel de Rothschild) elected to Parliament	1847
David Salomons elected to Parliament, votes without taking the oath, and is fined	1851
Jews' College founded	1855
Alderman Salomons chosen Lord Mayor of London	1855
Jewish Emancipation adopted	1858
The first Jewish Q.C. (Francis Goldsmid)	1858
Jewish Board of Guardians established	1859
The admission of Jews to either House of Parliament legalised	1866
Branch Sephardi Synagogue opened in West London	1866
Benjamin Artom appointed Haham	1866
United Synagogue established	1870
Anglo-Jewish Association founded	1870

INDEX

INDEX

THE END

Printed by BALLANTYNE, HANSON & Co.
Edinburgh & London